THE EVOLUTION OF A BUILDING COMPLEX

THE EVOLUTION OF A BUILDING COMPLEX

Louis I. Kahn's Salk Institute for Biological Studies

JEFFRY KIEFFER

Artifice

CONTENTS

SALK INSTITUTE CHRONOLOGY OF KEY EVENTS RELATED TO DESIGN AND CONSTRUCTION

1959

17–21 Aug: Jonas Salk's first visit to La Jolla, including site visit.
14–16 Nov: Salk's second visit to La Jolla, including site visit.
Dec: Jonas Salk tours the Richards Research Center in Philadelphia.

1960

2–11 Jan: Salk's third visit to La Jolla and the site. He meets San Diego city officials.
Feb: Kahn visits the Salk site with Salk, and Basil O'Connor and begins work on the project.
15 Mar: Kahn presents site model to the San Diego Mayor and City Council. They approve the scheme.
24 Mar: City agrees to allocate land intended for UCSD La Jolla to the Salk Institute.
7 June: Voter approval of land transfer to the Salk Institute.

1961

July: Kahn signs contract with the Salk Institute.
19 Dec: City of San Diego formally hands land over to the Salk Institute.

1962

Apr: Jonas Salk discards Kahn's double garden scheme. Contractor agreement signed April 1.
June: Kahn presents revised single garden scheme to Salk, after which the construction phase formally kicks off.
13 June: Salk asks that final decisions on the design of office and library wings be delayed.
26 July: Kahn letter to August Komendant requesting engineering for stairway, service and mechanical rooms. A second letter, same date, from Salk to Kahn explains the hiring of Earl Walls as lab consultant.
9 Aug: Kahn receives the design program for the scientists' studies.
28 Aug: Meeting in Kahn's office with Jack MacAllister, Marshall Meyers, Dale L Harvey and Earl Walls to discuss functioning of the service blocks.
Dec: Structural calculations for laboratory building completed.

1963

18 Jan: Full architectural/structural package for the laboratory building delivered to site.
21 Mar: Salk letter to Kahn, indicating lab construction drawings, is completed and construction is underway.
Aug: Kahn's contract amended to stop work on the Meeting House and resident housing.
28 Aug: Kahn letter to August Komendant, concerning desire to engineer open stairs.

1965

July: Major construction work completed.
Dec: Kahn visits architect Luis Barragán at his garden home in Mexico City.

1966

23 Feb: Barragán comes to La Jolla. He comments on keeping the plaza open by removing planned landscaping.
19 Dec: Kahn writes a letter to Salk indicating five different approaches to designing the courtyard. He also mentions Halprin's attempt to modify Barragán's bare plaza idea.

1967

Summer: Paving installed at the center courtyard. Laboratory building completed in construction.

PREFACE

I first became aware of Louis I Kahn's architecture through the illustrations in Robert AM Stern's book *New Directions in American Architecture.* This book was published in 1969 during my senior year in high school. The images of Kahn's work of the Salk Institute totally belied the theory of Walter Benjamin concerning the loss of the aura in his essay "The Work of Art in the Age of Mechanical Reproduction". The image auras of Kahn's work were more intense than those by such architects as Paul Rudolph, Robert Venturi and Charles Moore, which were also presented in Stern's book. Three years later, as an undergraduate in the Cooper Union School of Architecture under Prof. Richard Henderson, I was confronted by the perennial analysis problem: Pick a well-known building from a list of contemporary works and "analyze" it; study its spatial, functional and formal aspects; present the results of this research. As a young student, I was enamored of the work but could not adequately explain the fascination with it or for it. We can never explain our fascination for anything or anyone; we can only adequately or inadequately describe the aspects of things or persons. It has taken almost a lifetime for me to appreciate Kahn's achievement. He was not the architect of the architectural 'one-liner'. His entire oeuvre is the context for assessing the architecture of the Salk Institute.

There is the famous saying, "There are very few architects worth leaving home for", and like many other architectural students in the United States and internationally, I wanted to enter the Master's program at the University of Pennsylvania where Kahn was teaching. Unfortunately, Kahn passed away suddenly in 1974. Instead, after graduating from Cooper Union in 1975, I headed to Houston, Texas to attend the Graduate Program in Urban Design at Rice University, escaping the architectural recession of late 1970s New York. Meanwhile, Kahn's inspiring work persisted in my mind. When in 1979 my former Rice classmate Mario Noriega invited me to give a lecture at the University of the Andes in Bogotá, Colombia, I returned to Kahn and in restudying his work there was a revelation: the floor plan of the Salk Institute laboratory building resembled the image of the Torah! This discovery became the basis of several years' research and writing on the Judaic element in his work, which included a consideration of Kahn's architecture as a "deconstruction" of tradition. How else can we understand Kahn's comment that he was "unhistorical by nature". In the early 1980s my early research was shared with Prof. Vincent Scully at Yale University, and aspects of this research are presented in this book. However, later I wanted to return to a more purely architectural evaluation and presentation of Kahn's work—to return to the 'things themselves' as the phenomenologists used to say. This concern was supported by my intensive and extensive personal tour of the Institute in 1988. I had made shorter visits there in 1972 and 1983, and would return there in 1998 and 2006.

There were a handful of critical voices concerning Kahn's work from the 1950s through the 1980s: Colin Rowe, Reyner Banham and Manfredo Tafuri. His work was either compositionally "retarded" (Rowe), too fraught with latent symbolism and not utilitarian enough (Banham) or too isolated from the realities of American urban and suburban development (Tafuri). I have always felt that their resentments were misplaced. This is not a question of a return to an 'outdated' concern for purity in architecture. Kahn's architecture, more radical and greater than the critics were willing to admit, is worth exploring and returning to again and again.

INTRODUCTION

There is nothing equal to the delight in coming to realizations about architecture itself.

Louis I Kahn[1]

We will return to the subject of Kahn's typological invention, (which is simply his dialectic between Form and Design), but what distinguishes this process from its rationalistic expression, as in the well-known text by Quatremère de Quincy, is its understanding of the subject, not through reason, but through feeling, according to the norms of the bourgeois aesthetic of feeling from Hume to S.K. Langer. The way of art is in fact a 'different' way from that of reason. It is the expression of feeling, the safety valve of the individual immersed in a divided and alienating society.... It is formalism, but above all, a 'meta-language', a distanced reasoning process whose roots lie in fantasy and dream. It is re-creation of the mausoleum as a place inhabited by silence, a strange dwelling place in which architecture remembers itself....

....Kahn represents more dramatically than many other contemporary artists, the gratuitousness, the fragility, the helplessness and the drama characteristic of architecture as art in our culture today.

Ignacio de Solà-Morales I Rubio[2]

The Salk Institute for Biological Research was the most important biomedical research institute founded in the last half of the twentieth century.[3] Its development was based on the vision of two men: Dr. Jonas Salk (1914-1995) and the architect Louis I Kahn (1901-1974). The 'epic' of its founding was a complex affair of persons and institutions that rivaled the effort of Jonas Salk and his team in discovering the cure for polio itself. Yet 60 years later the Salk team's achievement has been largely forgotten even among the current generation of biomedical researchers.[4]

Jonas Salk, building on the momentum of his team's work on polio and being highly aware of the revolutionary developments in biomedical research, sensed that a new beginning could contribute to continuing this 'adventure'. But Salk was also highly cognizant of the need to engage non-scientists in this adventure as a necessary support for scientific activity. This support had two aspects. Firstly, Salk desired that a place be created where scientists, scientist-humanists and non-scientist humanists could interact for the benefit of science. Secondly, there needed to be a place where this community of 'specialists' could interact with the public. Public health policy formation was to be an important offshoot of the scientific research mission.

At the time Salk was envisioning his Institute, his vision was severely put into question when a nasty quarrel broke out between two British intellectuals. This was the famous Two Cultures debate initiated by CP Snow, who became one of the founding trustees of the Salk Institute, and while it was one polemic among many in the twentieth century, it was the one most pertinent to the founding of the Institute.[5] CP Snow was a Cambridge graduate with a PhD in chemistry and physics, and his critique was aimed at segments of the academic world lacking in any acquaintance with scientific learning, which was a necessity in a world of increasing scientific and technological development.[6] At least scientists had to write well to communicate the results of their work. Snow was also a novelist and came under the scrutiny of FR Leavis, one of Britain's leading literary critics.

CP Snow's central characters were model citizens of the new technocratic-academic regime. It was exactly this order that FR Leavis attacked:

> **But while Snow thought that the meritocracy would work through existing institutions to extend material prosperity, Leavis intended for it to foster a critical minority capable of exposing—and opposing—the values embedded within precisely those goals.[7]**

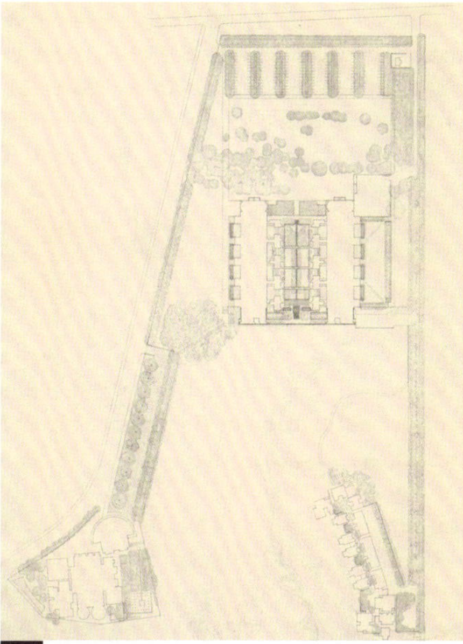

FIG.1

FIG.2

FIG.3

Leavis was no Marxist critic.[8] He lamented the cultural decline of England in the post-Shakespeare era as the sundering of popular from high culture and took up the cause of Blake against the social-intellectual effects of Newtonian science. The irony of this position was that Jacob Bronowski, one of the founding resident fellows of the Salk Institute, and the author of a book on William Blake, tried to bridge the Two Cultures divide.[9] Leavis shared with Heidegger a skepticism concerning science in a consume-oriented society. However, CP Snow's attack had an important practical effect. It was a wake-up call to Britain to meet the Soviet and American technological challenge. During the years of the Salk Institute's founding new science colleges were founded at Oxford and Cambridge.[10] The founding of the Salk Institute was another response to the politics of this Cold War period.[11]

The Salk Institute for Biological Research, on the cliffs of La Jolla, California overlooking the Pacific Ocean, was also what Louis I Kahn had sought in the post-World War Two era: a new expression of architectural monumentality. The project began without a detailed program and evolved into a three-building complex: the Laboratories, the Meeting House and the

FIG.1 | **Salk Institute final master plan (1965)**
FIG.2 | **Salk Institute current site plan**
FIG.3 | **J Salk and J Bronowski at the Salk site (c. 1964)**

Visiting Fellows Housing. By 1966 only the Laboratories building was completed in construction; Salk and Kahn's vision was compromised by lack of funding and lack of will. Once the north laboratory was occupied the focus was on the establishment of scientific work at the Institute, not the completion of the architecture.

Yet Salk and Kahn prepared a detailed master plan for this project. This book is a reassessment of all three buildings in the master plan for the Salk Institute based on a study of the design development drawings at the Architectural Archives at the University of Pennsylvania. We maintain that Salk and Kahn's vision for the Institute was realized in the master plan.[12] **FIGS.1,2** However, there is a difference between a narrative on the development of the Salk Institute as an institution, which is the substance of Suzanne Bourgeois' recent important book, and a narrative on the development of its architecture.[13] As the architect Robert Venturi stated, "form does not follow function", but "form should accommodate function".[14] Is architecture an 'expression' of an institution or a mask for one? Kahn had said: "Our institutions are rotten to the core."[15] What is concealed? What is revealed? Or is an institutional history a mask for architecture blocking perception of its physical order? What is the nature of the physical order?

Kahn too sought to bridge the Two Cultures gap. First he distinguished between the nature of art and that of science (or his notion of science):

> Seeing something again, is an important aspect of art. You don't ever see it all at one time. You could see it indefinitely, and there would always be something you haven't seen, because art is the product of the intuitive—the most powerful instrument within us. The intuitive is the most accurate sense we have. Science can never reach it. Knowledge can never reach it.[16]

Jacob Bronowski expressed a different conception of science's relationship to the arts:

> Science is nothing else than the search to discover unity in the wild variety of nature—or more exactly, in the variety of our experience. Poetry, painting and the arts are the same search... to discover a hidden likeness.[17] FIG.3

But in the continuation of Kahn's statement he sought other grounds for intuition, perhaps contradicting the earlier part of his statement:

> The beautiful thing that the intuitive gives is a sense of commonality, a sense of human agreement which is agreement without example. Something can be produced for the first time, and somehow it has a quality of having always been there. That is the quality of human agreement.

Earlier Kahn stated:

> **A great building, in my opinion, must begin with the unmeasurable, go through the measurable means when it is being designed, and in the end must be unmeasurable... But what is unmeasurable is the psychic spirit. The psyche is expressed by feeling and also thought and, I believe, will always be unmeasurable...**[18]

Louis I Kahn's office had over the years obtained several commissions for medically related or scientific research institutions. In the years 1944 to 1946 Kahn and his partner Oscar Stonorov, with their hospital consultant Isadore Rosenfeld, worked on schemes for new expansions at the Philadelphia Psychiatric Hospital.[19] By 1953 the Pincus Therapy Building and the Radbill Psychiatric Hospital projects were constructed. Kahn's AFL Medical Service building commission (1954-1956, but torn down in 1973 to make room for an expressway) was followed by the Martin Research Institute (1955-1957) project in Fort Meade, Maryland–although this project was not constructed.[20] This architectural activity of the 1950s culminated in the design and construction of the Richards Research Building (1957-1964) on the campus of the University of Pennsylvania. The Richards Building brought Kahn to the attention of an international audience by being honored with a 'one building' exhibition at the Museum of Modern Art in New York City in 1961.[21] However, this sequence of institutional 'types' were not the only important influences on Kahn's work at the Salk Institute–the composition and designs for his house commissions played an important part in the design development of the Institute.[22]

Louis I Kahn had graduated from the School of Fine Arts at the University of Pennsylvania in 1924. His Beaux-Arts instruction in architecture was led by professors like Paul Phillipe Cret, who was a direct heir of Julien Guadet at the Beaux-Arts Academy in Paris. Guadet's *Éléments et Théorie de l'Architecture* (1904) devoted two books to building types. Book one was dominated by ancient, Christian and modern funerary architecture. Book two included military architecture, rural architecture, gardens, architecture in gardens, public ways, bridges, aqueducts and viaducts. In Guadet's text the new urban building types of the nineteenth century were neglected: railway stations, hotels, apartment buildings, museums, libraries, factories, office buildings and laboratories.[23] But perhaps this attempt to classify architecture by functional types to imitate was and is misleading. At the beginning of the nineteenth century JNL Durand, professor at the École polytechnique in Paris, had already published his didactic display of building elements as geometric permutations. He never used the word 'type'. **FIGS.4, 5** The 'model' was a 'system' for planning and construction choices open to the known and unpredictable requirements of the city.[24] Durand's work 'systematized' and reduced the classical order of architecture. As Edgar Morin had stated: "...system oscillates between the ideal model and the descriptive reflection of empirical objects, and it is really neither one nor the other".[25]

> **The concept of type is almost completely missing from the architectural doctrine of Kahn... Is it a case of concealment or of minimization?–Jacques Gubler[26]**

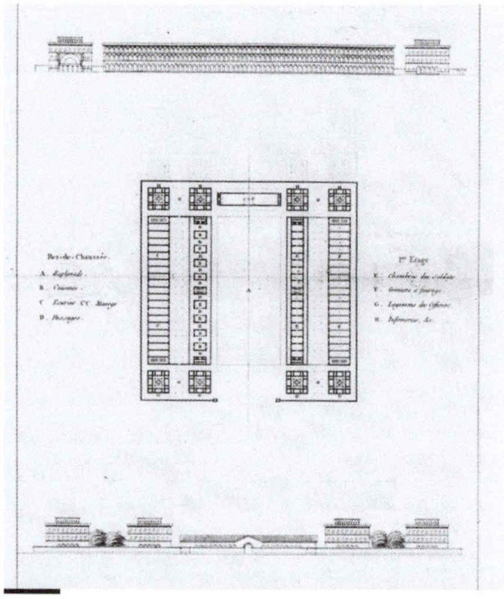

FIG. 4

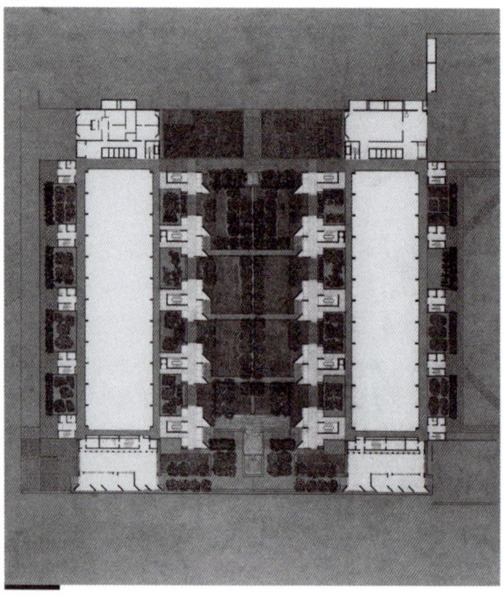

FIG. 5

In Louis I Kahn's famous 'Form and Design' diagram, which he did while he was working on the Unitarian Church, just before the Salk commission, he questioned the typological conception of architecture or form. It is classical planning reduced to a centralizing, layered diagram. **FIG.7** Design is the series of circumstantial design decisions on a project that either confirms the initial form diagram, deforms it or destroys it. Here one is reminded of Karl Popper's principle of falsifiability rather than verifiability of hypotheses and theories.[27] Linked to Form and Design is Kahn's concept of served and servant space–the functionalist remains of classical hierarchy.

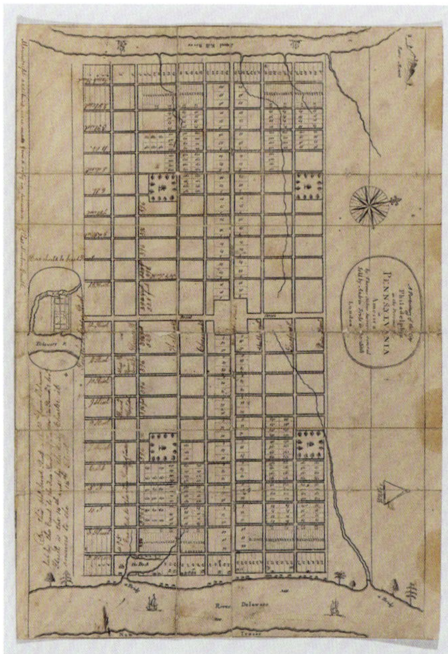

FIG. 6

The modern biological research laboratory as institution emerged from two lines of development. First the development of coastal marine research stations in nineteenth-century France represented the shift in biological research from natural history museums with their collections and "silence of the cabinet".[28] It was necessary to remove researchers from the urban environments and bring them to the actual source of study. A key component of these research stations was how domestic living arrangements were provided for. Two of the greatest coastal research stations founded in the United States were the Cold Spring Harbor facilities (1890) on the north shore of Long Island and the Scripps Institute of Oceanography (1903) at La Jolla. Both facilities eventually expanded their agendas beyond their original missions as marine research stations. Cold Spring Harbor brought together the world's leading life sciences specialists through its teaching and seminar programs. It was through Cold Spring Harbor that connections were

FIG.4 | **From JNL Durand's *Précis* (1809)**
FIG.5 | **Salk Institute laboratory final plan (1965)**
FIG.6 | **William Penn's Philadelphia Plan (1682)**

established with scientists at the Pasteur Institute in Paris, some of whom later became key scientists at the Salk Institute–another coastal research station of a different kind.[29] Meanwhile, Scripps expanded its programs to include astronomy and planetary science (the search for extraterrestrial life).

The second line of development which led to the modern biological research laboratory emerged from the private workshops and laboratories of the early nineteenth century. The father of the great German biological chemist Justus von Liebig, for example, was "a dry salter and hardware merchant who compounded and sold paints, varnishes and pigment".[30] This practical 'field' was at the basis of Leibig's conception of scientific research and was also why his efforts to establish a scientific research laboratory within the university setting failed.[31] As René Dubos indicated, the rise of laboratory science–for example, the founding of the Pasteur Institute in Paris (1888)–was also separate from clinical practice.[32] In the United States the Hoagland Laboratory, founded the same year as the Pasteur Institute, and the first American laboratory to focus on bacteriological research, was privately endowed.[33] Suzanne Bourgeois traces the development of independent laboratories to the founding of institutions like the Kaiser Wilhelm Institutes in Berlin in the 1920s.[34] This tradition of founding independent research laboratories continued when J Robert Oppenheimer advised Jonas Salk to found the new institute completely independent of the UCSD.[35]

There is very little direct correspondence between Jonas Salk and Louis I Kahn at the Salk or Penn Archives regarding the early-to-mid stages of this design development. Certain key decisions made by Salk are known from the Kahn literature. Peter Salk, Jonas's eldest son, has stated that his father was highly aware of all the changes that transpired in the evolution of the project.[36] In this regard Kahn made this statement regarding his working relationship with Dr. Jonas Salk:

> Dr. Salk listened closely to my speculations and was serious about how I would approach the building. He listened more carefully to me than I did to myself, and then he recorded these things in his mind. During the time for our study, he constantly reminded me of premises which were not being carried out. These premises, which he thought were important, were also the basis of questioning in his own way of thinking. In that way, he was just as much the designer of the project as myself.[37]

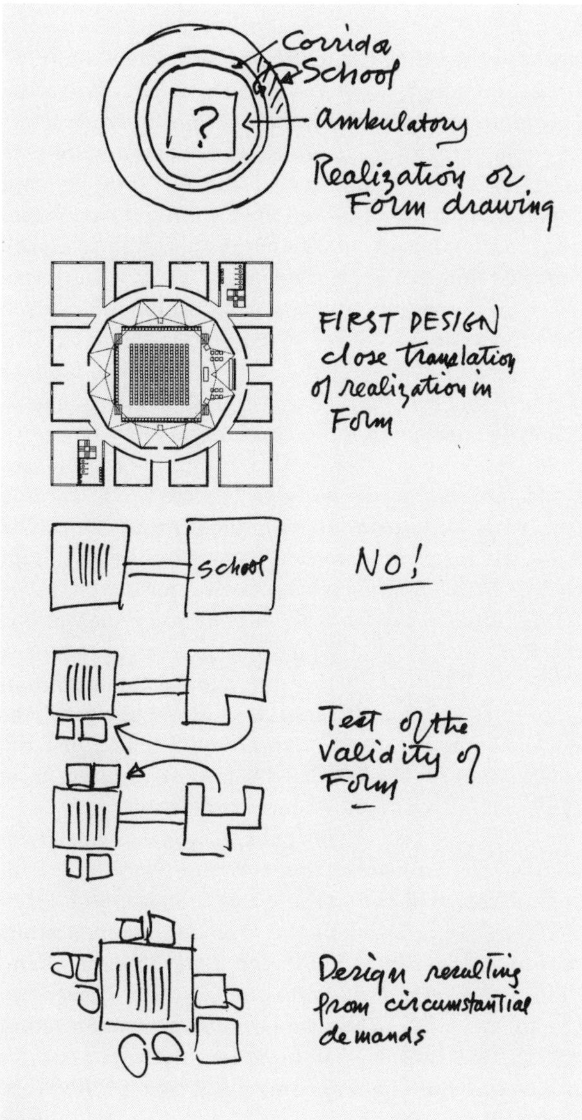

FIG. 7

FIG.7 | Kahn's Form and Design diagram (1961)

This book is a study of the shifts in Kahn's design development of the Institute. The apparent rigor of the Salk Institute architecture was an outcome of labyrinthine design procedures and decisions in response to the constantly changing demands of the commission. The drawings and models are important sources of information for understanding the architectural outcome that is the Salk Institute, and we ask some elementary questions: In what way did Kahn's earlier work influence the development of the Institute? In the evolution of the project how did three buildings emerge from the welter of possibilities offered by the initial minimum program requirements?[38] What 'crossover' relationships developed in the ordering of the three buildings of the Salk Institute: the Laboratories, the Meeting House and the Visiting Fellows Residences? What were Kahn's realizations concerning the Institute site, and how were the structures adapted to it?

The conception of Kahn's architecture as 'objective and verifiable' is valid only for those willing to engage with his work.[39] Louis I Kahn's 'types' were not deployed or imposed but 'elicited' from the work situation. To elicit means to 'draw out'. Louis I Kahn's unique contribution to twentieth-century architecture was based on his response to natural light. When he raised the joint as construction principle to a compositional principle in his 'spacings', to create an architecture of connection, he not only reinvigorated the wall but made light the 'theme'.[40] Kahn returned again and again to a small number of 'figurations' to 'enlighten' his commissions, and that is why we must situate the Salk Institute within his total architectural production. The Salk Institute is a temple to science unlike any of its famous predecessors such as the Pasteur Institute, the Johns Hopkins laboratories, Rockefeller University, the Rutgers University laboratories, the Institute of Advanced Studies at Princeton or Jonas Salk's original laboratories at the Universities of Michigan and Pittsburgh. We study the total vision of Salk and Kahn in the master plan for the Institute: "...that strange dwelling place where architecture remembers itself".

Chapter One of this book presents the development of the Salk Institute, starting with the initial consideration of the site and the site planning. From there an examination of the Meeting House is given before the presentation on the Laboratory building because the latter finds its compositional origin in the former work. Then we move on to a much more detailed perspective on the various elements of the Laboratory building–the only building built from the master plan–and the planning and composition of the Visiting Fellows Residence is reviewed. We close the chapter with a critique of the 1992 addition to the Laboratory building.

Next, Chapter Two reviews key Kahn buildings designed before the Salk Institute, stressing Kahn's concern for natural light, culminating with another look at the Laboratory building in this context. Chapters Three and Four deal with issues of critical, historical and biographical content that could not be divulged from a purely descriptive approach to the 'experience' of Kahn's Salk master plan and the Institute as built. Finally, Chapter Five will focus on the themes developed at the Salk Institute that found new resonance in four later projects by Kahn, two of which involve very complex institutional programs of an even larger scale than the Salk master plan.

INTRODUCTION ENDNOTES

1 Source unknown.
2 de Solà-Morales I Rubio, Ignacio: "A Lecture in San Sebastian", *Arquitecturas Bis*, 41-42, January-June 1982.
3 The most important biomedical research organization founded in the twentieth century was the Rockefeller University in New York City (1901).
4 Robert Redford's film on the Salk Institute (which became part of the documentary *Cathedrals of Culture*), was premiered in October 2014 at the Architecture Design Film festival in New York City. During the post-screening talk, Richard Saul Wurman stated that he once conducted an informal poll before an audience of two thousand at the University of Chicago. He asked how many in the audience knew who Jonas Salk was. Very few members of the youthful audience raised their hands. Redford, who had an early brush with polio and grew up in southern California, was an admirer of the architecture of the Salk Institute from the early years of his stage and screen career.
5 Among some of the scientific and social scientific debates in the twentieth century were the following: Einstein and Bergson, Einstein and Bohr, Cassirer and Heidegger, Popper and Wittgenstein, Popper and Feyerabend, Crick and Polanyi, Chomsky and Skinner, Chomsky and Piaget, Chomsky and Foucault, Derrida and Searle.
6 It is somewhat shocking even today to read the disdainful comments of Francis Crick, co-discoverer with James Watson of the molecular structure of DNA and for many years a key scientist at the Salk Institute. He was well aware of the Two Cultures controversy. He even thought CP Snow did not appreciate the extent of the divide between the two cultures. From his book *Of Molecules and Men*, pp 93-94: "It is not possible to see one's way clearly in the modern world unless one grasps this division between these two cultures and the fact that one is slowly dying and the other, although primitive, is bursting into life. University administrators should try to see that their universities become centers for the propagation of the new culture, and not merely homes for propping up an aging and dying one."
7 Ortolano, Guy, *The Two Cultures Controversy*, Cambridge, UK: Cambridge University Press, 2009, p 89. Also see: Kimball, Roger, "The Two Cultures Today", *New Criterion*, vol. 12, February 1994.
8 Ortolano, *The Two Cultures Controversy*, p 84: "Leavis loathed socialism."
9 Bronowski, Jacob, *William Blake and the Age of Revolution*, New York: Routledge and Kegan Paul, 1965. For Bronowski's other writings consult the bibliography.
10 This included the founding of Churchill College at Cambridge, which was based on a winning scheme in the 1964 competition by Richard, Sheppard, Robson and Partners. Every major British architect competed for this commission, including Stirling and Gowan, whose scheme was supported by Colin Rowe. Stirling and Gowan's scheme was deemed not buildable because it could not be phased in construction. The relationship of Kahn's work to that of Stirling could be a whole separate essay. Stirling's Leicester Engineering Building was designed at the same time the Richards Medical Center was being constructed. Although relying on Russian Constructivist architecture the overall building formation owes highly to the tower over 'shed' concept of Frank Lloyd Wright's Johnson's Wax headquarters, and its use of service towers should be compared to the Richards Building. Mention should be made of the possible influence of Kahn's Dominican Sisters' Convent on the conception of Stirling's Wissenschaft Zentrum (Social Science Research Campus) in Berlin and the influence of the Salk Institute laboratory building on Stirling's Bayer Research Complex in Mannheim.
11 Suzanne Bourgeois, in her book on the *Genesis of the Salk Institute*, Berkeley and Los Angeles, University of California Press: 2013, p 65, makes clear that the development of the entire Salk site, which was originally part of the much larger new campus of the University of California planned at the same time, and indeed the entire San Diego area, was amenable to the development of institutions devoted to science and technology. San Diego was already a Navy town—the base for the Pacific Fleet. General Atomic, a division of General Dynamics, was already based in La Jolla to the north of the Salk site. Roger Revelle, the first president of UCSD, had stated in response to the orbiting of Russia's Sputnik that "The nation's youngsters must learn either science or Russian!"
12 Michael Merrill, in his study, *Louis Kahn on the Thoughtful Making of Spaces—The Dominican Motherhouse and a Modern Culture of Space*, Basel: Lars Müller Publishers, 2010, p 7, emphasized Kahn's comments on the value of uncompleted things: "The value of uncompleted things is very strong.... If the spirit is there and can be recorded, what is lost? The drawing is important, the incomplete scheme is important, if it has a central gravitational force which makes the arrangement not just an arrangement but something which gives a richness to the associations which are lost. Recording of that which has not been done must be made much of."
13 Thomas Pollard, a Yale developmental and cell biologist and former president of the Salk Institute (1996-2001) made the following comments in a Tanner Lecture in the fall of 2008 (archived online): "If you Google Salk you get thousands of images of the courtyard but hardly any of the labs." There is a difference expressed in the structure of the Salk Institute between areas of 'scenic' value and areas of experimental work. Thomas Leslie's writings on the Salk Institute focus on the latter.
14 Cf. Venturi, Robert, "Accommodation and the Limitations of Order: The Conventional Element", *Complexities and Contradictions in Architecture*, New York: Museum of Modern Art, 1966. Louis I Kahn attended Venturi's thesis review at Princeton in 1950 and later employed Venturi, who had worked on the Richards Medical Research building.
15 Gutman, Robert, "Human Nature in Architectural Theory: the Example of Louis Kahn", *Architect's People*, Russell Ellis and Dana Cuff eds., New York, Oxford University Press: 1989.
16 Wurman, Richard Saul, *What Will Be Has Always Been—The Words of Louis I Kahn*, New York, Rizzoli: 1986, p 251. Statement made in 1974.
17 Bronowski, Jacob, *Science and Human Values*, New York, Harper and Row: 1965, p 16.
18 Wurman, *What Will Be Has Always Been—The Words of Louis I Kahn*, p 89.
19 Brownlee, David, and David G DeLong, *Louis I Kahn: In the Realm of Architecture*, New York, Rizzoli: 1991, pp 46-47.
20 This building was reviewed in Randy Swanson's PhD, referred to in the bibliography.

21 See the MoMA catalog edited by Wilder Green in the bibliography.
22 Cf. Marcus. George H, and William Whitaker, *The Houses of Louis Kahn*, New Haven, Yale University Press: 2013.
23 Cf. Eigen, Edward, *Between Stations and Habitations—the Architecture of French Science at the Shore 1830-1910,* MIT PhD thesis, February 2000, p 15, "This study proposes an understanding of the emergence of the laboratory as a modern building type. Writing after the fact in 1901, the academic theorist Julien Guadet noted that creating a composition which answered to the highly specific program of the laboratory deprives the architect of the crutch of symmetry or any other seductive design device." Also see Eigen's essay "The Place of Distribution in Architecture and the Sciences", in *Exchanging Metaphors.* Randy Swanson, in his PhD on four laboratory designs of Louis I Kahn, mentions that well into the twentieth century the laboratory building as functional type was excluded from major architectural texts such as Hamlin's *Form and Functions of Twentieth Century Architecture* and Pevsner's *A History of Building Types.* See Swanson p 41. In addition, Reyner Banham mentions Guadet's scientistic view of architectural training. See Banham's *Theory and Design in the First Machine Age*, Cambridge, MA, MIT Press: 1980, p 18.
24 See Vidler, Anthony, "The Third Typology", *Oppositions* 7, p 290. From the early 1960s to the late 1970s the question of typology engaged authors such as Vidler, Argan, Colquhoun and Moneo.
25 Cf. Morin, Edgar, *The Nature of Nature*, New York, P Lang: 1992, p 140. As Bourgeois stated in her book on the Salk Institute, p 170: "Morin spent six months at the Salk Institute, from September 1969 to March 1970. A French philosopher and sociologist—*un penseur* (a thinker)—living in Paris, he was well known to John Hunt and to Jacques Monod, who had recommended him... More importantly, however, Edgar's stay at the Salk Institute had a great impact on him. In his own words, 'The year at Salk was a rebirth for me.' What he learned in La Jolla became for him the basis for years of intellectual productivity." As Wikipedia states, prior to Morin's Salk Institute visit, "French sociologist Georges Friedmann brought him and Roland Barthes together to create a Centre for the Study of Mass Communication that, after several name changes, became the Edgar Morin Centre of the EHESS, Paris... In 1968, Morin replaced Henri Lefebvre at the University of Nanterre. He became involved in the student revolts that began to emerge in France. In May 1968, he wrote a series of articles for *Le Monde* that tried to understand what he called 'The Student Commune'."
26 Gubler, Jacques, "Is the Bay a Type?", *Casabella 509/510*, January-February 1985, pp 76-83.
27 Popper, Karl, *The Logic of Scientific Discovery*, London, Hutchison: 1959. Popper was a Visiting Fellow at the Salk Institute in 1967, as Suzanne Bourgeois indicates in *Genesis of the Salk Institute*, pp 162-163.
28 See Eigen, Edward: "The Place of Distribution", *Architecture and the Sciences—Exchanging Metaphors*, New York, Princeton Architectural Press: 2003, pp 55-62.
29 Bourgeois, *Genesis of the Salk Institute*, p 71.
30 Wikipedia article on Justus von Leibig p 2 at https://en.wikipedia.org/wiki/Justus_von_Liebig
31 Ibid, pp 3-4.
32 Cf. Dubos, René, *The Professor, The Institute and DNA*, New York, Rockefeller University Press: 1976, p 7. Jonas Salk once considered Dubos to be a resident fellow at the Institute. See Salk Archive Box 350 Folder 5—undated letter from Salk to Basil O'Connor.
33 Ibid, p 19.
34 Bourgeois, *Genesis of the Salk Institute*, p 35.
35 Ibid, pp 20-26. Oppenheimer headed the Institute for Advanced Study at Princeton (1947-1966), and was wary of bureaucracies and advisory committees, which was only exacerbated by his experience as leader of the research team on the Manhattan Project.
36 From a conversation with Peter Salk in Feb.2014. Peter was a student at Harvard and Johns Hopkins Universities at the time of the Institute design and construction.
37 Wurman, *What Will Be Has Always Been*, p 131.
38 Ibid, p 89. As Kahn stated: "I believe the architect's first act is to take the program that comes to him and change it. Not to satisfy it, but to put it into the realm of architecture, which is to put it into the realm of spaces."
39 Tafuri, Manfredo, *Theories and History of Architecture*, New York, Harper and Row: p 56.
40 The most significant essay on the nature of the joint in Kahn's architecture is "Louis Kahn and Venice: Ornament and Decoration in the Interpretation of Architecture" by Dostoglu, Frascari and Vivoni, in *Louis I Kahn—l'uomo, il maestro,* Alessandra Latour ed., Rome: Edizioni Kappa: 1986. This essay focuses on the unbuilt Palazzo dei Congressi project for Venice (1968-1974). There has been considerable scholarship and presentations on Kahn's unbuilt works by authors such as Kent Larson, Susan Solomon and Michael Merrill. The unbuilt projects were among the most significant in Kahn's career.

CHAPTER ONE

THE DESIGN DEVELOPMENT OF THE SALK INSTITUTE FOR BIOLOGICAL STUDIES

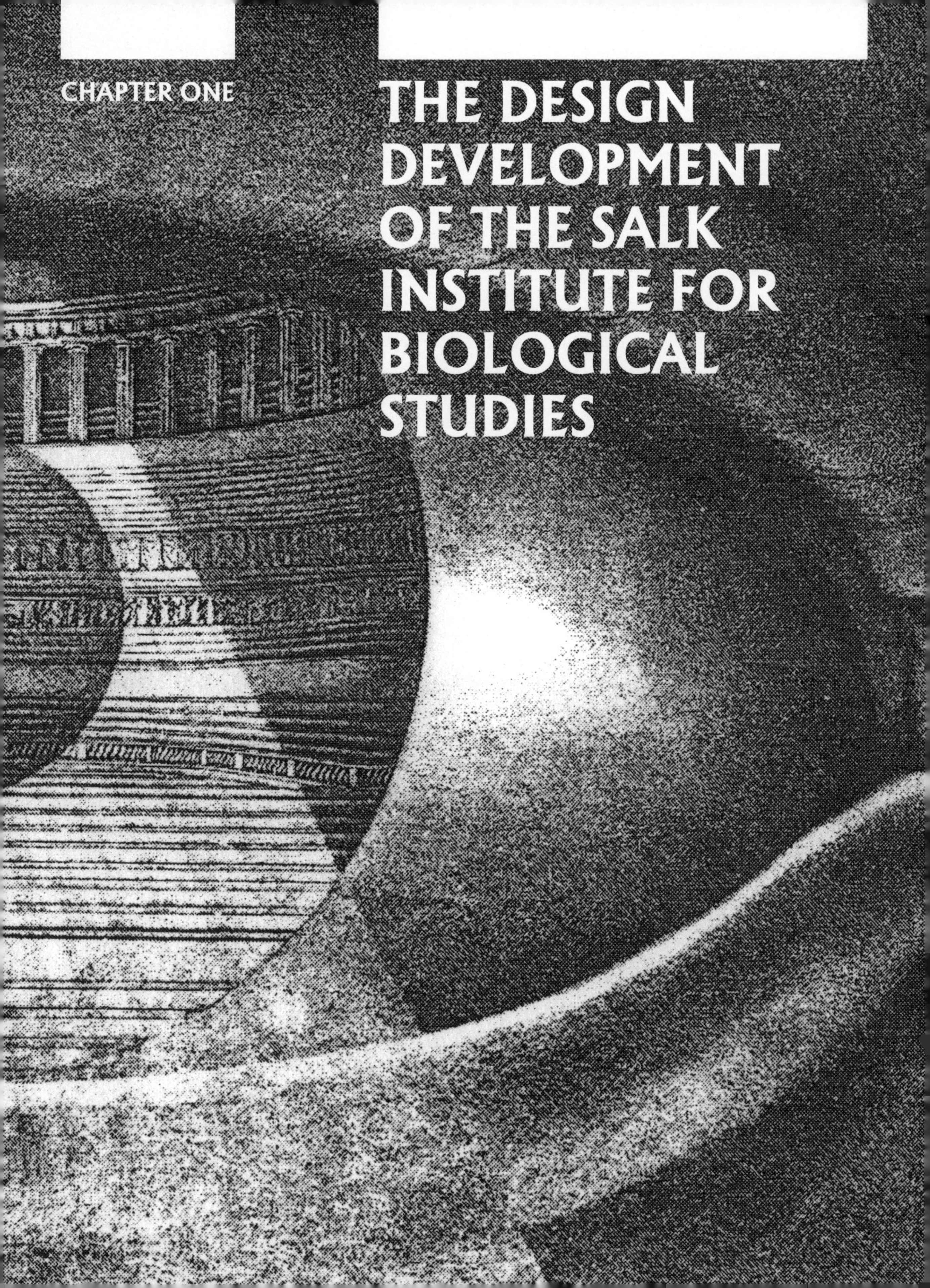

Chapter One

THE BEGINNINGS OF THE SALK INSTITUTE

I love beginnings.

Louis I Kahn[1]

The wish in the fairytale is the beginning of science.

Louis I Kahn[2]

FIG. 9

FIG. 10

OPPOSITE
FIG.8 | J Salk, E Roosevelt and B O'Connor at the NFIP Hall of Fame, (2 Jan. 1958)
FIG.9 | View–Georgia Warm Springs Foundation (erected 1928)
FIG.10 | FDR in the water therapy pool (c. 1930)

The Salk Institute site consists of 27 acres that was broken off from the master plan for the new University of California San Diego (UCSD) at La Jolla campus that has been developed and constructed over many years from 1960 until the present.[3] The site was originally a part of the pueblo lands ceded by Mexico to San Diego when California became a state in 1850.[4] In the late nineteenth century and into the early twentieth century the land to the north of the Salk site was given over to the Torrey Pines State Reserve to protect the unique pine named after botanist John Torrey. By 1940 the San Diego municipality leased the rest of the land of the Torrey Pines Mesa to the US military as a World War II training ground. What later became the Salk site was occupied in part by a municipal golf course and a city-owned glider port.

Behind the founding of the Salk Institute came the National Foundation for Infantile Paralysis (NFIP). This was the parent organization of the March of Dimes campaign, which was the major funder for the construction of the Institute. FIG.8 Franklin D Roosevelt, born in 1882, who became the governor of New York in 1929 and was to become President of the United States in 1933, was a polio victim from the age of 39,[5] and a friend of FDR's, George Foster Peabody, recommended that he try the 'cure' at Warm Springs, Georgia–80 miles south of Atlanta. FIGS.9,10 Peabody was part owner of this "rundown" resort as Suzanne Bourgeois has described it.[6] FDR first visited Warm Springs in October 1924, and treatment was provided at the large pool fed by the warm spring water high in minerals. By 1926 FDR had purchased the resort with his law partner Basil O'Connor's backing and rehabilitated it. They turned it into a non-profit organization, The Georgia Warm Springs Foundation, which was to become the precursor of the NFIP,[7] and O'Connor would be the president of the NFIP until his death in 1972. Jonas Salk met Basil O'Connor for the first time in 1951 during the voyage home from the Second International Poliomyelitis Congress held in Copenhagen,[8] and Salk announced the breakthrough cure for polio in April 1955. Then, in August 1959, Jonas Salk and Basil O'Connor toured the new UCSD site in La Jolla, accompanied by Roger Revelle, who was the director of the Scripps Institute of Oceanography (SIO) and local administrator for the University of California system, which the SIO was a part of.

For a while Salk vacillated between founding his new Institute in a number of locations: Pittsburgh, San Francisco, Palo Alto or La Jolla. He also considered spectacular sites in San Francisco like the Presidio and Treasure Island. But the physicist Leo Szilard had written a letter to Salk advising him to not to establish the new institute in Pittsburgh: "Frankly, I see no possibility of getting many first-class people to move to Pittsburgh."[9] Szilard, nearly twenty years earlier, had written another even more important letter to FDR. That was the letter Einstein signed which eventually led to the Manhattan Project. Szilard was hoping to get Salk to move to La Jolla where Szilard was already a research scientist with General Atomic, designers and manufacturers of atomic reactors whose headquarters was just north of the proposed site for UCSD La Jolla. Szilard was one of the key scientists who shifted their research interests from physics to the life sciences.[10] This shift was partly motivated by Szilard's own guilt complex from his association with the Manhattan Project and the subsequent atomic destruction of Hiroshima and Nagasaki. Also, a former associate of Salk in Pittsburgh had just moved to La Jolla and was also working for General Atomic,[11] while one of Jonas Salk's brothers lived in Palm Springs, California.[12] The mayor of San Diego, Charles C Dail—himself a polio victim—encouraged Salk to make the move, and the establishment of the Institute would contribute to the economic development of the area.

FIG. 11

FIG. 12

Jonas Salk became aware of Louis I Kahn through his friends Ann and Alex Lowenthal of Pittsburgh, who had heard Lou give a talk at the centennial of Carnegie Tech (now Carnegie Mellon University) in October 1959.[13] Two months later, just before his third tour of the UCSD La Jolla site, and while on a trip between Pittsburgh and New York, Salk visited Kahn's office in Philadelphia, and Kahn gave Salk a personal tour of the Richards Research Center, then under construction. In its 'raw' state, and without the later knowledge of its 'operational' shortcomings, the Richards building must have seemed to Salk a radically new vision of what a scientific research laboratory could be. The building and Kahn himself suitably impressed Salk, who invited the architect to visit La Jolla soon after. Simultaneously, the core group of founding scientists for the future Salk Institute gave their blessing to move to the La Jolla area.[14]

Kahn visited La Jolla in early February of 1960, just after Salk's third visit. He began sketching the site and began work on the project without a contract.[15] Only five weeks later, on 15 March, Salk and Kahn presented the initial project site model to the San Diego mayor and City Council. It was then that it became evident to Roger Revelle, who was to soon become the first president of

FIG.11 | Kahn's earliest known drawing—Para, Brazil (1913)
FIG.12 | Kahn's early Salk site drawing (Feb. 1960)

UCSD La Jolla, that Salk and Basil O'Connor were seeking the most desirable plot of land from the UCSD dispensation–the 27 acres west of North Torrey Pines Road overlooking the Pacific Ocean. Revelle was not pleased, and a rift developed between Salk and O'Connor.[16] Salk's visit to impressive sites in the Bay Area influenced his decision to obtain the most desirable part of the future La Jolla campus. By 24 March, the City Council agreed to transfer the land to the new Institute, and voter approval for the land transfer occurred on 7 June.

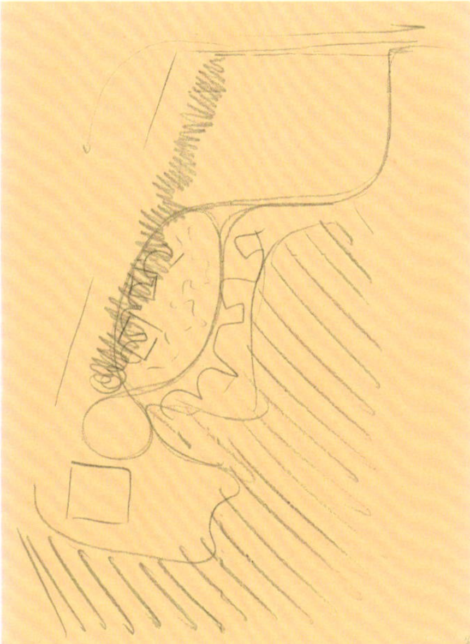

FIG. 13

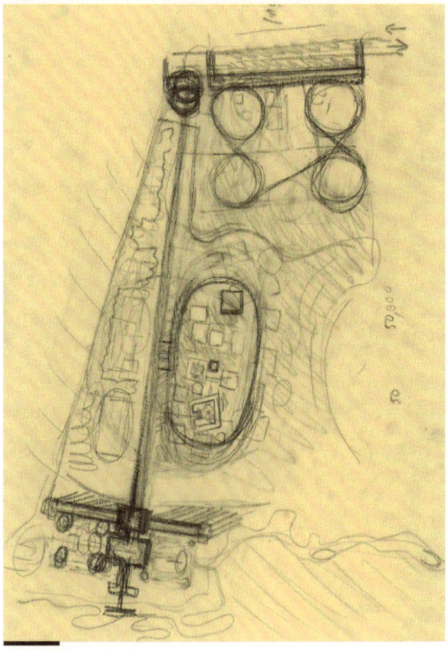

FIG. 14

EARLY PLANNING

Louis I Kahn's first sketches of the La Jolla site ranged from calm to enervating, like an abstract expressionist work. **FIG.12** The topography suggested lines of force which defined the spatial character of the site. Kahn was very familiar with coastal sites from the time of his childhood; his first known sketch, created while a student at Central High School in Philadelphia, was a copy of another work showing the coast of Para, Brazil. By the 1920s he had sketched the Amalfi coast and by the 1930s, on several trips to Canada, had done numerous sketches of village coastlines in Quebec and Nova Scotia. **FIG.11**

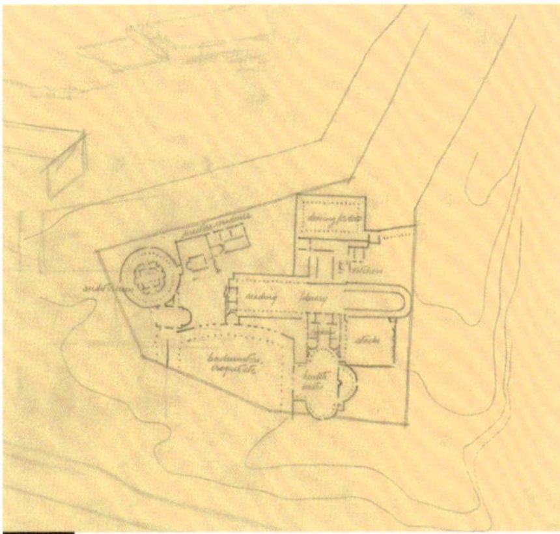

FIG. 15

In his earliest site plan for the Salk Institute (540.3) Kahn left out any suggestion of building on the part of the site where the laboratory building would eventually be constructed. **FIG.13** A sinuous line defines the north side of the site only. An east to west line of vegetation defines the road approach to the end of the site where Kahn juxtaposed a square and a circle. It is not at all clear in what manner Salk's program was to be accommodated in these 'Platonic' forms. Embedded on the north side of the ravine appears a continuous structure, which again is undefined. The 'Platonic' forms will survive the design process to become the unbuilt Salk Meeting House. Later Kahn assigned project architect Tim Vreeland to work out a schematic variation of the Meeting House. Without Kahn's prior knowledge Vreeland based the plan on a direct adaptation of the plan of Hadrian's Villa. **FIG.15** This was the scheme that architectural historian Vincent Scully had referred to as "a draftsman's joke" and which Kahn tried to deny in his comment that he was by nature "unhistorical".[17]

FIG.13 | Earliest Salk site plan drawing 540.3 (Feb.-Mar. 1960)
FIG.14 | Salk site plan drawing 540.6.1 (Feb.-Mar. 1960)
FIG.15 | Salk Meeting House plan–T Vreeland (Feb.-Mar. 1960)

In site drawing 540.6.1 Kahn begins to articulate the scheme that the San Diego City Council would eventually approve for development. **FIG.14** (The laboratories were sited on four circular cross-linked platforms occupying the formerly empty area of drawing 540.3.) The quadrapartite nature of these platforms will also survive in drastically modified form in the final plan of the Laboratory building. The road connecting the site entrance at the north east becomes a forceful east-west axis intersecting another axial path running north-south, which defines the approach to the Meeting House building with its broad face of elements

FIG.16

FIG.17

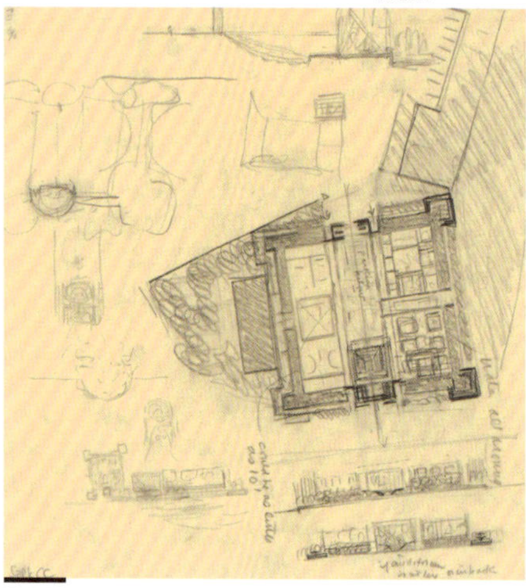

FIG.18

overlooking the Pacific Ocean. Kahn further developed what appears to be a village of structures that defined the scientists' long-term living quarters south of the east-west road/axis.

In drawing 540.137 Kahn established the design for the Meeting House building, which eventually would become what Robert McCarter has called an adaptation of an ancient Roman fortress: Diocletian's Palace at Split.[18] **FIG.16** But at this stage of development the scheme is more reminiscent of the Erdman dormitory project for Bryn Mawr College, which was an ongoing project in Kahn's office. **FIG.17** Like at Bryn Mawr, Kahn positioned three components aligned along a parallel path. Two programmatic elements flank the central entry module, which resembles one of the laboratory loft floors of the Richards Medical Research Center. The frames of the flanking elements are peripheral circulation corridors with panoramic views of the sea, within which programmatic elements have been inserted like the organs within a body. To the south Kahn developed what will become the Salk Institute director's house. To the north of the entrance hall he inserted an assembly hall and presumably what would become a library, kitchen and dining halls within the frame of the corridor overlook. In time Kahn would unpack the programmatic elements confirming his Form and

FIG.16 | **Salk early Meeting House drawing 540.137 (Feb.-Mar. 1960)**
FIG.17 | **Main entry level plan Erdman Hall, Bryn Mawr, PA (1960-1965)**
FIG.18 | **Salk Meeting House drawing 540.127 (Feb.-Mar. 1960)**

Design dialectic and his served-and-servant conception of architecture. There is a continuous dialectic of the inside and outside as his architecture developed towards greater exteriority.

THE MODEL OF THE MASTER PLAN APPROVED BY THE SAN DIEGO CITY COUNCIL

Louis I Kahn's office was required to prepare the master plan model for a city council review by 15 March 1960. FIG.19 That was less than six weeks after Kahn's first site visit. That he had adapted his Richards Medical Center

FIG. 19

FIG.19 | J Salk (left) and L Kahn present to the San Diego City Council (15 Mar. 1960)

tower scheme for the Salk Laboratories on two of the four circular platforms could only have been a rush decision necessitated for the official review. The casual placement of a variety of low-level structures, based on a courtyard typology intended as scientists' residences and recreational facilities, was also part of this expedited presentation requirement. The most formal part of the scheme was the 'Split', like two level terraces of the Meeting House with its broad elevation facing the Pacific Ocean.

The crossover–or exchangist and quadrapartite character of the circular platform work areas defined by the interconnecting paths (what Thomas Leslie described as a "pulley system")–would survive the design development process in drastically modified form in the Laboratory building as built. This early scheme was in fact a model of the exchangist or crossover procedure that Kahn would utilize to develop the architecture of the Salk Institute. He would also develop the positive/negative, or solid/void, character of the architecture of this scheme. The apparent 'free-form' composition of the residential/recreational facilities vaguely resembles, in a much more minor key, the juxtaposition of buildings in Piranesi's fantastic reconstruction of ancient Rome in his Campo Marzio. **FIGS.20,21** This could have been behind Kahn's thinking, since only a few years earlier he had sketched his Penn Center urban design scheme for Philadelphia over the plan of the Campo Marzio, which was then in his office. Little did anyone know, at that City Council meeting in March 1960, to what extent the master plan would be radically revised over the next few months. Kahn's placement of the scientists' residences south of the ravine would be developed further, and the rectangular terraced layout of the Meeting House would be displaced to the laboratory site, becoming the double garden quadrapartite enfilade of laboratories that was to preoccupy him. New, more centralized schemes would be worked on for the Meeting House.

FIG.20

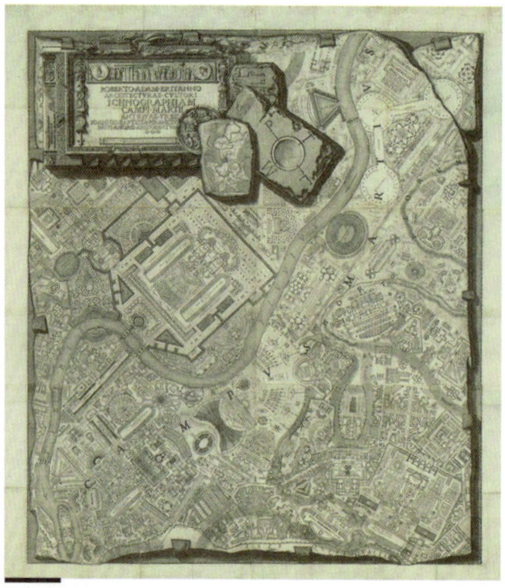

FIG.21

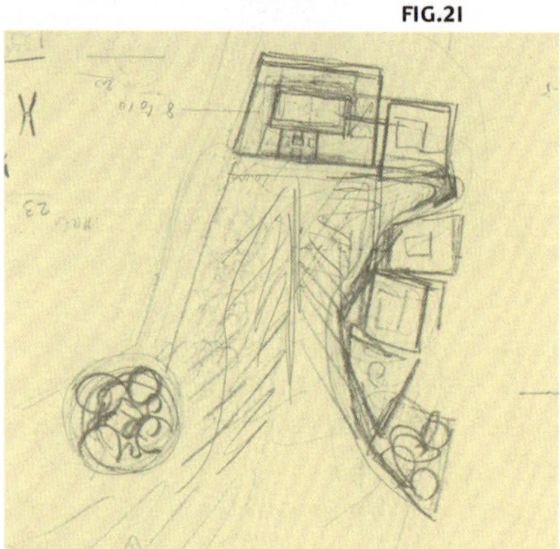

FIG.22

EARLY SITE PLANNING SCHEMES

With drawing 540.11 one begins to understand the final laboratories, as built, as an architecture of incorporation where exterior elements dispersed over an entire site are gathered within the building's limits.[19] **FIG.22** It suggests an entirely new way of understanding aspects of the Laboratories as built and of key elements of the unbuilt Meeting House. The Laboratory building is now conceived as a courtyard with a laterally attached structure also possessing a courtyard. Multiple courtyard structures continue along the south ravine from east to west. It is not clear from this sketch what the secondary courtyard structures are, programmatically. Did Kahn begin to consider the Laboratory organized as a double courtyard plan? And, regarding the three other courtyard structures wedged into the south contour: are those to be considered living quarters for the scientists or multiple extensions of the Laboratories? Kahn's spacing of architecture, evident in the multiple voids separating the scientists' studies from the Laboratory wings proper

FIG.20 | **Master plan site model presented to the San Diego City Council**
FIG.21 | **Plate–G Piranesi's Campo Marzio (1762)**
FIG.22 | **Salk site plan drawing 540.11**

and the multiple voids between the service blocks at the north and south flanks of the building, defines 'garden' courts at the basement level.[20] **FIG.22** These repetitive courts contract Kahn's site courtyard typology. This is the relationship of the distant to the near, or the contraction of space and time. The west office façades of the Salk Institute, as built, climax this process by incorporating the 'emergent' scientists' studies.

The Meeting House now appeared as a bubble diagram with the centralizing character that was to be retained throughout the design development process. The final scheme for the Meeting House was developed around multiple courtyards or framed spaces, from the ambulatory arcade defining the terminus of the stream, to the director's house, to the introduction of a double-height space solving the served/servant relationships in the library, to the void as multiple-use space at the heart of the complex. Again, there is an almost unconscious repetitive influence or obsession through Kahn's drawing 540.11 with its repetitive courtyards on the outcome of the Meeting House plan.[21] But perhaps the most important aspect of this drawing is the center of the shallow ravine, where Kahn draws two parallel lines suggesting a drainage channel which begins to orient the laboratory courtyard to the sea beyond. The water channel would make its first appearance in the Meeting House scheme, before becoming incorporated in the final Laboratory building. However, what is astonishing is how Kahn uses sketch 540.11, which defines the entire building, and displaces and condenses it into the cistern and stream as built at the center of the Laboratory building. **FIG.23**

FIG.23

FIG.23 | Cistern feeding water course at the courtyard

DESIGN DEVELOPMENT OF THE MEETING HOUSE

When Salk asked me to do the laboratories in San Diego, he said that he wanted a hundred thousand square feet of space to give to ten scientists who wanted each ten thousand square feet of space. Then he said, *I would like to add one more requirement. I would like to be able to invite Picasso to the laboratories*. That really electrified me. I proposed to him at the next meeting a laboratory of a hundred thousand square feet, but a meeting place which amounted to almost a hundred thousand square feet in addition. These were laid out in a manner which would suit the unmeasurable qualities—and the laboratories were dedicated entirely to measurable qualities. The contrast was between law, which is unchangeable, and rule, the law of the artist, which is changeable. And he bought it. To this day it's on the agenda as something that must be done.

Louis I Kahn[22]

The plan is a society of rooms.

Louis I Kahn[23]

The unbuilt Meeting House at the Salk Institute was probably the most highly differentiated building Kahn had worked on in his career. The final scheme integrated various aspects of his work of the previous ten years, adapted to the humanist program at the heart of this project. This program emerged as Kahn's composition evolved. Unfortunately, the schematic design drawings, as collected at the Kahn Archive, are not dated and the catalog numbers assigned to them are not necessarily in chronological order.[24] Therefore the sequence of drawings is marked by discontinuities and reversals not necessarily of Kahn's making. For example, drawing 540.137 is ordered later than 540.127 but perhaps it should be considered earlier chronologically. **FIGS.16,18** Kahn discarded the tripartite scheme of 540.137 with its cross-axial oblong orientation in favor of the obliquely oriented square organization of the Meeting House of 540.127, adjusting the latter to the fan-like boundaries which characterize the site. The assembly hall in the latter scheme is located at the western side of the Meeting House, terminating a circulation axis at the neck of the fan which would have continued to the Laboratory site. Only the swimming pool directly adjacent to this structure can be identified. The other programmatic elements of the Meeting House remain undesignated. In hindsight one begins to understand that the staircases flanking the cascading pool off the end of the Laboratory courtyard as built may have been indebted to the placement of the terminating auditorium in drawing 540.127.

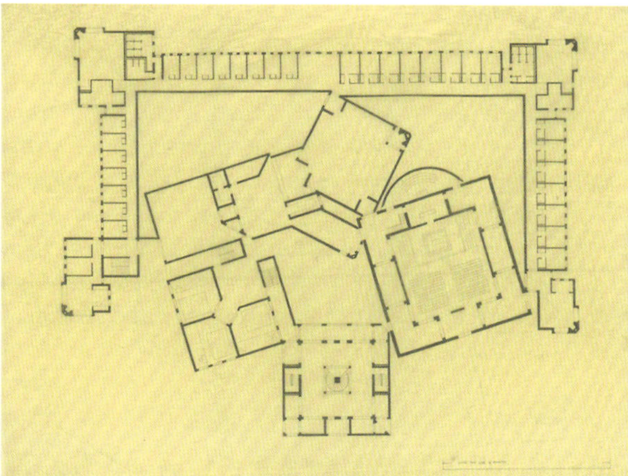

FIG.24

Vincent Scully, the author of the first book on the work of Louis I Kahn, later analyzed Frank Lloyd Wright's work in an essay comparing Wright's work to Freud's conception of the dream work.[25] Scully may have thought that these same concepts of condensation and displacement could have been used to explore Kahn's own 'dream work'. Drawing 540.127 is a displacement and enlargement of one of the framing pièces (the director's 'house') of drawing 540.137 which became the compositional frame for the entire Meeting House. This 'frame' is then reduced and the composition reversed to become the courtyard typology of drawing 540.132. **FIG.26** Programmatic elements are schematically shown exterior to the void rather than within the framed void. This 'withdrawal' and shift is most forcefully indicated in the solid/void relationship of the pochéd square to the courtyard void. The disarticulation of this element marks the repositioning of the auditorium to the neck of the fan, which is the entry area off the long axis from the laboratories. The dramatic terminus of the sea view is sacrificed by positioning the assembly hall as a public gathering place between the Meeting House and the Laboratories. For all intents and purposes drawing 540.132 is the scheme that Kahn adopted for his final version of the Meeting House. Several years later Kahn would reutilize the encompassing frame of drawing

FIG.24 | **First-floor plan of the Dominican Sisters' Convent (1965–1968)**

540.127 in fragmented form in his final scheme for the also unbuilt Dominican Motherhouse project.[26] **FIGS.18,24**

The concealment of the typological nature of Kahn's work at the Salk Meeting House is due to its exasperated development of form and the multiple crossover relationships that he had developed between all of his projects. Concealment was already evident in his completed project for the Unitarian Church, where the Roman or Carcassonne-inspired 'thick' enveloping walls are expressed as deep-shadowed compressed voids concealing the two floors of the ancillary spaces serving the congregation area. The quadrapartite light hoods that define the congregation ceiling were displaced from the more prominent corner positions, as indicated in the earlier model of the Unitarian Church. **FIG. 28** The power of the early model inspired Kahn's final decision to organize the laboratory as a quadrapartite formation where key mechanical spaces and the administrative offices occupied corners of the building.[27] For the Salk Meeting House final scheme the programmatic elements and the peripheral nature of the building/site dissolve or fragment this quadrapartite typology. The four 'corners' of the Meeting House are defined by the skewed assembly hall, the split between the ambulatory arcade and the director's house, the dining halls with kitchen wing and the exercise space. **FIG.29** The differentiation of the architecture was the outcome of the specialization of labor applied to the slowly evolving nature of the program. The pièces were worked on individually and then tested against other pièces in a continual process of assembly and reassembly.

The assembly hall of the Salk Meeting House could be viewed as a version of the original ambulatory/congregation area at the Unitarian Church, split in half and thrown out of its quadrapartite formation. The skewed nature of the assembly hall disposition enhances this notion of instability or 'thrownness'.[28] In an earlier version of the assembly hall at Salk, Kahn presented an 'eye'-like organization of the seating within a square plan disposition of walls. **FIG.27** This scheme is clearly indebted to Ledoux's Theater at Besançon (1775). **FIG.25**

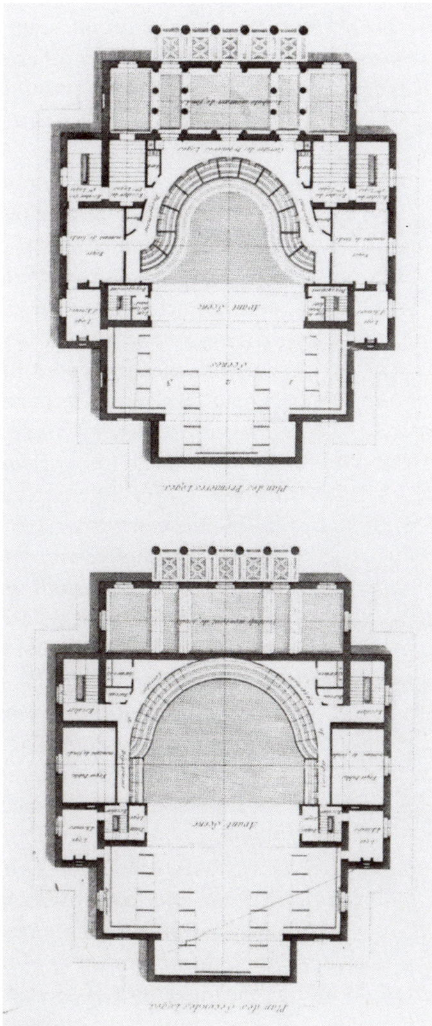

FIG.25

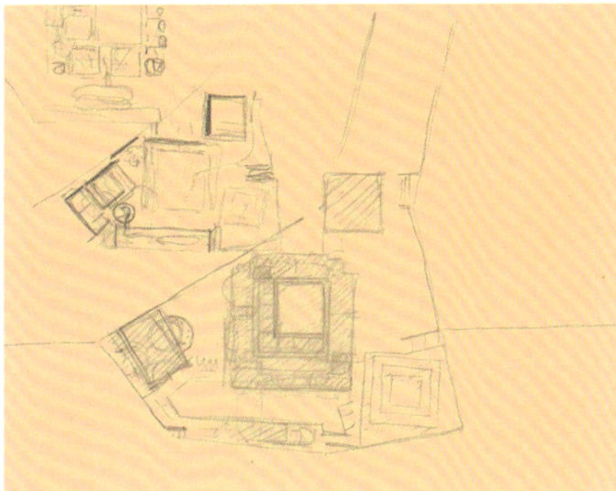

FIG.26

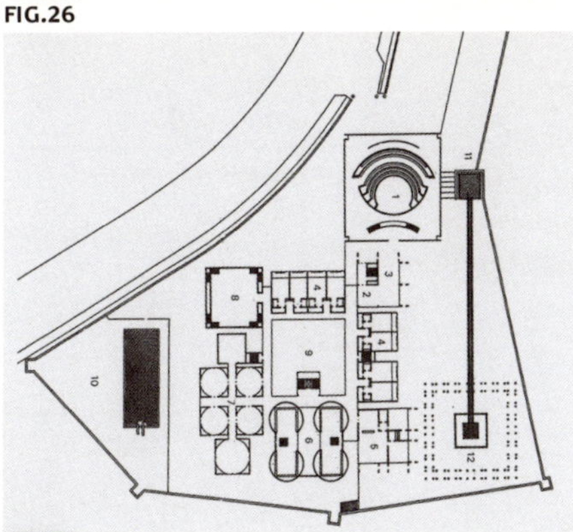

FIG.27

FIG.25 | Plans from CN Ledoux's Theater at Besançon (1784)
FIG.26 | Final Meeting House plan 540.132
FIG.27 | Meeting House intermediate phase plan

The concept of 'circular form' within its frame would have been consistent with the assemblage of dining halls diagonally opposite. Instead Kahn developed the assembly hall as a large hemicycle amphitheater of classical inspiration under a radially organized roof structure. The semi-cylindrical bounding wall of this assembly hall allowed the approach to the complex to be split between service and pedestrian access. The radially organized structure gestures towards the more public side of the overall site by emerging like an unfolding fan out of the lobby volume it is attached to. The indented nature of the assembly hall back wall defines the projected stage area, but also expresses the insertion or attachment of it to the entrance lobby. The assembly hall would have functioned both for professional meetings of Salk's "academy" and as a public space of invitation. The assembly hall, the south wing of the Meeting House proper with its apartments for visiting scientists and humanists, the director's house, the arcaded ambulatory and the linear flow of the stream would have defined the entrance area to the Meeting House as a topos—a place responding to the southern California environment opened to the view of the Visiting Fellows Residences across the ravine with partial views of the laboratory building and the sea. **FIGS.30, 32**

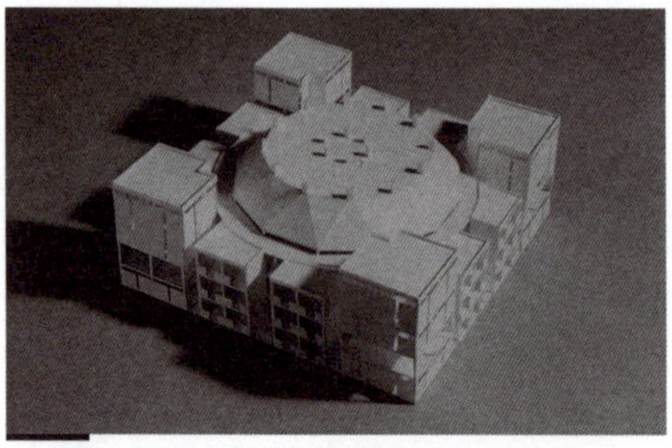

FIG.28

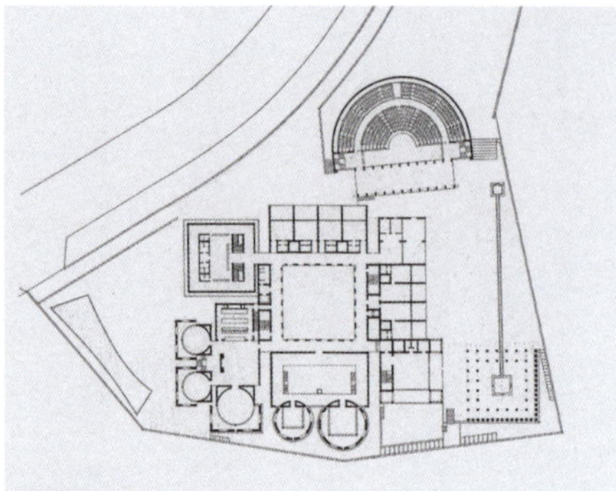

FIG.29

FIG.30

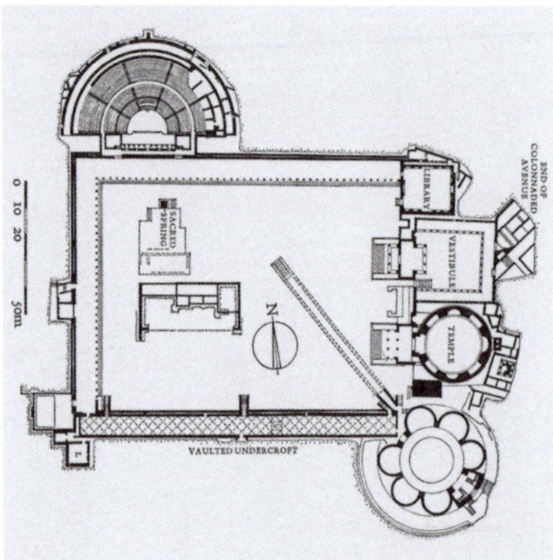

FIG.31

The three-story director's house, of which two floors only are visible from the entry plaza, occupies a strategic corner of the Meeting House site. The protruding south east corner would have allowed surveillance over the plaza. **FIG.30** The uppermost level containing the bedrooms is bounded by a *chemin de ronde* (walk path) defined by crenellation blocks between corner 'towers'. The massive teeth-like nature of these blocks is reminiscent of the bollard blocks that lined the entry area to the Richards Medical Research Center, and in a more massive treatment became the defining walls of the FDR Four Freedoms Memorial, completed in 2012, 38 years after Kahn's death. But perhaps these crenellations less resemble medieval battlements than immense classical dentils.[29]

FIG.28 | Unitarian Church first scheme model photo (1959)
FIG.29 | Meeting House final plan
FIG.30 | Meeting House main entrance model photo
FIG.31 | Aesclapius Sanctuary (2nd cent. BC)

OPPOSITE
FIG.32 | Kahn rendering showing Laboratory viewed from Residences

What is the plan of the director's house but a remnant of drawings 540.127 and 540.137? It is juxtaposed between two other square spaces with ambulatories: the interior courtyard and the exterior arcade. All of these spaces are defined by an A-B-A grid. This A-B-A pattern is also a basic musical form. Kahn's montage of elements is the breakdown of his more formal use of the A-B-A grid in his seminal Trenton Jewish Community Center and in the only building built from that complex, the Bath House.[30] This pattern was introduced by Kahn in an earlier Meeting House scheme, as indicated in drawings 540.142 and 540.143. Here the Meeting House is organized by an A-B-A grid with its broad face to the sea view. In the final Meeting House composition the east and west corridors of the ambulatory around the central court extend to the north with connections to the exercise building and the kitchen/dining wing, suggesting the fragment of a larger gridded movement system. The corridor to the exercise space repeats the organization of the stream flowing from a cistern at the plaza entry stairs to the arcade around the terminating pool. In other words, it is the incorporation of an element outside the frame of the architectural ensemble.

FIG.33

Kahn's "building wrapped in ruins" was the description applied to the most prominent part of the Meeting House: the cylindrical sunscreen walls enveloping the seminar volumes which are the served elements to the library proper which was to house 50,000 books. **FIG.33** This expression was originally applied by Kahn in reference to his own US Consulate project for Luanda, Angola. Kahn's analytical sketch shows how he arrived at these walls as anti-glare filters for the seminar reading areas. The contrast of these elements with their reversal in the dining hall areas, which are defined by cylindrical walls within framing rectangular walls, originate from ancient Roman antecedents—whether it be the pavilions at Hadrian's Villa, the market pavilion of ancient Leptis Magna (in Libya) or the dialectics of the circle/square theme at the floor of the Pantheon.

The seminar spaces of Kahn's Meeting House, each a stack of three floors, were originally not organized on squares but on rectangles with their long axes oriented to the sea. In two schematic designs, done prior to Kahn's final design for the library, different juxtapositions of square-to-circular organized spaces are offered. **FIGS.34A,B** In the first design the overall library is entirely defined by a single square layout embedded within a quadrapartite formation of cylinders which in turn suggest spaces formed by cellular division. Square layouts of shelving appear within each cylinder. But what constitutes the reading area seems to be merely the residual space left over from this ordering. In the second of these penultimate schemes Kahn sensed this lack of definition. He tested this layout against his served and

FIG.33 | **Kahn rendering–Meeting House library (1961)**

servant idea of architecture and introduced an asymmetry by having one larger cylinder for book shelving, only served by three smaller cylinders which encompassed square reading areas. This asymmetry is preserved in the final design, which has now been reduced to two cylinders attached to book stacks organized around a double-height space. **FIG.34C** One formal/programmatic decision suggests another formal/programmatic decision, as Kahn finally arrived at the clear expression of his served and servant concept of architecture. The assemblage of served library volume, with the servant seminar spaces encircled by sunscreen walls, is a variation of the 'blind' service core of the Richards Research Building, **FIGS.69,70** with its garden facing quadruple brick intake/exhaust shafts. The plans of the Salk library seminar volumes not only reproduce the sense of the shafts at Richards but they collapse the plans, as we shall see, of the study structures at the Salk Laboratory building. The 'perforated' cylindrical screening walls not only modulate the sun's effect on these spaces, but they 'protect' these volumes from the exposure of the 'infinite' space beyond. Bracketed, ringed or embraced, these forms are honorifically framed by Kahn. They are citations similar to how he cited and enlarged the geometry of the tetrahedral ceiling system in the triangular roof structure of the cylindrically enclosed stair at his earlier Yale University Art Gallery. And in the differing size of the cylindrical screening walls we have that 'oscillation' of forms that will be found at the courtyard of the Salk Laboratory building. This perceived oscillation is the result of a planning principle used by Kahn in his constant rescaling of events in his work, and is the trace of that oscillation between the "measurable and the immeasurable", as he had often stated.

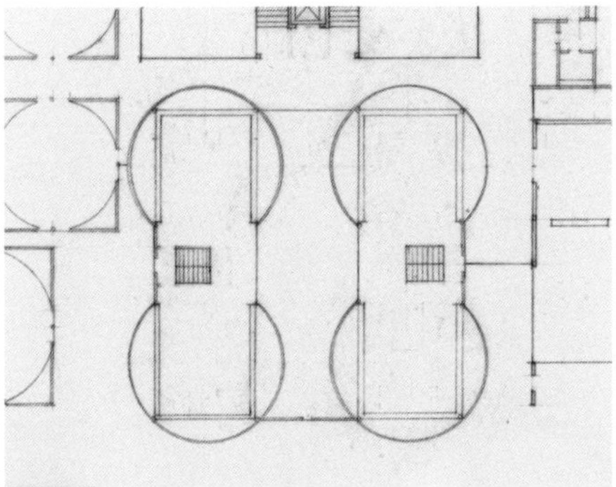

FIG.34A

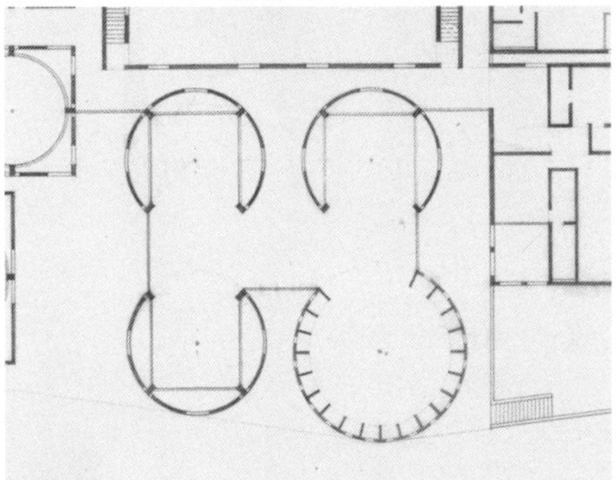

FIG. 34B

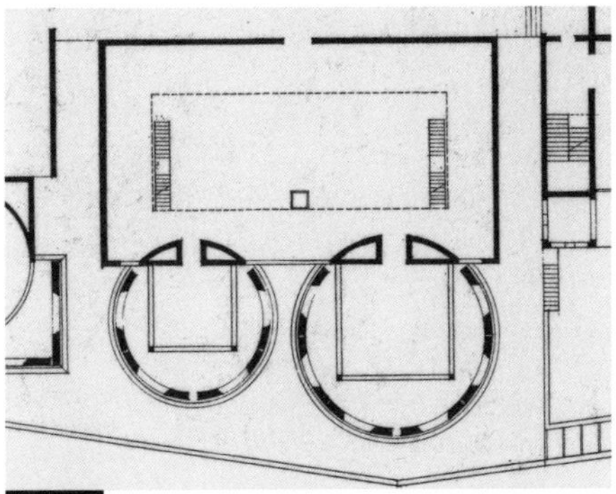

FIG. 34C

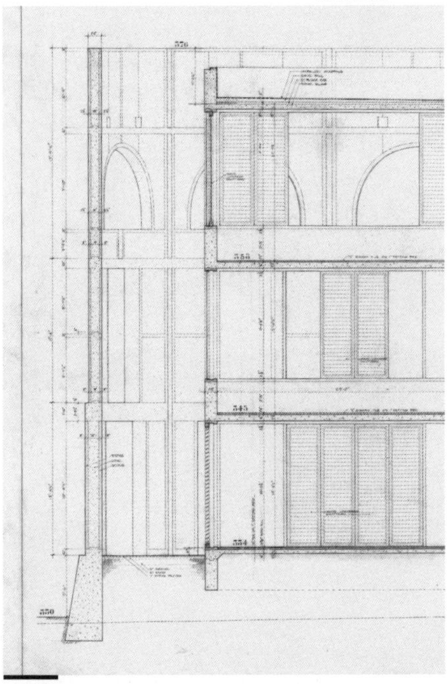

FIG.35

FIG.34 | Detail–Meeting House library plan first (A), intermediate (B) and final (C) schemes
FIG.35 | Meeting House section library seminar volume

The double cylindrical screening walls are mediators between the seminar rooms, the sun and the panoramic views of the ocean. **FIG.35** The movements of the sun would have been captured and diffused by the inside surface of the cylinders and would have animated the environment of the seminar rooms. Further control of the natural lighting was offered by the sliding floor-to-ceiling shutters facing all sides of the seminar volumes. Episodic views of the ocean, from within the seminar rooms, are offered through various cut-out openings in the segmented cylindrical walls. The segments are in rotational symmetrical relationship. They are an iterative series–the return of the more opaque piers of the laboratory courtyard. The

ancient Roman-inspired arches, in their eye-like repetition, scan the horizon. Are they not in their outlines the vertical translation and rescaling of the assembly hall plan at the Meeting House? Didn't Kahn translate to the Salk site a more personal memory, not only from the upper levels of his own Fleisher House proposal (1959) but from the series of arched windows defining the apse end of Furness's Fine Arts Library at the University of Pennsylvania—the same building in which he ran his Master's studio? **FIG.36** This is the same space, along with structures from Piranesi's Campo Marzio, that could also have provided the solution to supporting the assembly hall roof with its radial disposition of structural beams. Kahn moves us from the interior theater of memory to the theater or spectacle of nature. The "building wrapped in ruins" is the ruin and mask of history. The radial assembly hall is a 'radiant' structure.

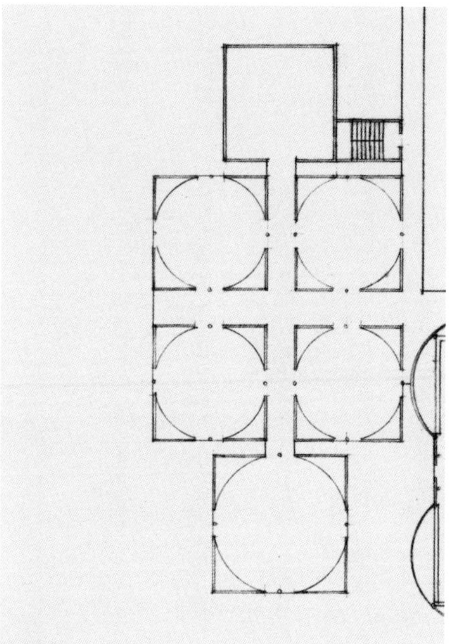

FIG.37A

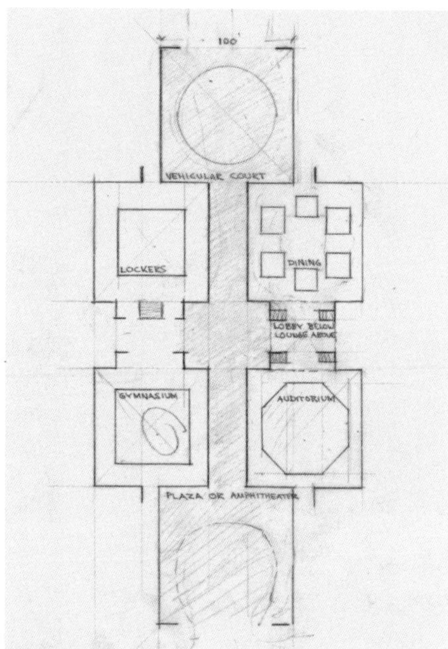

FIG.37B

The Salk Meeting House is a demonstration of the several ways to develop an architecture of connection. The assembly hall is an 'unhinging'. This contrasts with the 'hinged' formation of the monumental inflected piers defining the Salk Laboratory plaza. The south enfilade of elements at the Meeting House: the entrance hall, the scientists' apartments and the director's house forming one wing—all are elements which are adjacencies to the center courtyard. The double cylinders of the library just barely intrude on the rectangular volume of the library proper. The rectangular seminar rooms can be read as folds within the cylinders with an axial orientation outward toward the sea complemented and conjoined with the cylindrical enclosures. They are joined to the main body of the library by short-narrow, neck corridors. It is in these 'craft' decisions that Kahn worked out an architecture that went beyond its schematic origins. This is certainly the case when he went on to consider the organization of the kitchen/dining hall wing.

In two late schematic design development drawings for the Meeting House, Kahn developed a quadrapartite formation of dining halls, of round within square forms, separated by a 'Greek' cross corridor intersection. **FIG.37A** Four round dining halls each would have provided an intimate setting for eating

PREVIOUS PAGE
FIG.36 | Fisher Fine Arts Library main reading room. UPenn, Philadelphia—F Furness (1890)
FIG.37A | Detail of Meeting House kit/dining wing first scheme
FIG.37B | Detail early plan for the entire Meeting House

and conversing. The upper two levels of the dining halls were to be for table service. The garden level areas were to be a self-service cafeteria.[31] The round rooms would also have evoked a more ancient communal idea of eating. To this formation Kahn appended to the east the kitchen and to the west a larger dining hall with more direct views of the sea. Programmatic considerations also allowed this hall to be used as additional seminar space. There is another drawing in the Kahn archive which indicates that Kahn had once conceived of this assemblage of kitchen/dining spaces as the total parti for the Meeting House. **FIG.37B** It was retained in the dining hall/kitchen wing as memory trace, again demonstrating Kahn's freedom in scaling events. The leap to the final plan for the dining hall/kitchen wing shows Kahn's power of invention which yields a more palpably 'real' architecture, clarifies his notion of an architecture of served and servant spaces and reinforces the notion of architecture as compositional assemblage. **FIG.37D** Kahn broke the enclosing rectilinear walls encumbering the round dining areas. He eliminated the Greek cross corridor in favor of a common connecting space and he reduced the number of dining areas from five to three. The kitchen was enlarged. This entire 'assemblage' was then attached to the rest of the Meeting House complex by aligning the south side of this 'wing' through an extension of the wall to the north wall of the bathroom/stair volumes which in turn plugged the whole assemblage to the side of the courtyard corridor. This is a shear relationship of elements and a variation of his own planning for parts of the Fleisher House (1959). Because of the rotational nature of the northernmost dining halls Kahn was able to position entrances to these spaces off the corners of the common areas. Access is not dead center on these spaces.

The Salk Institute Meeting House presents Louis I Kahn's dialectic of the inside and outside in the positioning of the cylindrical elements: the dining halls within the broken screening walls and the "building wrapped in ruins". Of ancient Roman inspiration one thinks of the celli of certain Roman temples within

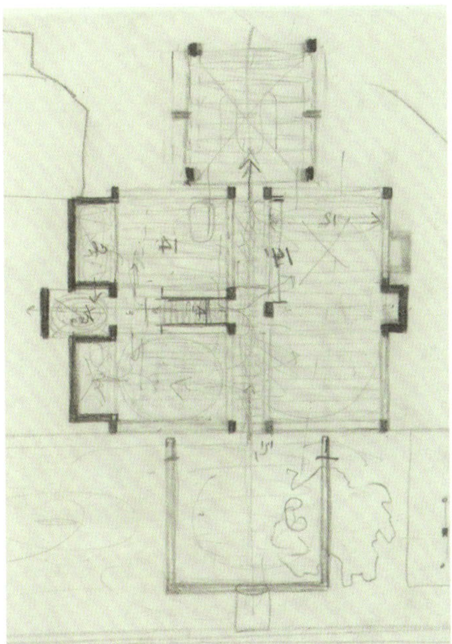

FIG.37C

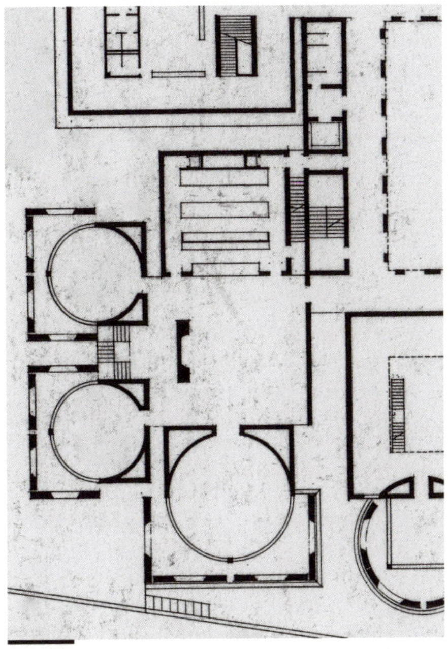

FIG.37D

FIG.37C | Early plan of Esherick House (1959)
FIG.37D | Detail–Meeting House kit/dining wing final plan

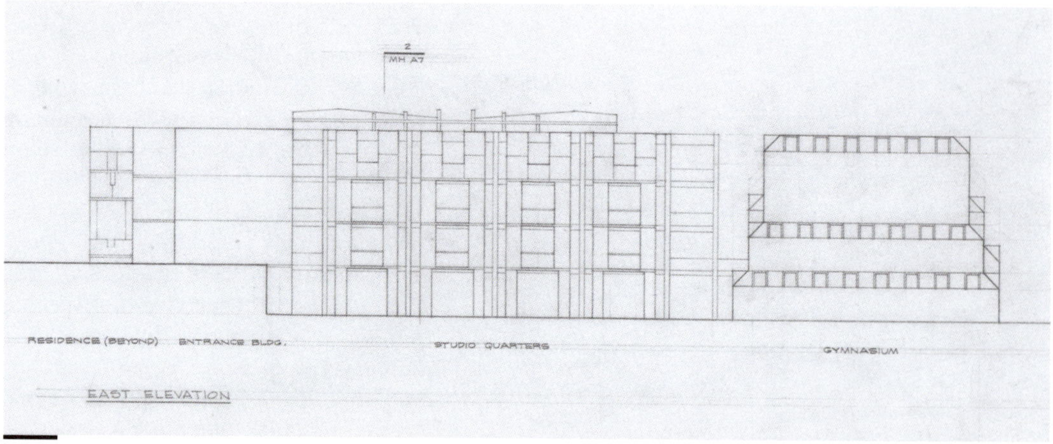

FIG.38

FIG.40

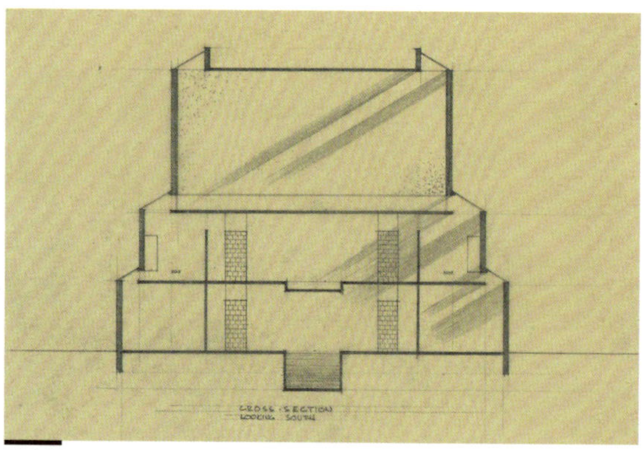

FIG.41

FIG.39

FIG.38 | Meeting House west elevation final scheme
FIG.39 | Kahn drawing–stepped pyramid Saqqara, Egypt (1951)
FIG.40 | Kahn sketch–Washington University Library competition (1956)
FIG.41 | Section–Meeting House exercise space

their cylindrical colonnades, or the floor of the Pantheon with its marble inlaid pattern of circles within squares and squares within circles. Kahn transformed this pattern in the base of his City Tower project for Philadelphia (1952-1957) where cylinders defining access, light and ventilation wells to subterranean parking are set within square cutouts. At the Salk Institute Meeting House this dialectic becomes a commentary on the institutional meaning of the place as the relationship of the inner to the outer circles which was precisely the dilemma of the 'Two Cultures'.

In his musings on 'silence and light', Louis I Kahn was a metaphysician. He reinvoked Le Corbusier's definition of architecture as "the masterly, correct and magnificent play of masses brought together in light". The play of light is the play of light, shade and shadow. The deep voids of Kahn's works express the tactile (one might say almost erotic) nature of his architecture; the library double cylinders when viewed obliquely touch–they rotationally rub against each other. **FIG.38** When viewed more frontally, perhaps from the imaginary vantage point of the sea, they seek tangency but remain apart with the curving walls disappearing into the shadows. This relationship of physicality to light is intensified in the design for the exercise building. Kahn adapted a stepped pyramid form for this area from his competition project for the Washington University Library (1956). **FIGS.40,41** The lower levels of locker rooms and service areas support the upper level of the exercise space proper, which appears extruded up from these lower levels. There is very little evidence of an extended design development process for this area. There is a conflict, however, between the section and elevation drawings done by Kahn's office for this structure. The section shows continuous sloped skylights at the ceiling level of each 'step'. Yet the elevation drawing and the Matt Wargo photo of the wood model at the Penn Archive show the continuous skylights interrupted by notched forms, relating this exercise building to the crenellations of the director's house. **FIG.38** This mis-coordination would have been resolved if Kahn's office had continued to work on the Meeting House project. The fully concentric form of the exercise building offered the only space at the Salk Meeting House with 360-degree light penetration which included an orientation to the morning sun. Kahn displaced a library program from a stepped pyramid form to accommodate the exercise building. Activities promoting human health, the mission of the Salk Institute, would have been accommodated in a powerful form whose origins monumentalize death as a place of ascension.[32] **FIG.39** The stepped pyramid evoked the Babel problem at the heart of the Salk Meeting House, which was to be the place of communication between scientists, non-scientist humanists and the public.

The stepped profile of the exercise building reappears immediately adjacent in the fenestration of the block of twelve fellows' studios distributed over three floors, the fenestration frames projecting balconies at each level. The visitors' suites facing south at the entry plaza were to be triplex apartments with three bedrooms each. The balconies there were to be defined as top-lit cutout shaft enclosures presaging the design of the library "wrapped in ruins". These shafts are displacements of the buried lightwell/mechanical access shafts flanking the entry area to the laboratories as built, which in turn were transpositions of the vertical brick "servant" shafts from the Richards Research Building.

Jonas Salk had visited the Convent of St. Francis in Assisi in September of 1954 after he had left a medical conference in Rome and was on his way to Florence.[33] **FIG.42** The architectural experience left an indelible mark on Salk.[34] Louis I Kahn had sketched the convent during his visit in 1929. **FIG.43** A number of other 'typological' precedents could be adduced for the Meeting House, from Hadrian's Villa (second century AD) to the Monastery of St Gall (tenth to eleventh century AD). However, there is one precedent that must be mentioned without any proof of Kahn's 'intentions': the Hellenistic Sanctuary of Asclepius (second century BC). Asclepius was the ancient Greek god of medicine, one of whose daughters was Hygieia. **FIG.31** The comparison of the sanctuary plan—with its enclosing stoa, theater, spring and library—to the final Salk Institute Meeting House plan is striking. Vincent Scully described this sanctuary in his *The Earth, the Temple and the Gods*, published the year Louis I Kahn's office was finalizing the construction documents for the laboratory building:

FIG.42

> The site is absolutely quiet; it is a place intended to eliminate distractions, scenes and upsets. There is no sound but the gentle murmur of the healing water which flows through it. The theater, the colonnade, the round temple on the slight rise, and the splendid Roman fountain house below it are all contained in the arms of an earth which seems here, if one may use the only word that applies, understand-

FIG.42 | Courtyard at the Convent of St. Francis of Assisi, Italy

OPPOSITE
FIG.43 | Kahn drawing—Convent of St. Francis of Assisi, Italy (1929)

ing. The patient is brought in touch with it, and from the vaulted fountain house, partly underground, he may walk up through a cryptoporticus down the center of which runs the water of the sacred spring. Emerging from the cavern he is at the spring itself and before the theater, with the bulk of the temple above him to his right. Though now a new architectural vocabulary, both Greek and Roman, has created and arranged the forms of the buildings, the observer can still feel himself in touch with a tradition of harmony with the earth that goes back to Minoan times.[35]

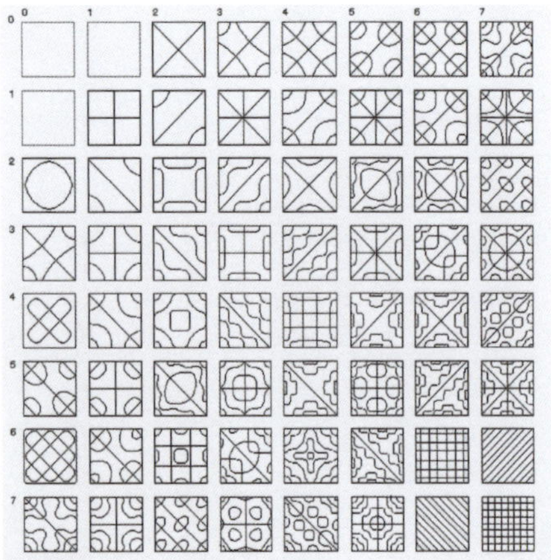

FIG.44

But all these 'sources' would already have been filtered through Kahn's own architectural activity in the immediate years before the Salk commission. Besides the Unitarian Church with its centralized congregation area, Kahn had worked on the Goldenberg House (canceled 1959) which was organized around a courtyard. **FIG.46** This space was conceived less as an inhabitable space than as a 'light' void that would have allowed the daily movements of the sun to animate the house interior. This light void and the total organization of the Goldenberg House with its outwardly sloping roofs is the inversion of the four-sided hip roof with oculus of any one of the pavilions at the unbuilt Trenton Jewish Community Center or the built Bath House. **FIG.45** The domestic program of the Goldenberg House is wedged into the diagonals and the exterior walls are folded, varying the purely orthogonal geometry of the Trenton 'cells'. Kahn had conceived of the Salk Meeting House courtyard as a space of occasional inhabitation or perambulation open to the Mediterranean climate of La Jolla. The early models of the Meeting House show the courtyard open at the roof line. Client demands, however, modified the space to become multifunctional, requiring that the courtyard be protected from direct sunlight. A schematic solution is indicated in the model at the Architectural Archive at the University of Pennsylvania for covering over this space. Kahn devised a translucent roof supported by a Chladni-inspired ordering of structure just before this part of the Salk project was canceled.[36] **FIGS.44,47**

FIG.45

FIG.46

FIG.47

In our imaginary circumambulation of the Meeting House site we return to the entrance plaza—to the 'beginning'. Kahn's arcaded ambulatory evoked his own beginnings as an architect. The inner double layers of the ambulatory were to be constructed from 'simple' concrete beams spanning over widely spaced concrete columns. The stream of water flowing toward the Pacific Ocean was to be a vector caught by the pool

FIG.44 | **Chladni patterns**
FIG.45 | **Model—Goldenberg House (1959)**
FIG.46 | **Kahn rendering—Trenton Jewish Community Center (1954-1959)**
FIG.47 | **Model photo—final Meeting House scheme**

at the center of these double arcades open to the sky. Two sides of the arcade are a phalanx of much thicker T-shaped concrete columns anchoring the entire Salk Meeting House to its site. This outer arcade evokes imagery from Kahn drawings from the earlier and later stages of his career. One thinks of the drawing Kahn did for the Sesquicentennial International Exhibition Building for John Molitor, the City Architect for Philadelphia in 1925. **FIG.48** Or a major work by one of Kahn's own Beaux-Arts teachers at the University of Pennsylvania: Paul Philippe Cret's American Battle Monument Memorial at Château-Thierry, France, completed in 1928. **FIG.49** This memorial was based on a thick wall of monumental pilasters. At the time of his tenure at the American Academy in Rome (1950-1951) Kahn had visited ancient sites in Greece and Egypt where he sketched ruined colonnades. More importantly the

FIG.48

FIG.49

double arcade creates an ambulatory around the center pool. It collapses the 'arcades', which are the passages below the scientists' studies that bracket the entire stream at the laboratory building, yet it is a radical expansion of the square shape of the 'cistern' repeated at the Meeting House entry sequence. But this 'oscillation' has a deeper significance. In adapting the architecture of his mentor and teacher, Paul Phillipe Cret, Kahn commemorated the memory of the Pacific War which had ended only 20 years earlier. As mentioned earlier, the site during World War II was a military training ground. Kahn does something similar at the Salk site in La Jolla, but in grander fashion than at Point Loma over 12 miles to the south, where there is a naval cemetery overlooking the Pacific Ocean. Is Kahn's work at the Meeting House pastiche?[37] No, this is an architectural eclecticism totally absorbed into Kahn's composition and translations of squares and half-squares.

FIG.48 | Sesquicentennial International Exhibition Building, Philadelphia, Kahn rendering (1925)
FIG.49 | American Battle Monument, Château-Thierry, France—Paul Philippe Cret (1928)

DESIGN DEVELOPMENT OF THE LABORATORIES

Perhaps the key lesson to be learned in the design development of the laboratories is that the early and intermediate schemes which are based on the double gardens are based on the discarded early schemes of the Meeting House with its broad side facing the Pacific Ocean.

Little correspondence survives—either at the Kahn Archive at Penn or the Jonas Salk Archive at UCSD La Jolla—between Kahn and Salk concerning design development issues. However, Peter Salk stated that his father was highly aware of all the changes that Kahn proposed.[38] Jonas Salk made two key architectural decisions that moved the project forward. Firstly, of course, he hired Kahn, but secondly, he reduced the laboratory scheme from a two-garden to a one-garden scheme, thereby reducing the isolation of one set of laboratories from the other. Salk felt that this isolation would have also bred an unwanted competitiveness within the Institute. He was always aware of that quality of 'emergence' in Kahn's work. The idea or concept of 'emergence' was a development in the recent history of biology, just as the concept of life was.[39]

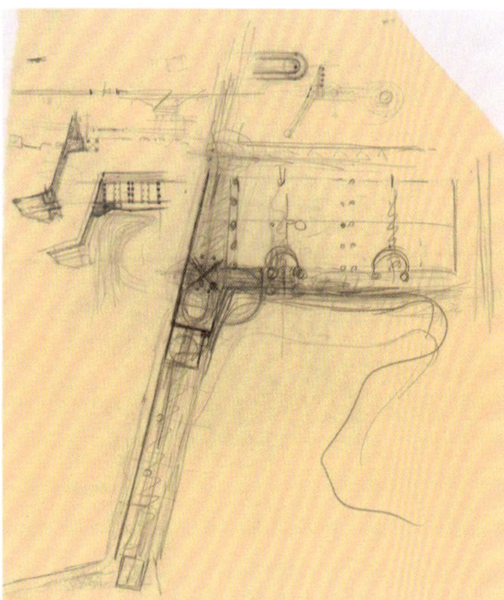

FIG.50

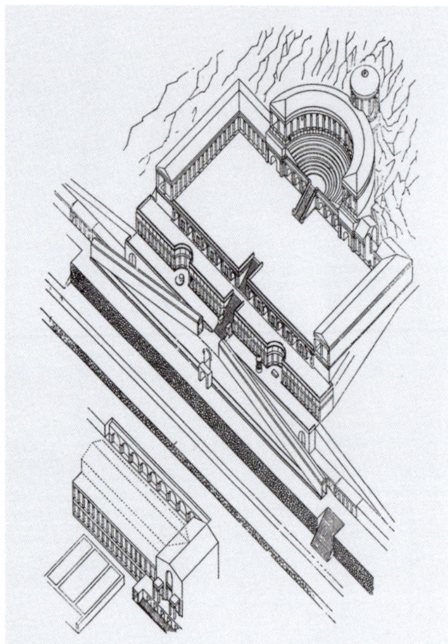

FIG.51

The double garden scheme for the Salk Institute laboratories is suggested in drawing 540.11, but only partially emerges even in drawing 540.13. **FIGS.22,50** Axes for the later gardens were established, leading to two classically inspired niches that open to the ocean view. As Kahn developed this scheme the niches were multiplied in a lower-level terrace building stretching from the north to the south edges of the laboratories where the ancient Roman sanctuary of Fortuna Primigenia (80 BC) was clearly referenced. **FIG.51** Occupying the terrace center was to be the main technical library flanked by administrative offices. Kahn filled the garden voids with his Hadrian-inspired scientist study structures, some of them connected at mid-garden by common conference areas.

FIG.50 | Early Laboratory building drawing 540.13
FIG.51 | Fortuna Primagenia Roman sanctuary (80 BC)

The overall 'parti', or schema, of the laboratories is a quadrapartite formation emerging from the shift from a common single-garden layout with double flanking labs. This reproduced the shift of the four vertical brick servant shafts at the rear of the Richards Research Center. **FIG.52** Views to the sea are restricted to the administrative wing and only the westernmost facing scientists' studies. Kahn's understanding that the full depth of the garden courtyard or plaza should be open to the sea views was only a gradual realization as he played with the various permutations of the scientists' study structures. The intermittent connections between the scientist studies are gradually broken, opening up the plaza as a landscaped garden, and the Hadrian-like configurations of the studies are replaced by a series of block/volumes. **FIG.54** Multiple studies were made for the scientists' studies. A stream feeding multiple pools is introduced at the center of both gardens, mainly for irrigation purposes.

FIG.52

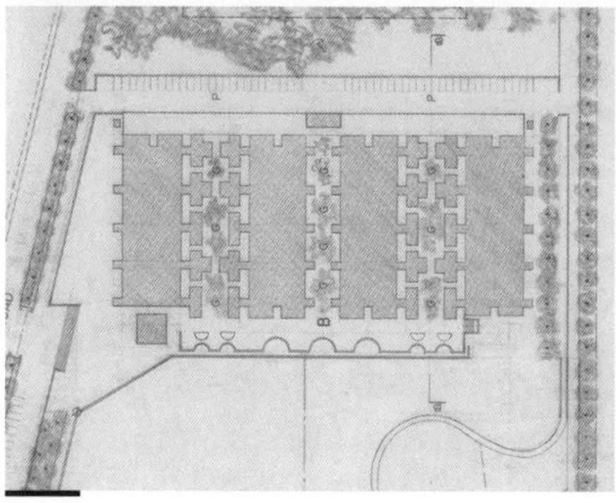

FIG.53

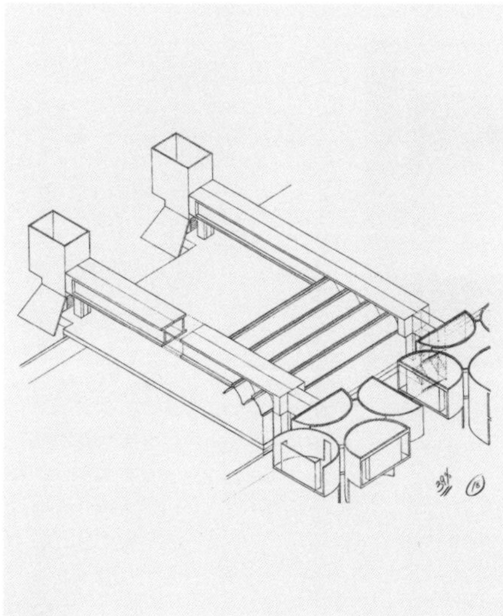

FIG.54

The double garden scheme was still a powerful expression of the laboratory as industrial workplace. The major functional advance of this project over all other biomedical research facilities was the creation of flexible 'open' laboratory spaces provided with required services from upper and lower interstitial spaces. Box beam structures spanned the north and south flanks of the laboratory building, linking the scientists' study structures and the giant exhaust hood structures. **FIG.53** Folded concrete plates were to span between the box girders, defining the parallel runs of services to supply the various liquids and gases required by the scientists as well as for exhaust requirements.

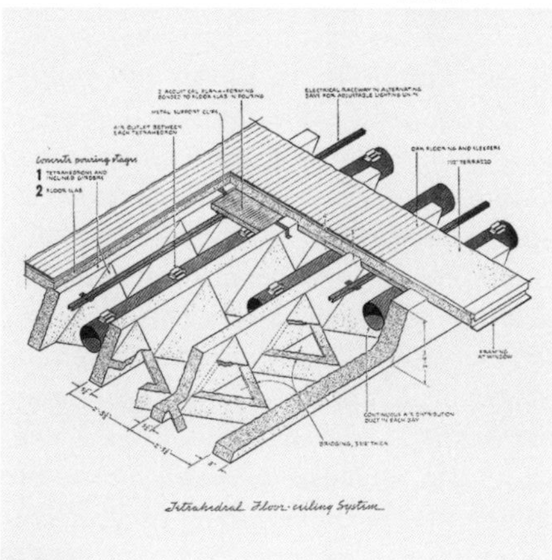

FIG.55

For the decade prior to the Salk commission, Kahn had been involved with structural investigations on other projects which led to his work at the Institute. As Thomas Leslie pointed out already at the Yale University Art Gallery, the clients George Howe (Dean of the School of Architecture) and Charles Sawyer (Director of the Division of Fine Arts) recommended that the gallery "adopt factory-like loft construction allowing flexibility".[40] Kahn's use of the complex cast-in-place tetrahedral concrete ceiling, which concealed required mechanical and electrical services, was adapted from experimental work done by his office colleague Ann Tyng who was inspired by the work of Buckminster Fuller.[41] **FIG.55**

FIG.52 | Rear view–Richards Research Building (1957–1964)
FIG.53 | Intermediate quadruple Laboratory plan
FIG.54 | Isometric section drawing–intermediate laboratory scheme
FIG.55 | Isometric section drawing–Yale University Art Gallery floor/ceiling

In his design for the Richards Research Building, Kahn—relying on the work of his engineer August Komendant—developed a very complex pre-cast post-tensioned structural system for the initial cluster of lab lofts whose openness allowed the needed servicing of the laboratories from overhead.[42] Richards is perhaps Kahn's most powerful expression of his served-and-servant concept of architecture. The glazed towers with their servicing are revelations of, and cluster about, the more hidden, more immense blind-walled core which houses the main mechanical equipment and the animal quarters where historian Vincent Scully said you could hear the shriek of animals.[43] The open loft arrangement of laboratories, 45 feet on each side, was stacked seven stories high with an additional basement level using the open structural frame of the loft above to allow subterranean light penetration. **FIG.56** We will not elaborate here on the various problems that were perceived to be the fault of the architect.[44] One problem at Richards that was effectively eliminated at the interstitial spaces for the Salk Institute was the possibility of dust gathering in a complex structural/services system over the scientists' laboratory spaces. Yet at Richards Kahn and Komendant offered a new architectural language based on a notion of 'spacing' that would become the ordering principle for the Salk Institute Laboratories. The use of glass at the initial towers for Richards is no longer based on the conception of framed window—be it individual frame, strip or gridded curtain wall. The laboratory loft glazing covers the gaps in a structure. Richards was the first laboratory building with inoperable 'windows'. The voided quality of the stacks of laboratory lofts is emphasized within repetitive low brick walls, and an anthropomorphic skeletal suspended structure supports the complex weave of servicing conduits. **FIG.57** But perhaps this notion of spacing had an origin that lay deep in Kahn's memory. We are thinking of the exploded views of gothic rib vaults that Viollet-le-Duc had done in the late nineteenth century. **FIG.58**

In one of the final developments of the quadruple-lab double-garden scheme for the Laboratories Kahn came to the realization of the garden or plaza as void. This is indicated in drawing 540.32 where Kahn proposed double-membrane defined spaces which ordered the

FIG.56

FIG.57

FIG.58

FIG.56 | Richards Laboratory corner ground level
FIG.57 | Richards laboratory tower model photo
FIG.58 | Viollet-le-Duc from his *Dictionary* (1854)

scientist studies along curves. **FIG.59** This suggested that Kahn considered these spaces as diaphragms or lungs. Kahn wanted to insert spaces into his 'rationally' ordered elements, spaces mimicking the act of breathing which can be found in the ancient concept of pneuma, which is spirit. This gesture paralleled his own statement that he "wanted to give to the wall a consciousness."[45] But perhaps just as remarkable is the origin of Kahn's double-diaphragm concept. Insofar as they occur in between the quadruple labs, they are inspired by the quadruple supply and exhaust shafts at the rear of the Richards Research Building, whose mechanical core is basically a "breathing machine".[46] Although these double diaphragms or lungs may have been too literal a statement of intentions the rhythmic nature of breathing is retained in Kahn's eventual solution to the scientists' studies at the Laboratories with their shifted inflected/deflected minor and major piers, which brought to the courtyard plaza the ebb and flow of the ocean beyond.

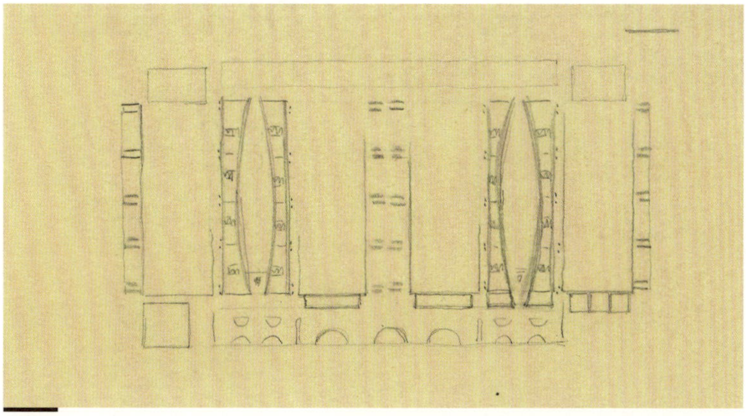

FIG.59

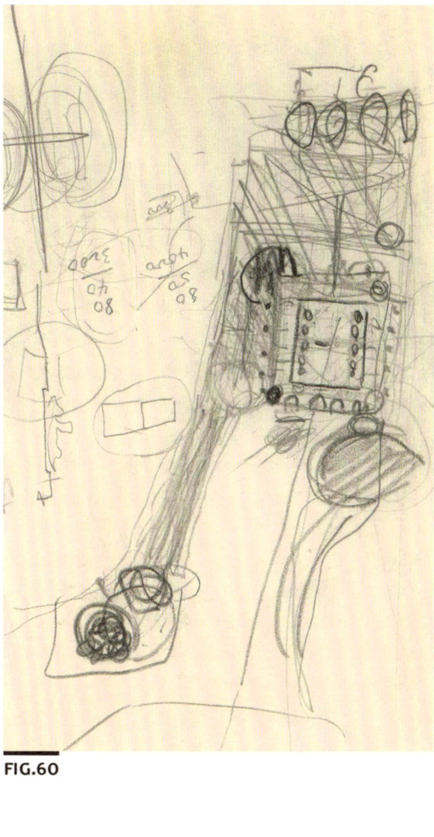

FIG.60

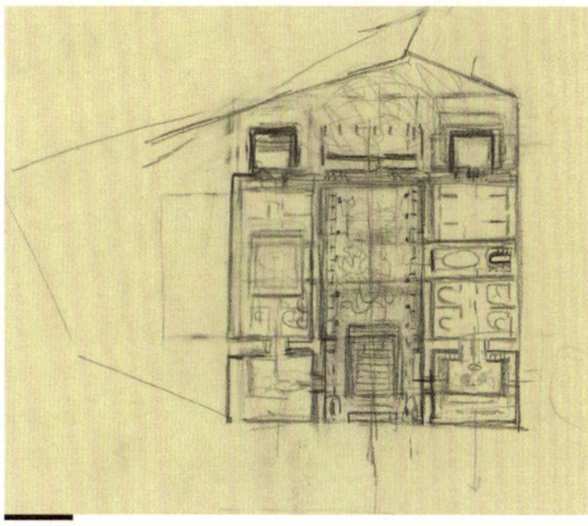

FIG.61

If the archive chronology is correct, drawing 540.11.2 indicates that Kahn had considered a single-courtyard scheme for the Laboratories before the double-garden scheme of 540.13 emerged. **FIG.61** Drawing 540.11.2 also indicates at this early stage the final parti of the Meeting House as two structural blobs connected back to the laboratory site by an arm-like axis. **FIG.60** Yet in drawing 540.166 for the Meeting House Kahn develops a triple enfilade of elements within a quadrapartite formation that is quite different from the eventual solution for the Meeting House. It is not clear if Kahn was trying to repeat the ordering of the Laboratory building on the Meeting House site or if he was trying to simplify the Meeting House design in itself, or if this sketch is meant to be considered earlier in the Meeting House design development. Whatever the case, 540.166 becomes the final parti for the Laboratories as built: a double flank of elements around a ceremonial axis within a quadrapartite formation highly reminiscent of the Durand's early nineteenth-century permutations and of Kahn's own discarded scheme for his Unitarian Church.

FIG.59 | **Salk Laboratory plan 540.32**
FIG.60 | **Salk site plan 540.11.2**
FIG.61 | **Salk Meeting House plan 540.166**

DISCARDING THE DOUBLE-GARDEN SCHEME AND THE BEGINNINGS OF CONSTRUCTION

Two radical changes were made to the Salk Institute Laboratory scheme. The double gardens were reduced to one centralized space, and the folded plate interstitial structure was replaced with a different system. Jonas Salk realized that four laboratories on two levels, organized around two gardens, would exaggerate the divide between groups of scientists and overly encourage competition at the expense of pure scientific research. Therefore, the scheme was changed to two laboratory areas ordered around a single garden/plaza.

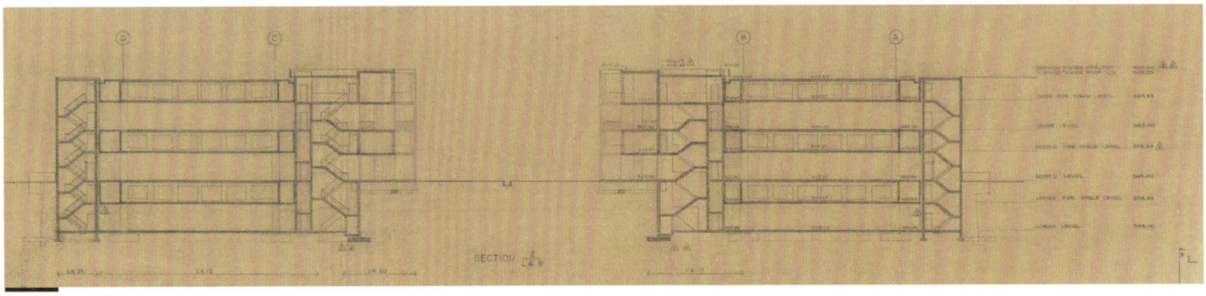

FIG.62

The loss of area resulted in three levels of laboratory spaces, with one level sunk into a basement to meet the height restrictions of the California Coastal Commission.[47] Salk and Kahn also realized that the folded plate interstitial spaces were too complex and not as accessible as needed for maintenance purposes. The interstitial structure would be changed to a 9-foot-deep Vierendeel truss arrangement.[48] Meanwhile, the perimeter mechanical spaces/exhaust hoods were displaced from the north and south flanks of the building to the east ends of the laboratories, where their forms would be modified considerably. Stanford Anderson presented an important critique of the outcome of the design development phase at the Salk Institute.[49] His critique focused on the changed nature of public access to the Laboratory building when the double-garden quadruple-lab scheme was discarded. **FIG.62** The Laboratory building as built placed the parking lot to the east of the building with an intervening garden through which one approached the courtyard/plaza on center without any formal reception. One is prohibited from entering this space by a wide marble bench, and one does not know whether to move left or right to access the labs proper.

FIG.62 | Salk Laboratory section as built

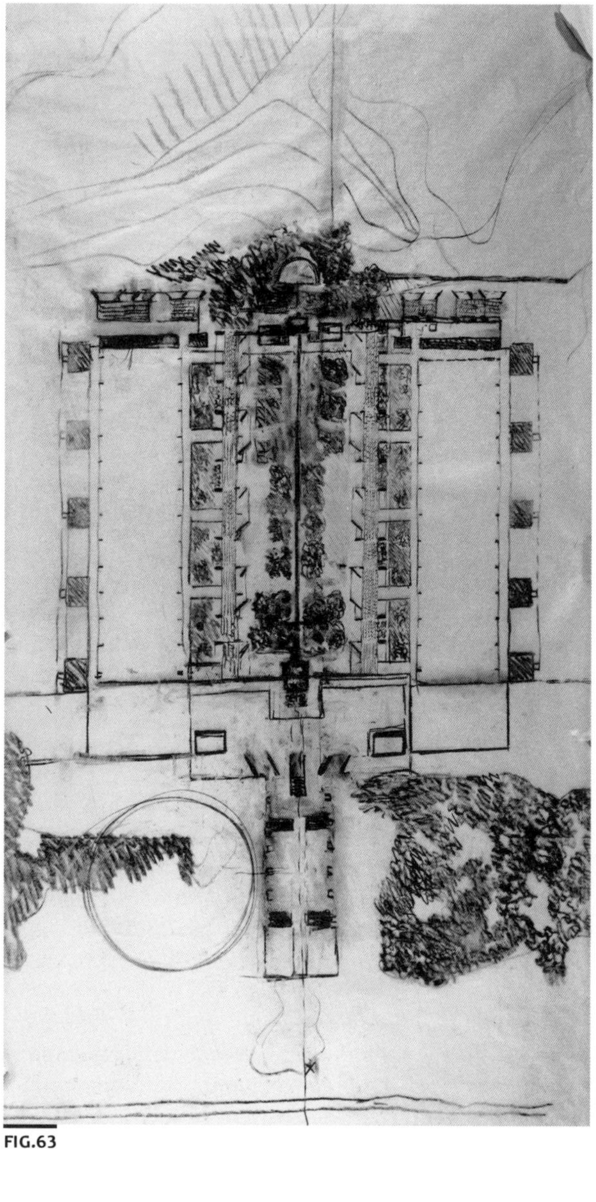

FIG.63

FIG.63 | Salk Laboratory final plan with unbuilt garden pavilion

In the earlier scheme there was no intervening garden but instead a low wing of animal quarters abutting the east end of the entire laboratory extent served by a parallel access road. Service spaces for the Institute would have been below grade running the full extent of the animal quarters. Circulation into the lab complex was to be from the north west from the parking lot defined by an allée of trees defining the approach to the Meeting House. At the north corner of the administrative/ library terrace there was to be a reception space allowing access to a circulation corridor paralleling the full extent of this terrace which connected to the circulation corridors feeding back to the peripheries of all the lab wings.

The Laboratories as built still have parking to the north west without the formal landscaping Kahn had intended. However, the approach to the northernmost administrative block was not provided with a separate reception structure. As opposed to the earlier scheme, where all public and employee access was from the north west through a secure area, the Laboratories as built had multiple points of access from the east, multiple entrance/exits at the service blocks at the north and south flanks of the building and the approach from the north west. Anderson not only lamented the changed circulation pattern, but also the loss of a powerful image of the quadruple laboratories as industrial workplace.

Jonas Salk's decision to discard the double-garden quadruple-laboratory scheme with its folded plate interstitial structure was made in April 1962.[50] On 9 June that year, in Salk's office, Kahn presented a radically revised scheme based on organizing flanks of labs and scientists' studies around a single courtyard/ plaza. This is scheme 540.25.1 as presented in the Kahn Archive publication. FIG.63 After the numerous design studies of the scientists' study structures, Kahn quickly settled on primarily double-bay ordering with double oblique piers, and oblique piers were introduced into the west office blocks. The final dispositions of these piers was to be worked out in the subsequent weeks. Landscaping was still included at the center courtyard and at the lower courtyards flanking the labs. The June 1962 construction 'kick-off' date arrived but without a final completely resolved plan for the Salk Institute. By March 1963 construction documents for the laboratory buildings were completed, allowing construction to move forward.[51] It was not until the end of 1963 that all design aspects for the building were resolved. This included the final designs for the administrative blocks facing the Pacific Ocean, the scientists' study structures, the exterior stairs linking the studies to the labs, the east-facing mechanical/service blocks and the service blocks defining the north and south elevations of the building.[52] The north laboratory wing was occupied by early 1966, and the final disposition of the plaza was not agreed on until 1967.[53]

"Operative criticism" was defined by Manfredo Tafuri as the "forcing of a future" leading to a distorted reading of current and past events.[54] For example, Bruno Zevi's advocacy of Frank Lloyd Wright's work had nothing to do with the urban realities of mid-twentieth century Italy. Too utopian or not utopian enough? Perhaps Colin Rowe's critique of Kahn and other American architects in his essays on "Classicism and Neo-classicism in Modern Architecture" was more than describing a trend–it was trying to influence the future direction of architecture.[55] In his 1950s critique of Kahn's work, Rowe found Kahn's use of the A-B-A grid at his Trenton Jewish Community Center to be regressive. **FIG.64** Rowe found no benefit to Kahn's adaptation of the 'tartan grid' compared to the aesthetic and planning benefits offered by the free plan as developed by Le Corbusier. This criticism took place, as Robert McCarter indicated, just after Rowe and Robert Slutzky had visited Kahn's office at the time the Center was being designed.[56] They had given Kahn a copy of Rudolf Wittkower's book on Palladio: *Architectural Principles in the Age of Humanism*; perhaps they thought that Palladio's typologies could be of use to Kahn.

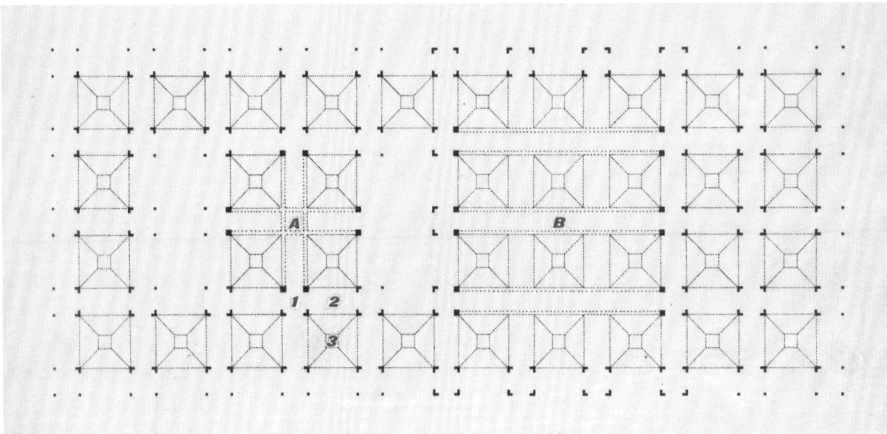

FIG.64

Earlier in the March 1947 issue of *Architectural Review*, Rowe published his essay comparing Le Corbusier's Villa at Garches to Palladio's Villa Rotunda. In a formal comparison he stressed Le Corbusier's use of an A-B-A grid to Palladio's own use of this grid over three hundred years earlier. There was a deep contradiction in Rowe's views of Kahn's work. One moment he was trying to influence Kahn and the next moment he was criticizing Kahn for maladapting Le Corbusier's concept. But Kahn's use of the A-B-A grid was in its own way as 'flexible' as Le Corbusier's use of it. It was the mark of an open architecture procedure: the establishment of an open urban grid at the scale of architecture which was to be an important organizing device for some of Kahn's most significant projects.[57]

Rowe's criticism was shared by others who considered Kahn's architecture too dogmatic, too restricted, based on latent Beaux-Arts prejudices.[58] At the Salk Institute Kahn's adaptation of a Durand-like compositional parti–an assembly of pièces, in fact–allowed the building to start in construction without resolution of all its design components. It also allowed Kahn to develop an architecture of openness, connection and void, unlike anything in the Beaux-Arts tradition.

FIG.64 | Trenton Jewish Community Center intermediate plan (c. 1955)

THE LABORATORY BUILDING COURTYARD

The beginning is a breakthrough. There is no precedent. It is from the feelings of beginning that one measures man.
Louis I Kahn[59]

The movement of silence to light, light to silence, has many, many thresholds. Each threshold is a singularity. Each one of us has a threshold in which the meeting of light and silence lodges. The threshold is the position or the aura of the inspirations.
Louis I Kahn[60]

FIG.65

FIG.66

FIG.67

FIG.65 | **Salk Laboratory view from original garden**
FIG.66 | **Laboratory courtyard west view**
FIG.67 | **Court of the Lions, Alhambra, Granada, Spain (late 13th cent.)**

The Salk Institute Laboratory building marks a site between a vast Pacific Ocean, a vast continent laying behind it and the vastness of the earth below and the sky above it. The 'overdetermined' structure of the building incorporates this vastness. The courtyard void is a 'breakthrough' space—a eureka moment for the scientists and whoever else visits the site. The main approach to the Salk Institute was originally through a garden of low eucalyptus trees with multiple paths converging on a single path which centered us on a low gate. **FIG.65** Our first perception of the building is an oblique view of the first scientist study structures juxtaposed to the end of mechanical blocks left or right. We will discuss later how this approach was changed with the 1992 construction of a subterranean auditorium with its new entrances in the garden. We ascended four steps on axis between two raised planter areas incorporating trees within the complex. We continued, and descended four steps to be confronted by a wide marble bench blocking our way into the courtyard/plaza paved in travertine and split by a steam running from the cistern to a pool at the far end. **FIG.66** The Pacific Ocean is seen beyond the building, and as we move left or right into the access ways below the enfilade of the scientists' studies, the dominant recessionary view to the sea gives way to oblique views of the scientists' studies. The doubled full-height inflected concrete piers almost seem to flutter as the gaps are revealed between the structures.[61] **FIG.68**

The courtyard/plaza repeats the sense of the ravine to its west. Kahn's served-and-servant concept of architecture, which are the scientists' study structures, linked to the 'marginally' located laboratories, dissolves in the play of light, shade and shadow and a play of architectural elements that can only be called contrapuntal in nature. Kahn's drive to perfection to create a space of simultaneity—a space that seems unconditioned—was the result of numerous design decisions.

FIG.68

Kahn and his office staff did numerous design studies for the scientists' studies when the Laboratory building was still based on the double-garden plan. One of the last versions (SIL7) showed a sequence beginning and ending with two bay structures with three three-bay structures in between. The two bay structures included one bay for access and one study per level. The three bay structures had two scientists' studies served by a common access bay. Eight scientists' studies would have served each lab level. In the final design each lab level is served by nine study bays beginning with a single bay at the head of the court, then marching towards the end of the courtyard/plaza in double formation. In the earlier scheme there were gaps between the study structure volumes themselves and gaps flanking the bridge/stair connections between the studies and the continuous lab space. When the lab levels became three levels—with one in the basement—the intervening lightwells became larger in area. This is when Kahn realized that the gaps should be merged. In the Laboratory building as built, the lightwells match the area of the study structure/bridge connections creating a figure/ground relationship with the central void that is the courtyard/plaza.[62] **FIG.70** Kahn created a determinate relationship between the flanks of buildings and the courtyard/plaza through the notion of composition as joint. The cross grain of Kahn's architecture alluded to by William Jordy many years ago is to be found in the play of this jointed-ness, with the shifting composition of the actual structural supports.

FIG.69

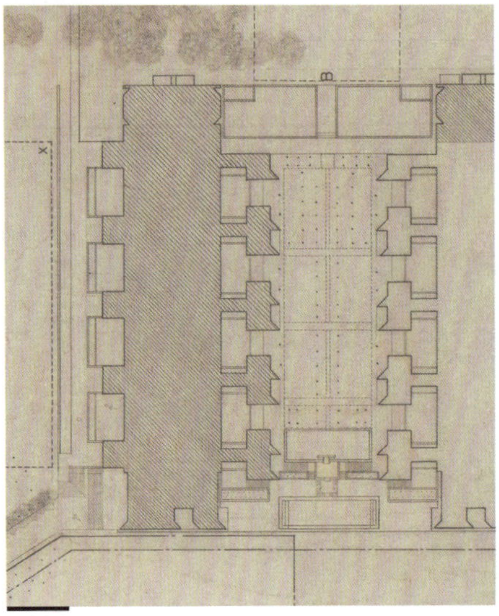

FIG.70

FIG.68 | Salk north studies/ laboratories oblique view
FIG.69 | Apartment buildings for Philadelphia Mid-town City Center project (1947–1948)
FIG.70 | North laboratory figure/ground plan

This is enhanced by Kahn's introduction of a minor and major order of deflected piers clearly opening the views from the studies toward the sea.

The voids articulating the scientists' studies are patterned on voids found years earlier in the garage base for his City Hall Tower project (1956) in Philadelphia, where cylindrical forms within square voids connect to the periphery of the project. **FIG.71A** These cylindrical forms are lightwells and at the corners of the project define vehicular down ramps. The plan of the Yale University Art Gallery (1951-1953), which is a binuclear attachment to the original Art Gallery if its elements were evacuated, maintains the profile of this voided figure. **FIG.162** Kahn's Goldenberg House, commissioned at the same time as the Institute, is organized around a connecting entrance oriented toward a light court or void. **FIG.71B** As the Salk Institute was design-developed, Kahn had worked on the interlocking room order of his Erdman Dormitories at Bryn Mawr College (1960-1965). **FIG.71C** The structural order there is similar to the interlocking order at Salk. **FIG.70** At the same time Kahn obtained a commission to design a new Chemistry Building on a site not too far from Thomas Jefferson's original campus for the University of Virginia. The arcade-connected pavilions at Jefferson's campus, framing the lawn centered on the library inspired by the Pantheon, served as multifunctional units with professorial residences above and teaching space below at arcade level. There can be no doubt that Kahn was thinking of Jefferson's work when he was re-considering the work on the Salk scientists' studies.[63] However, the most likely influence from the University of Virginia can be found in the side garden walls to the pavilions which are formed very much like the Salk lightwells. Beyond this influence, however, or that of the solid/void relationships of Kahn's beloved Scottish castles, the figure/ground order at Salk may be indebted to a more ancient source: the individual tombs of Etruscan burial mounds. **FIG.72** It is possible Kahn might have been aware of these structures from his time as fellow at the American Academy in Rome and from the lectures given by Frank E Brown at the Academy. This same motif appears in the seminar volumes of the Salk Meeting House as well as at the City Tower scheme and at the Bryn Mawr dormitory.

The Salk scientists' studies are a sandwich of elements suspended within their structural supports

FIG.71A

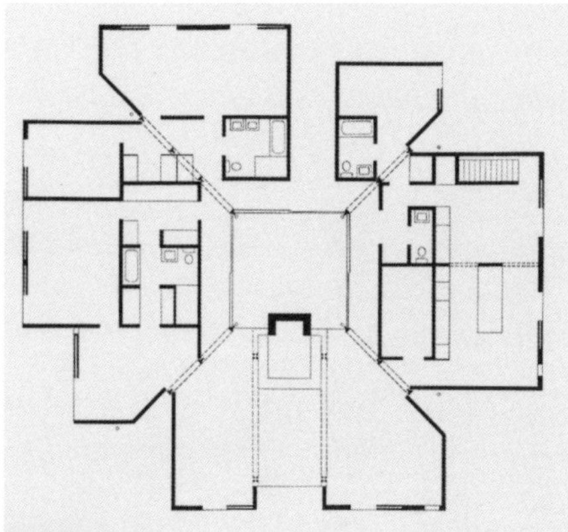
FIG.71B

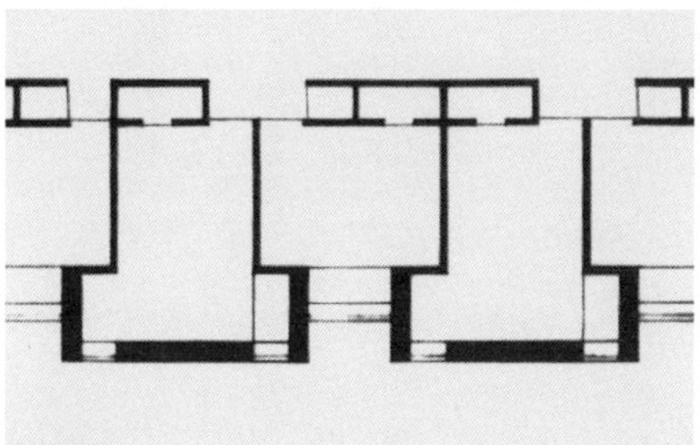
FIG.71C

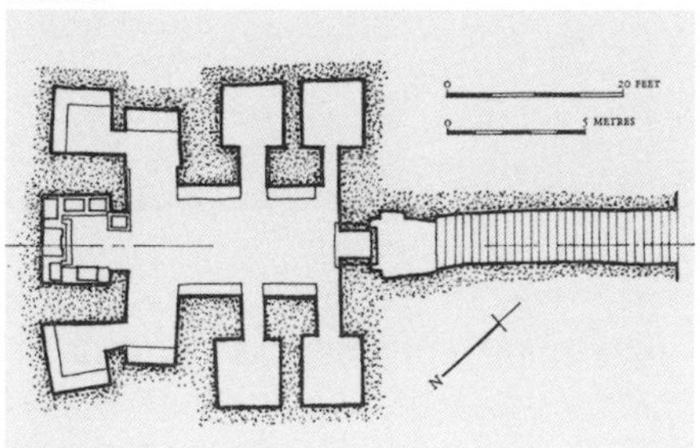
FIG.72

FIG.71A | Detail plan of lightwell at City Tower project (1952-1957)
FIG.71B | Goldenberg House plan (1959)
FIG.71C | Detail plan of dormitory rooms Erdman Hall (1965)
FIG.72 | Etruscan tomb plan (c. 500 BC)

which includes the double order of giant 'hinged' piers. Kahn freely adjusted these elements within his conception of architecture as spacing. The individual scientist study rooms are very raw spaces, defined as they are by concrete structure and the raw wood framing backing the teak infill panels. The latter allowed final interior finishes to be determined by the scientists or the Institute. Many of these studies were used by the scientists for storage rather than spaces for active study or contemplation. They are level with the upper two interstitial spaces over the laboratories proper. The courtyard/plaza level, and the open terrace two levels up, remain open, allowing views from inside the labs through the study structures across the courtyard/plaza.[64] **FIG.73** Kahn's free adjustment of spacing is expressed with the greater ceiling height of the upper-level studies, which suggests a gravitas of architecture, a fall of architecture, over the open terrace and the lower level of scientists' studies which are in more compressed form. **FIG.73** The same effects are produced in the horizontal direction where the larger hinged pier defines a narrower bay of studies behind while the front narrower pier stretches the front bay forward. Kahn's intuition here touches on the relativistic contraction of length. This syncopation of elements is enhanced by the disposition of the windows in each teak infill panel of the studies. Windows are laterally

FIG.73

FIG.73 | **Salk studies/laboratories north view**

forward or behind the piers. The windows themselves suggest discontinuous verticals; they form a quadrapartite formation which translates the building plan into the elevations. The teak infill panels articulated on the ends from the concrete structure by glass slots are teak panel frames in four rows, themselves infilled by vertical sawn teak members, highly reminiscent of both the sawn delicately scaled wood floors and the horizontal coursing of the main façade at the Yale University Art Gallery.

Kahn also translated another horizontal to vertical: the discarded folded plate structure of the earlier laboratory scheme is preserved in the courtyard/plaza in the piers as broken folds. **FIGS.54,74** The difference in width of the piers had already been reflected in the varying depths of the original folded plates. The scientists' studies are structures that are *generated* from the folded but encased elements that articulate the vented mechanical blocks at the east ends of the lab building. They *emerge* from these volumes which supply heating, ventilation and cooling to the complex as well as the hot water, steam and distilled water required by the laboratories. **FIG.65** But the studies are also the *generations* of scientists in time confronting the void and the future. From them emerge the narrower hinged piers that articulate the diagonal ordering of the administrative volumes overlooking the Pacific Ocean. The oblique hinged pier structures also originate from a drawing Kahn did (PMC.3) for large apartment buildings for his Mid-Town City Center project for Philadelphia (1947–1948). **FIG.69**

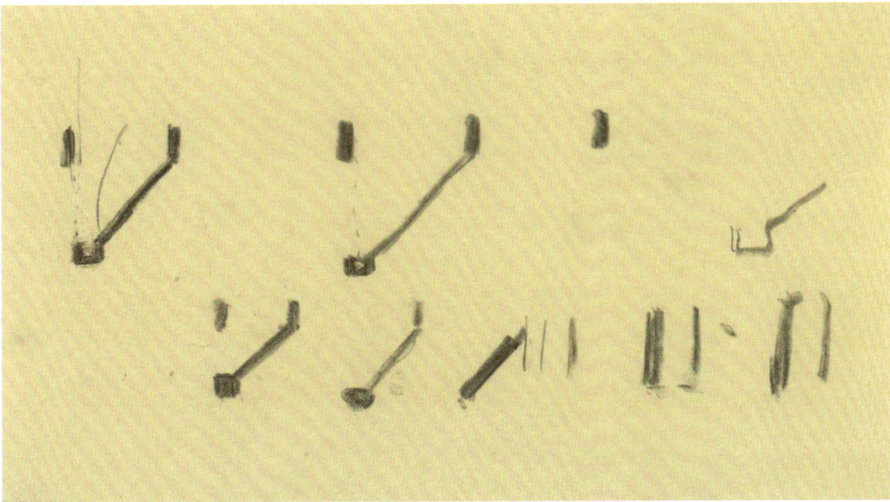

FIG.74

The courtyard/plaza at the Salk Institute is a level space or datum at a sloped site. The scientists' study structural piers are embedded at the flanks of this courtyard/plaza. They extrude downward, expressing the depth of the basement-level labs and sub-courts below. Across the center of the courtyard/plaza is the stream, which is a continuous channel that forms a split in the plaza floor. It is an originary groove at the base of the great void which is the opening of the lab complex to the horizon beyond. Lingering memories of the water courses in Islamic gardens may have influenced Kahn's design decision here. **FIG.67** However, Kahn had since the 1950s, in his urban studies for city-center Philadelphia, been interested in movement

FIG.74 | Kahn late sketch for studies structure

'systems'. At the same time as the design development of the Salk Institute Kahn was working on his plan for the Midtown-Market Street East proposal (1961-1962). Kahn stated:

> A street wants to be a building. The new spaces that want to be will emerge from the designs drawn from an order of movement. An order of movement that distinguishes staccato from go movement and includes the concept of stopping. The zoning of streets for characteristic movement must precede the zoning of the land they serve. Expressways are rivers that need harbors. Streets are canals that need docks.[65]

FIG.75

The courtyard/plaza is a giant passage, a street, a giant flow closed by the garden behind and open to the sea, sky and horizon ahead, articulated at the margins by a staccato structure.[66] None of this would have become evident if Luis Barragán had not made his famous recommendation on what this 'space' wanted 'to be'– devoid of the poplars and other landscaping as originally intended. **FIG.77**:

> This should be a plaza of stone, not a garden ... If you make this a plaza, you will gain a façade, a façade to the sky.[67]

FIG.76

FIG.77

There are movements of pedestrians, of vehicles, of water and even an 'order of winds'.[68] Kahn's parallel flows at the Salk Laboratory are the dispositions of its architectural elements: the exterior corridors around the 65-foot x 245-foot open lab lofts, the scientists' studies and the plaza stream. The center stream is parallel to the concealed flows of the piping servicing the laboratories from the overhead interstitial spaces. **FIG.75** The center stream is the poetic transformation of these more utilitarian flows.

The 'openness' that defined Kahn's spacing of architecture in the development of the scientists' study structures allowed the Salk Institute staff to have views across the courtyard/plaza while responding to Jonas Salk's requirement for enhanced privacy for the individual studies themselves. This openness was also a response to La Jolla's Mediterranean climate. Kahn had already demonstrated this climatological awareness in his earlier project for the US Consulate in Luanda, Angola (1959-1961). **FIG.76** There, Kahn raised a sunscreen roof over the Consulate offices below. The interlayer of air was to be open to breezes, providing natural insulation to the structure below. At Luanda Kahn surrounded

FIG.75 | Laboratory building interstitial space
FIG.76 | US Consulate project in Luanda, Angola (1959-1961)
FIG.77 | Original landscape concept for the Laboratory courtyard

the Consulate with immense raised pools of water to mitigate the semi-arid breezes. The pool terminating the stream at the west end of the courtyard/plaza at the Salk Institute is a recessed pool with a recessed seating area before it. Its function is more poetic than climatic. **FIG.92** It foregrounds the Pacific Ocean, bringing a slice of the distant sea into the courtyard/plaza, and it spills out beyond into a raised pool which is a fragment of the larger raised pools at Luanda. The deflected piers become part of that 'order of winds' that Kahn had spoken of. Meanings changed as Kahn and others responded to new and different inspirations. Originally, the function of the stream was to irrigate the courtyard/plaza landscaping. As built it suggests the remnant of a once flooded space where the recession of the waters, back toward the sea, reveals the building as an eroded geological formation. The center stream is the 'spine' of the Institute, flowing with 'healing' waters entering a pool, evoking the institutional origins of the Salk Institute itself. [69]

THE LABORATORIES THEMSELVES

Architecture for Kahn was thus the expression of timeless ideals through contingent circumstances, and it was in his view the architect's task to approach as nearly as possible the realms of Order through work that sprang from the messy realities of everyday life.
Thomas Leslie[70]

God is in the details.
Mies van der Rohe[71]

The Salk Institute for Biological Studies has an on-site research and support staff of approximately 850 persons. Current research areas include: aging and regenerative medicine, cancer biology, immune system biology, metabolism and diabetes, neuroscience and neurological disorders, and plant biology. The major technical innovation of the Institute was the concealment of the support services (gas, fluid, electrical systems) in interstitial spaces above the laboratories. Kahn and his project team constantly reassessed the technical requirements for the Salk Institute project. In light of the functional problems that plagued the Richards Research Center, Kahn reversed course with the Salk project. No longer desiring the blatant public exposure of the scientists' laboratories with their exposed mechanical servicing, as at Richards, Kahn at Salk set the lab floors back below the cantilevers of the overhead interstitial service spaces which Jonas Salk called the mesenchyme spaces.[72] This gesture was certainly a response to the climatic differences between Philadelphia and La Jolla. The laboratory wings would be protected from direct sunlight while still being fully accessible. From a construction point of view, as Leslie points out, the folded plate elements defining the original double-garden laboratory scheme were preferable to the Vierendeel system eventually used. **FIGS.78,79** The folded plates formed individual pre-cast elements, precisely Kahn's concept of "building with hollow stones",[73] which were to be lifted in place (much like the pre-cast/post-tensioned elements at Richards) onto the giant box girders spanning between the scientists' studies and the exhaust hood structures. The folded plate or corrugated elements, as Leslie referred to them, could provide services from above or below. As Leslie noted: "The deep corrugations of the ceiling would have added a visible order to the functionally necessary chaos of a lab environment, particularly at the top level where the recesses would have been flooded with daylight from above."[74] **FIG.54** But this system was abandoned as unworkable. The hollow folded plate sections could not accommodate all services and they were difficult to access. Instead Kahn and his structural and mechanical design team developed the nine-foot-high interstitial space structured by the more difficult to construct cast-in-place post-tensioned Vierendeel trusses placed twenty feet on center. These trusses allowed complete flexibility and access to mechanical ducts and piping. The eight-inch-thick pre-cast hollow-core floors of the interstitial spaces were perforated with eight-inch-wide slots, five foot on center parallel, to the major extent of the labs allowing service runs to the lab spaces below. **FIG.80** Each slot was closed by a thin steel plate on support angles. Where points of service are required to the labs below the plates are cut back. The north and south laboratory spaces at the Salk Institute are column-free spaces, 65 feet wide by 245 feet long, with 11-foot-high ceilings completely glazed at their perimeters floor to ceiling. **FIG.82** Kahn and his staff closely coordinated work with the lighting and workbench manufacturers, and also designed and had fabricated the original movable partitions for the laboratory spaces. The glass and special doors to the surrounding corridors are framed by stainless-steel brake-formed components. **FIG.81** The corridors that surround each open laboratory on each floor are open at their long sides to the exterior light. The laboratories are hermetically sealed environments occupying the margins of a building which frames nature.

FIG.78

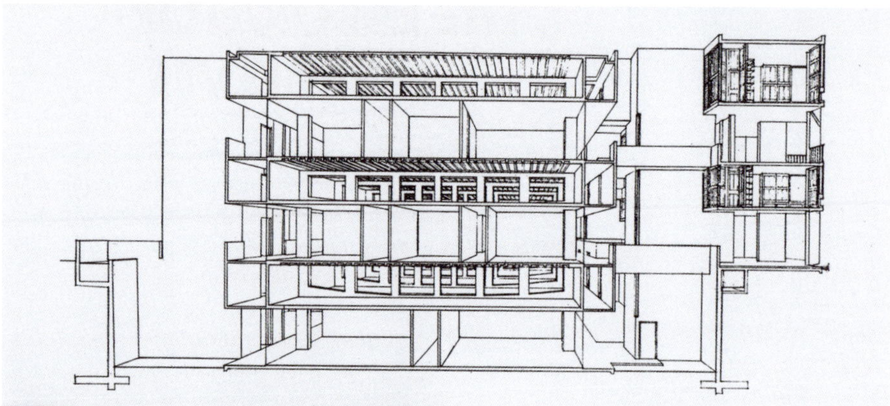

FIG.79

FIG.80

FIG.78 | **Salk Laboratory plan with surrounding landscape**
FIG.79 | **Salk Laboratory building section perspective**
FIG.80 | **Salk Laboratory interior view**

During the early phases of the formation of the Salk Institute Jacob Bronowski was the lead coordinator of those scientists in Europe who would become the initial group coming to La Jolla.[75] During the construction of the Salk Institute, Bruno—as Jonas liked to call him—was the 'go-between' between the core group of scientists and Earl Walls the laboratory consultant. He was involved in the discussions concerning the planning and fitting out of the laboratories, as well as the library being considered for the Meeting House and the technical library for the Laboratory building.[76]

FIG.81

FIG.82

FIG.83

Laboratories are dangerous work environments. Explosive blasts, fire, and chemical, bacteriological and viral agents are potential hazards. Early in the laboratory planning Francis Crick had requested that due consideration be given to working with radioactive elements.[77] Great care had to be given to worker safety. Planning for the perimeter service blocks at the north and south flanks of the Laboratory building included provision for emergency showers within the bathrooms. **FIG.83** The service blocks contained emergency stairs, large elevators to bring lab carts up to the upper lab levels and, at ground level, the emergency exits from the building which also doubled as entrances. The design of the stairways in between the scientists' studies and the laboratories proper must also be seen in the light of safety requirements. **FIG.84** In the original double-garden lab scheme the stairways were a relatively simple affair. They were walled their full height up to just handrail height at the second level. One of the problems Kahn's office dealt with was whether they could eliminate sprinkler requirements for the external stairs.[78] This certainly helped with the budget and reduced technical requirements for the project. The results are the stairs as seen at the Institute today. The stair landings closest to the labs

FIG.81 | **Salk Laboratory north exterior corridor**
FIG.82 | **Salk Laboratory interior view before occupation**
FIG.83 | **Salk Laboratory building south elevation**

FIG.85

OPPOSITE
FIG.84 | North studies, stairs, lower courts and laboratories
FIG.85 | North service shaft/ lightwell

OVERLEAF
FIG.86 | North flank of the Salk Institute

are supported by a stack of vertical piers the full width of the stairs, acting as structure and protective barriers. The bridge connections from the open terraces and the plaza level to the laboratory levels are supported by T-shaped extensions of the vertical piers which run to the underside of the short roofs resting on top of the low parapets of the uppermost interstitial space. One enters the stairs protected by concrete just open enough to meet code requirements. By emphasizing the profile of the bottom run of stairs and the voided character of the stair enclosures Kahn developed the three-story stair towers (six stories if you consider the interstitial spaces) as decomposed elements in descent completely consistent with the staccato structure of the scientists' study structures. The 'origins' of the stairs are from the buried lightwell/mechanical access shafts flanking the entrance to the Salk Institute courtyard. **FIG.85** It is as if Kahn had pulled the stairs out of the Richards brick 'servant' shafts to expose and multiply them.

THE LABORATORY BUILDING WEST FAÇADE

One of the most intriguing aspects of Kahn's entire architectural output is the final design at the Salk Institute of the administrative blocks facing the Pacific Ocean. **FIG.86** There has been very little comment on the asymmetric nature of these façades.[79] When the double-garden lab scheme was discarded in favor of the single-courtyard/plaza scheme there was a radical change to the nature of the circulation route that would have connected all the buildings of the master plan. From the Meeting House on the north side of the ravine to the proposed Visiting Fellows Residences on the south side the connecting route in the earlier scheme threaded itself between the administrative offices/ central library block and the ends of the laboratories. In the Laboratory building as built Kahn brought the connecting route under the office blocks now five stories high. The administrative/library block at the center disappeared to become the open terrace that we experience today. The library was reduced in size and incorporated within the north office block at the area level with the under-passage. It is the terrace that functions as the day-to-day meeting place for the Salk staff taking breaks from their scientific and other duties, and acts as the connecting space between the north and south office blocks. Given the positive weather conditions in La Jolla the loss of the roofed connecting corridor along the earlier administrative/library block was only a minor setback.

In the design of the terrace area Kahn integrated a movement system with a space of relaxation. In an earlier terrace scheme he retained the discarded classical niches of the even earlier administrative/library block in a layout of semi-circular pools flush with the terrace pavement. **FIG.88** Instead he decided in favor of a recessed area within the terrace flanked by groves of trees. The pools were reduced to one smaller square raised pool which accepts water from the spillway of the upper courtyard/plaza pool. This raised pool is the condensed and displaced version of the much larger pools that enframed Kahn's unbuilt US Consulate project in Angola. **FIG.94** In turn the raised pool spills water into a square pool flush with the terrace but enframed by travetine block seating. The stairs along the pool, to and from the upper courtyard/plaza level, would have played an even more important part in the movement system if the entire master plan for the Institute had been constructed. The passages under the flanking office blocks are raised versions of the even deeper connecting corridor that connects both lab wings below the eastern edge of the courtyard/plaza where it meets the entry garden. **FIGS.87,89** Meanwhile the travertine block seating enframing the pool is a reduced variation of the unbuilt Salk Meeting House with its courtyard.

FIG.87

FIG.88

FIG.89

In one of the penultimate plans for the west-facing office blocks Kahn's office defined the perimeter structure with a Bryn Mawr-like arrangement of piers. **FIG.92** However, at the Erdman Dormitories at Bryn Mawr the spacing of these piers occurs along an oblique plane providing considerable visual and organizational interest lacking in the transposition to the Salk scheme. Kahn eventually adapted the minor oblique piers from the scientist study structures and plunged them into the office façades, and so inverted the Bryn Mawr scheme. **FIG.92** The oblique elements are organized along more frontally organized limits when viewed from the planned Meeting House or Visiting Fellows Residences. They are true brise-soleils, significantly blocking direct light from the sunset condition that the office blocks face. Kahn's decision to articulate the four outer corners of the west façade blocks with the oblique piers splayed out reinforces the symmetry of the plan and implies an infinite opening to the horizon. **FIG.91** This design decision may have come from Kahn's earlier experiments for the scientist study blocks where a Janus-like ordering of Y-shaped studies was discarded

FIG.87 | **View under one of the office blocks**
FIG.88 | **Sketch 540.118.2 showing early pool concept**
FIG.89 | **Carver Court Housing by Howe, Stonorov+Kahn (1941–1942)**

in favor of studies with an orientation forward toward the sea. FIG.115 The splaying out of the corners of the office block may also have been indebted to Robert Venturi's North Penn Visiting Nurse Service building completed in 1960.[80] FIG.90

The oblique piers support structural beams, running the full depth of the office blocks from west to east so they become layered elements within the volumetric nature of the office blocks. FIG.87 Kahn and Komendant developed a complex order of elements in the west façades—a rich play of architecture that seems 'irrational'. The deep vertical voids across each façade are retained from deep voids that split undefined blocks that terminated the ends of earlier laboratory schemes. However, Kahn's design treatment of these voided shafts is also highly reminiscent of some of the work of the Italian architect Ignazio Gardella. FIG.93 Kahn would have been familiar with Gardella's work during his visits to Italy in the 1950s.[81] The deep voids are the absent increment of the teak-infilled vertical segments in the rest of the façades themselves, abutting against the doubled bays defined by deep spandrel beams. This effect should be compared to the design of the Biology Towers in the second phase of construction at the Richards Medical Center where vertical segmentation occurs.[82] In the west façade facing the south lab extent, the vertical segments visually collapse into, or extend out of, the spandrel-defined bays on their flanks, or they can be read as vertical segments structurally infilling the gaps between the flanking spandrel-organized bays. Some window infill panels are removed from the structural bays to create shadowed terraces below. However, there is no immediately evident logic to why the administrative office façades were organized in such a highly differentiated manner. There is nothing in the record that indicated whether complicating the structure at the Salk Institute had anything to do with mitigating the possible effects of earthquakes.

The play of light and shadow across these façades would have made the building more visible from other parts of the site or even from a vantage point in the Pacific Ocean. The deep vertical voids spatially pin the entire lab complex to its site, as well as indicate entry points into the office blocks. The full stack of window panels set back into these voids are traces of the removed segments. The doubled windows of the west façades unite the individual windows of the scientists' study structures in a play of multiple frames.

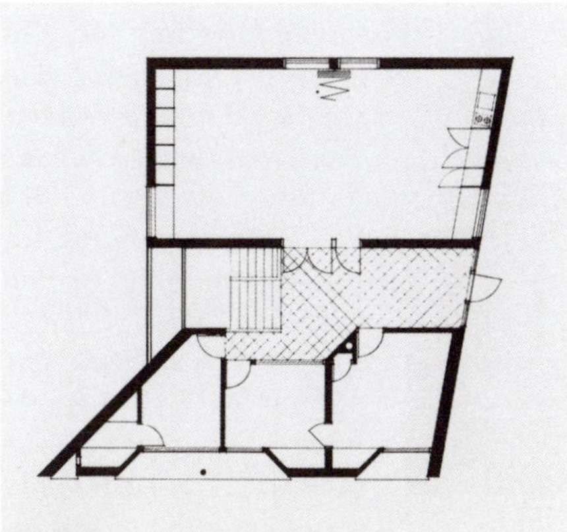

FIG.90

FIG.91

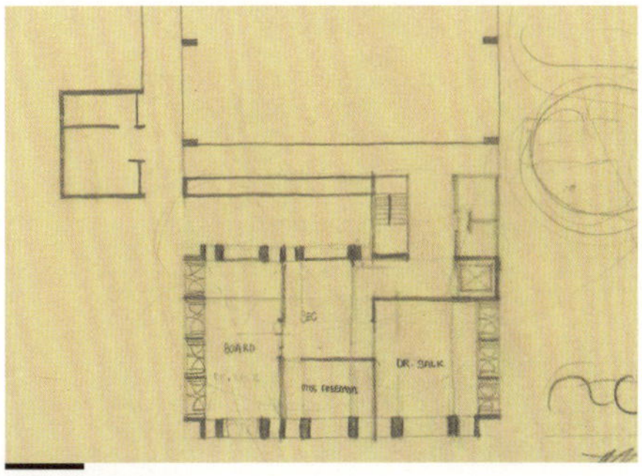

FIG.92

FIG.93

FIG.90 | Plan of North Penn Visiting Nurse Service building by R Venturi (1960)
FIG.91 | Drawing 540.40.2 of north office block
FIG.92 | Drawing 540.40 of north office block
FIG.93 | Apartments INA Case Quarter by I Gardella (early 1950s)

The oblique piers direct views to other site areas from the passages below the office blocks and from within the office spaces. Kahn developed a major and minor order of windows in the relationship of the teak panel windows, articulated from the structure by vertical slots of glass. From the interior these vertical slots of glass give the illusion of structure supported by white light and allow slivers of light to enter the office spaces during the sunset hours while the major window surfaces are protected by their exterior horizontal rolling teak shutter screens. **FIG.94** These screens evolved out of Kahn's earlier experiments for controlling sunlight and views, as developed at the Morton Weiss House and the Pincus Therapy building. He would later re-adapt the concept for the Yale Center for British Art (1969-1974).

FIG.94

FIG.95

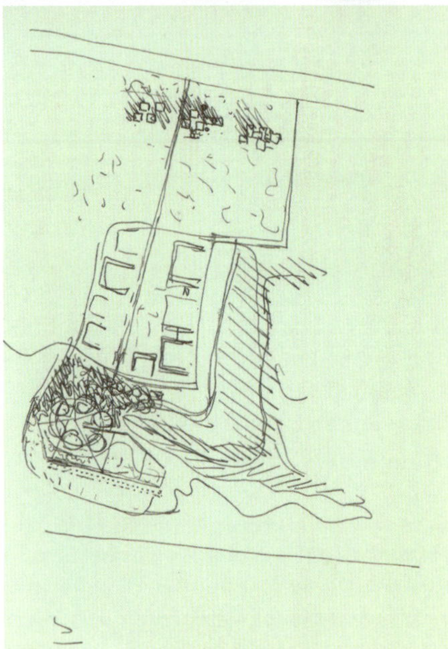

FIG.96

Viewed from the oblique path that would have connected to the Meeting House the office façades at Salk are doubled volumes, segments of a series in depth. **FIG.98** They are anamorphic transformations of the half-square plans of each office block. The splayed end of the wall surface that defines the north elevation of the office block establishes a perspective convergence onto this elevation. The double office blocks have a genetic relationship to each other. Rotating certain oblique piers in one block transforms it into its other. But even here the supposed 'lawfulness' is violated by Kahn. What is that small oblique pier, an odd 'man' out, doing below the spandrel at the south office block? **FIG.95** Is it perhaps an afterthought or making up for a structural oversight? The west façades at the Salk Institute express the 'fault' conditions of its site. They are an expression of the binding and liberation of architectural elements along a limit—a boundary.

THE VISITING FELLOWS RESIDENCES

The Visiting Fellows Residences is the forgotten part of the Salk Institute master plan. Attention (scholarly and otherwise) over the years has rightfully focused on the Laboratory building—the raison d'être for the founding of the Institute—and the Meeting House, which was the lost opportunity to 'symbolize' the needs of a scientific-humanist community. But the Visiting Fellows Residences is one of Louis I Kahn's greatest architectural efforts.

FIG.94 | Interior view—office block
FIG.95 | South flank—Salk Institute
FIG.96 | Early site plan—Salk Institute

OVERLEAF
FIG.98 | J Salk walking to his office (1988)

In one of the earliest site plan sketches for the Institute, the Visiting Fellows Residences is located between the labs and the Meeting House. **FIG.96** The residences are defined by a series of south-facing courtyards, each one opened on the southern side. The road connecting the lab area to the Meeting House would have bisected the resident areas. This scheme was then discarded in favor of another one where 'amorphic' clusters of small courtyard structures and pavilions were located to the north and south of the ravine. This scheme too was discarded in favor of the linear scheme along the south side of the ravine that was to remain the 'parti' until the completion of the project. Two points of access were offered to the residences. Firstly, a pedestrian path from the south side of the laboratory area snaked along the ravine and intersected the east end of the residential area. Secondly, vehicular access from the lab area was offered by a road lined with eucalyptus trees which led to the service road parking area behind the residences.

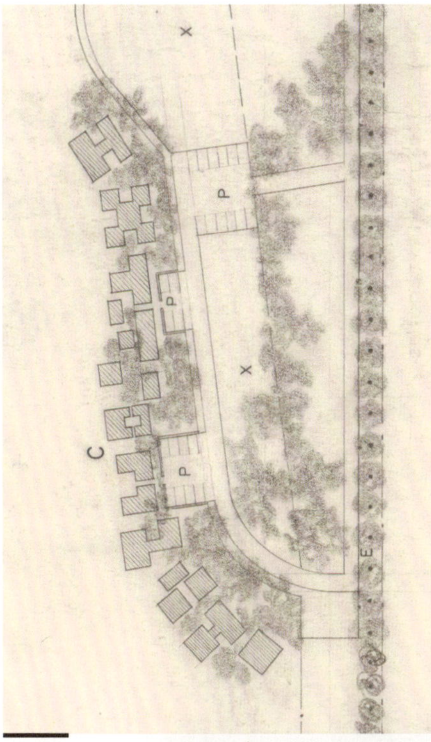

FIG.97A

FIG.97B

FIG. 97C

FIGS.97A,B,C | **Evolution–Visiting Fellows Residences**

In three early linear schemes for the residences all units were located to the north side of the connecting pedestrian walk. **FIGS.97A,B,C** One scheme was a looser play of units along this walk. In the second scheme Kahn began to articulate the spaces between the units as internal walks and small courtyards between block units. However, the spatial ordering remained claustrophobic and the pedestrian access confusing. In the third scheme Kahn reintroduced the courtyard typology from much earlier in the site planning process (540.11) and reinvigorated the spatial character of the scheme. The short connecting link of space that allows access to the courtyards is reminiscent of a long line of spatial developments in Kahn's work which reached a singular resolution in his Goldenberg House project (1959).

Only when Kahn pushed his work to conclusion was the proper balance found between openness and closure. This is accomplished in scheme SIH.2 where Kahn realized the importance of separating the pedes-

trian walk from the access driveway and parking to become a true pedestrian street by organizing the residential units as a double enfilade. **FIG.97D** All the units were duplex apartments with the smaller ones to the south of the street and the larger ones to the north. The south formation was tightly formed, like a continuous series of row houses with their entry areas overlapping the street. These areas were the lower part of the open shafts facing the apartment units which frame balconies. The shafts like the "building wrapped in ruins" at the unbuilt Meeting House would have caught the light from the southern arc of the sun behind the Visiting Fellows Residences, reflecting and diffusing it onto the balconies. If there is a 'type' form here, it is the open loft concept of the Yale University Art Gallery having migrated to this ravine in La Jolla. Intervals of space allow views toward the north from the rear housing units and from the pedestrian street which widens into small balconies overlooking the ravine. The street at the east and west ends widens to become small courtyards around which are organized larger living units. Three of the larger units have much larger balconies (two of them with corner balconies), responding to their prominent positions on the site. The entire SIH.2 plan on a schematic level is highly reminiscent of Kahn's layout for his Radbill Psychiatric Hospital (1950-1953) with its splayed plan organization. **FIG.100** But in the context of the entire master plan of the Salk Institute this adaptation relates to the 'hinged' piers of the Laboratory building, the 'un-hinging' of the assembly hall at the Meeting House, and is itself one of the hinge points that occur at key points in the site circulation offering multiple perspectives. But perhaps Kahn felt that the SIH.2 plan was still too rigid. He went on to develop alternative plans.

In plan SIH.3 Kahn returned to an earlier scheme where the residential units are deployed along an arc largely following the contours of the ravine. **FIG.99** Instead of one main point of access to the parking, Kahn developed four. The northernmost units are

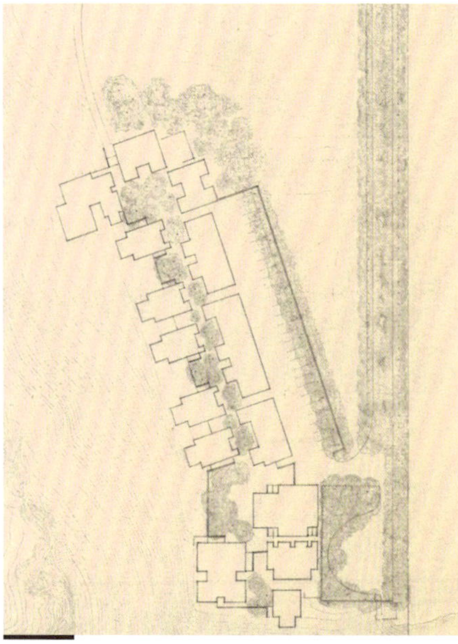

FIG.97D

FIG.99

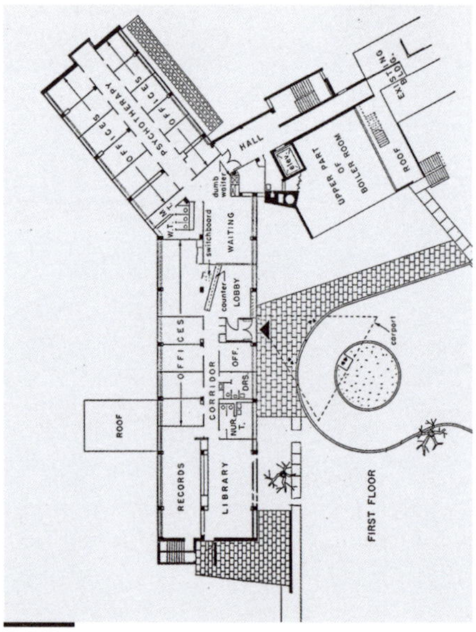

FIG.100

FIG.97D | Evolution—Visiting Fellows Residences
FIG.99 | Colored in intermediate plan—Visiting Fellows Residences
FIG.100 | First floor plan of addition to Radbill Psychological Hospital (1950-1953)

more individuated along the street. There is less pairing of units. The entrances to these units no longer overlapped the pedestrian street. Instead they became vestibules just touching the street perimeter. The only changes in elevation of the street occur at the north and south ends of the complex. It is here that the Visiting Fellows Residences most evoked the Italian hill towns that Kahn had sketched thirty years earlier. **FIGS.101,102** He eliminated the east end courtyard but retained the one to the west framed by housing units, taking advantage of the scenic views from this area.

FIG.101

FIG.102

The entire scheme was changed again, becoming the final plan of the Visiting Fellows Residences. **FIG.97D** A terrace and pool is introduced, interrupting the north tier of residences. **FIG.103** This 'loss' is made up for in the block, with multiple units facing the terrace and pool aligned with the southern tier of residential units. Kahn transformed the vestibule areas of the northernmost units. They are no longer individual points in series, but are flipped into paired units to frame T-shaped voids that spatially anchor the units to the pedestrian street. **FIG.103** These voids are like remnants of the earlier Visiting Fellows Residences organized around courtyards. A wider T-shaped void between paired units is a counter void in this interlocking order of elements. The northern tier of units is 'up against', and interlocked with, the pedestrian street, creating a compressive effect on the light shaft balconies of the southern tier of units. The T-shaped voids were adapted from the Meeting House scheme at the Salk Institute where they articulate the guest apartments at the entrance plaza, the voids between the northernmost dining halls and the access corridor to the exercise building. However, in the Visiting Fellows Residences this adaptation resulted in an interlocking system of voids as powerful as those at the Salk Laboratory Building or the earlier Erdman Dormitory at Bryn Mawr. The 'relaxed' arc-like formation of the units contrasts with the 'rigidity' of the workplace that is the Laboratory complex. This formation of elements suggests a 'spinal' curvature. But more importantly the arc responds to the curvature terminating the road access to the north side of the unbuilt Meeting House. And Kahn's response to the rest of the Meeting House plateau was to define its perimeter as a folded or unfolded continuous wall. He reinforced the character of a pre-existing landscape situation. Kahn's principle

FIG.103

FIG.101 | **Kahn drawing–Positano, Italy (1929)**
FIG.102 | **Kahn drawing–Visiting Fellows Residences**
FIG.103 | **Alternative model–Visiting Fellows Residences**

of spacing and folding worked not only at the building scale but at the site scale as well. And the double solutions to the residential planning–one based on the skew or fold, the other on the curve–suggests a principle of undecidability or incompletion at the heart of a totalizing site plan.

THE SALK INSTITUTE SITE, LANDSCAPING AND THE 1992 ADDITION

FIG.104

FIG.104 | Concept for Salk courtyard–L Barragán (1966)

From the moment of its founding the Salk Institute was in financial crisis. Because of the very success of the Salk and Sabine vaccines there was a decline of contributions to the March of Dimes (MOD, a division of the NFIP), which was the major backer of the Salk Institute. The Institute was to remain in financial difficulties for years to come. The scientists moved from their temporary lab barracks, which they had occupied for three years, into the newly completed north laboratory wing in the summer of 1966. As Suzanne Bourgeois recalls it, the central courtyard/plaza was still a "muddy mess".[83]

In August 1963 Louis I Kahn's contract was amended to stop work on the Meeting House and the Visiting Fellows Residences. By December 1965 Kahn had proposed that the courtyard/plaza at the Salk Institute be filled with a double row of poplar trees to be irrigated by a central stream. **FIG.97** The surface of the courtyard/plaza was to be grassed. However, Kahn was not totally convinced by his own proposal. He invited the Mexican architect and landscape architect Luis Barragán to La Jolla to consult on the project. In 1965 Kahn had seen some of his work in an exhibit at the Museum of Modern Art in New York.[84] In December of that year Kahn visited Barragán at his garden home in Mexico City and was inspired by what he saw: "His gardens have nothing but a trickle of water, and still are so immense that all the landscaping in the world couldn't equal it."[85] On 23 February 1966 Barragán visited the Salk Institute site as Kahn recalled **FIG.104**:

> **When [Barragán] entered the space he went to the concrete walls and touched them and expressed his love for them, and then said as he looked across the space and towards the sea, 'I would not put a tree or a blade of grass in this space. This should be a plaza of stone, not a garden.' I looked at Dr. Salk and he at me and we both felt this was deeply right. Feeling our approval, [Barragán] added joyously, 'If you make this a plaza, you will gain a façade—a façade to the sky.'[86]**

FIG.105

As Robert McCarter stated, this convergence of feeling between Dr. Salk and Kahn only reinforced their mutual admiration for the courtyard of the monastery of San Francesco at Assisi, which was a piazza paved with stone with a well at its center. **FIG.42** However, nearly a year after Barragán's visit, the decision concerning the design for the courtyard/plaza was still not settled with the project's contracted landscape architect, Lawrence Halprin.[87] Halprin's master landscape plan for the entire Institute was eventually accepted except for the courtyard/plaza area and the lightwell courts flanking both laboratory wings at basement level. For the latter areas Halprin provided a series of alternative designs which included landscaping and/or fountains. These courts as well as the main courtyard/plaza were to remain paved only, with the former in a light red Mexican stone tile and the latter in light Roman travertine. It was not until the summer of 1967 that construction began to complete the pavements. Funding was provided by the Gildred Foundation, named after Theodore Gildred, Sr, who was a pioneer developer and aviator in the San Diego area.[88] Budgetary issues have significant effects on the direction of an architectural project. The convergence of feeling that Dr. Salk and Kahn felt at Luis Barragán's suggestion may also have been a mutual sigh of relief because it resolved a problem in an economic way.[89] However, 'economies' could not prevent the cancellation of the Meeting House and the Visiting Fellows Residences. Salk and Kahn's vision on the ground was compromised.

FIG.105 | **Symphony gala at Salk courtyard**

One of the saddest stories that Suzanne Bourgeois mentions in her book on the founding of the Salk Institute is the selling off of the Szilard Memorial Collection. This was a library assembled by Jacob Bronowski which was part of the broader Archive of Contemporary Biology, and it documented the history of the neurosciences and included rare books from the sixteenth century. This library, as well as the Council for Biology for Human Affairs which was established at the Institute in 1970, were precisely the programs that Jonas Salk encouraged, fulfilling his vision for the Institute. After Bronowski's death in 1974, the same year as Louis I Kahn's death, these programs were terminated by the new president, Frederic de Hoffman.[90]

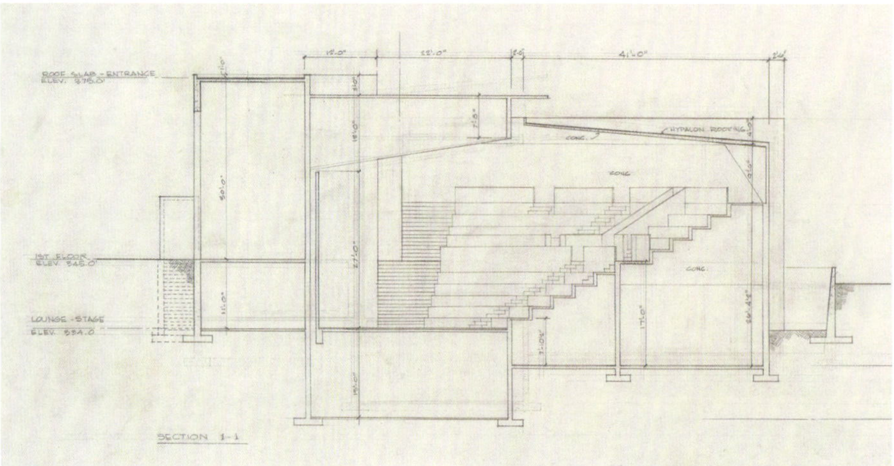

FIG.106

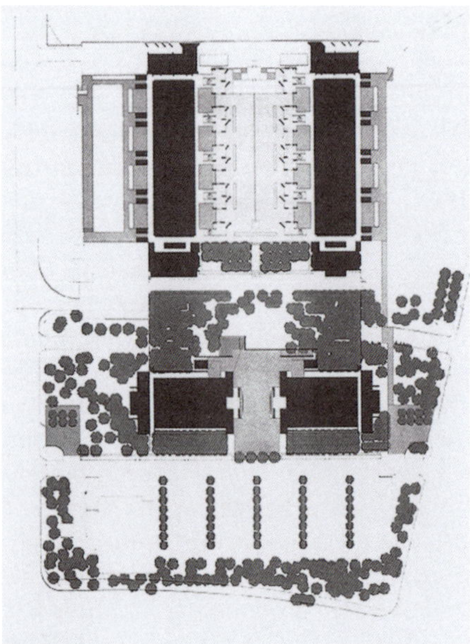

FIG.107

FIG.108

Compromises are the substance of everyday life and politics. The Salk Institute master plan may have been compromised in construction, but the creation of the Salk Institute Laboratory building was not—it was the result of Louis I Kahn's pursuit of architectural perfection. Yet this 'perfection' was short-lived. The south wing laboratories were not fully occupied until 1996. However, well before then the compromised master plan was affecting the operation of the Salk Institute. Cancellation of the Meeting House meant the elimination of the planned 350-seat assembly hall. **FIG.106** There was no large assembly area either for the Salk staff or the public at the Laboratory building. The Institute needed to be expanded to provide future laboratory space.

By 1992 the needed addition was under construction. Jack MacAllister and David Rhinehart—site architects for Kahn during the construction of the Salk Institute—were hired by Anshen and Allen Architects to work on the addition. Numerous studies had been done to resolve the problem of placing a laboratory addition with a sub-surface auditorium in the east garden that served as the main entrance point into the existing Laboratory building. **FIGS.107,108** However, none of the studies deviated from the basic parti: two lab wings of two levels flanking an entrance void on center with the main laboratory building beyond. The

FIG.106 | Section—Meeting House auditorium
FIG.107 | Laboratory/auditorium addition in garden
FIG.108 | Relationship of addition to existing laboratories

two flanking entrances would meet in a common space below the void which allowed access to the auditorium, meeting rooms, lab support spaces and bathrooms. The key siting issue that engaged the architects, in order to appease certain members of the public and the architectural community, was how far into the existing garden should the new structures be located, and what was the nature of the connecting space in between. Only part of the eucalyptus grove in the garden survived—just enough to screen the view of the new addition from the laboratory courtyard/plaza. However, the original approach sequence—from the parking lot, to the multiple paths merging into a double forked path, in turn converging on the single point of access—was destroyed.

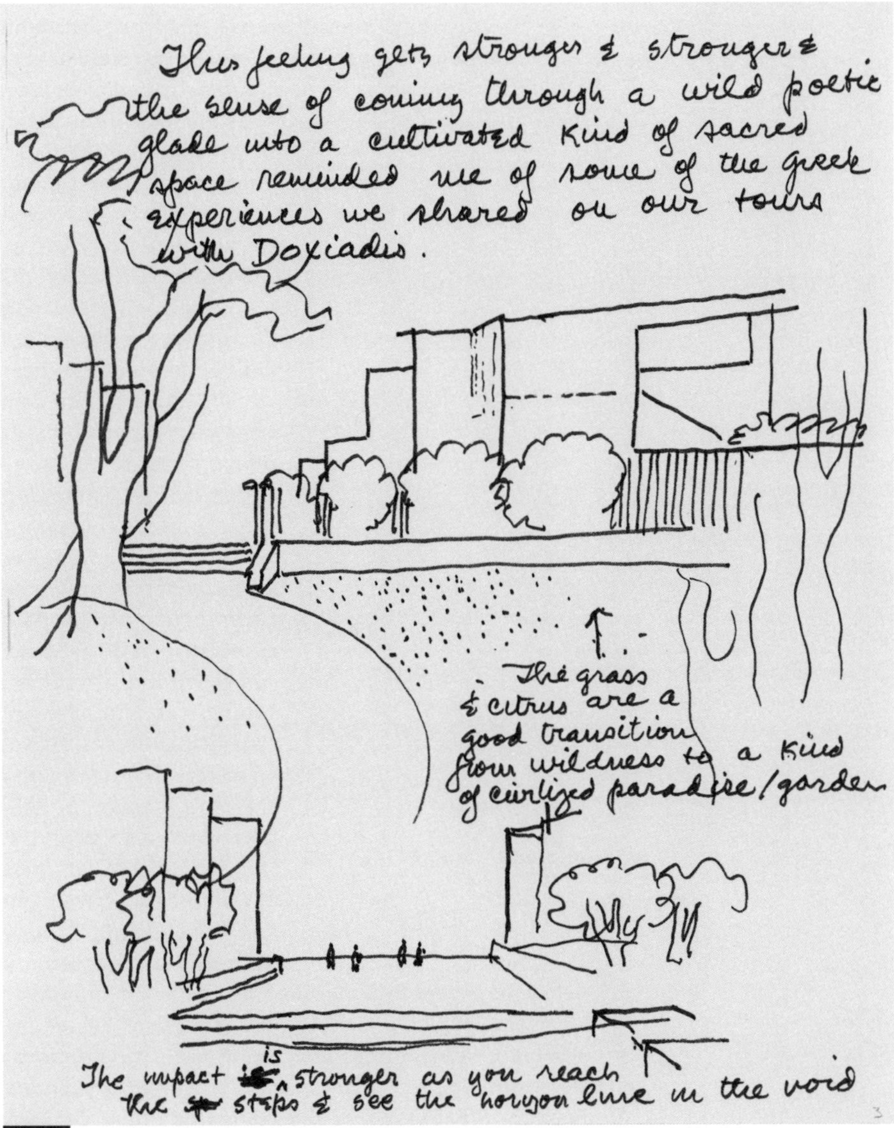

FIG. 109

Prior to the construction of the addition, and for the first time many years after completing his landscape work at the Salk Institute, Lawrence Halprin returned to the site. It was, for him, a new experience because the garden grove had matured. In his handwritten six-page letter of 10 October 1991 to Jonas Salk he explained, using his own analytical sketches, the beauty of the original spatial sequence and the inappropriateness of the addition then under consideration. **FIG.109** Halprin evoked his memories of the Ise Shrine in Japan and the Athenian Acropolis in his description of the Institute garden and Laboratory building. When one exited the parking lot and proceeded through the garden with its screening eucalyptus trees the appearance of the Laboratory building was very gradual, then upon entering the 'precinct' of the courtyard/plaza there is an explosion of space that engages the distant ocean horizon. Halprin understood that an appropriate structure might be one parallel to the axis to the great courtyard/plaza, not across it. When plans for the addition were submitted to the local and state regulatory

FIG.109 | L Halprin sketch (1991)

agencies it was assumed that the eucalyptus grove would be only minimally impacted. This was not to be the case. Jonas Salk was a strong advocate of the Anshen+Allen addition even though he was no longer in charge of the Institute. However, leading members of the architectural community were against the addition. By May 1993, as plans for the addition firmed up, the Kahn family began an international letter writing campaign to prevent its implementation.[91] The Louis I Kahn Preservation Group was founded in Los Angeles to continue the campaign.

During the design of the original Institute, Kahn had done two studies for structures introduced into the garden. **FIGS.110, 63** One scheme indicated a pavilion structure that would have acted as a point of orientation before entering the courtyard/plaza. The second scheme was to provide a 'service building' for the Institute. These additions were canceled during design development. In both cases the structures were aligned directly on axis with the courtyard/plaza beyond. In other words, instead of aping the laboratory courtyard/plaza void in a smaller 'fore-court' or 'fore-void'–thinking that this would respect the nature of the courtyard/plaza–the true solution to the problem should have been based on an effective contrast to the main space of the Salk Institute. Additionally, the program of the new addition could have been divided, allowing more of the laboratories to be sunk below the garden by removing the auditorium to another location. The Salk Institute could have constructed the assembly hall of Kahn's design for the Meeting House at its originally planned location. It was after all separate from the other elements of the Meeting House. Perhaps this structure could have been completed as funding became available. However, Salk and Kahn's original vision no longer had any influence on site planning decisions by the then current Salk administration. Utilitarian need trumped aesthetic considerations. As Louis I Kahn stated: "Need is so many bananas."[92]

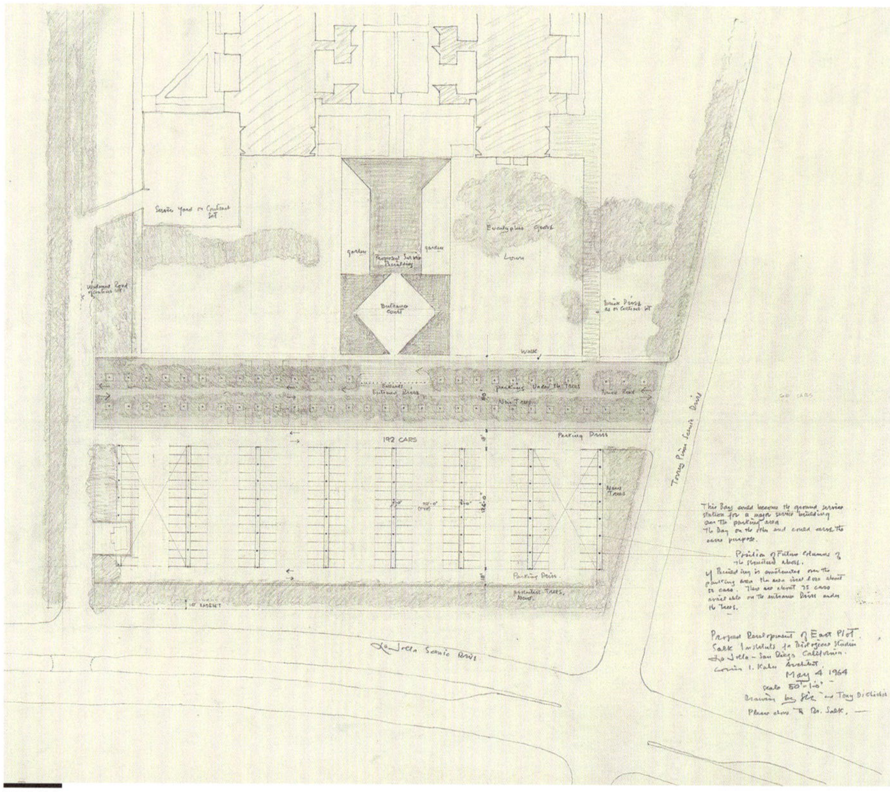

FIG.110

FIG.110 | Alternative scheme–service building in garden

THE DESIGN DEVELOPMENT OF THE SALK INSTITUTE FOR BIOLOGICAL STUDIES ENDNOTES

1 Wurman, *What Will Be Has Always Been,* p 150.
2 Ibid, p 185.
3 Charles Luckman and Associates were the campus planners and, with William Pereira, the architects of the Geisel Library where Salk's archive is located.
4 We summarize the more complex description offered in Suzanne Bourgeois' indispensable book, *Genesis of the Salk Institute–The Epic of its Founders.*
5 Bourgeois, *Genesis of the Salk Institute,* p 3.
6 Ibid, p 4.
7 Ibid, p 4.
8 Ibid, p 8.
9 Ibid, p 58. For a biography of Szilard, see: William Lanouette, *Genius in the Shadows–The Man Behind the Bomb: A Biography of Leo Szilard,* Chicago, University of Chicago Press: 1994. Szilard is also mentioned in Kati Marton, *The Great Escape: Nine Jews Who Fled Hitler and Changed the World,* New York, Simon and Schuster: 2006.
10 Erwin Schrödinger's book *What is Life?* (1948) was a key early expression on the subject by a physicist. Notable bio-researchers responsible for the revolution in biological research all had backgrounds in physics, chemistry and mathematics: Melvin Cohn, Francis Crick, Max Delbrück, Edwin Lennox, Linus Pauling, James Watson, etc.
11 Bourgeois, *Genesis of the Salk Institute,* p 54. "Jonas Salk, however, had been familiar with the name (La Jolla) since 1956. This is when a collaborator from his University of Pittsburgh laboratory, Lenora Brown, had left Pittsburgh for La Jolla with her husband, Massoud Simnad. Massoud had been offered a job he could not refuse at General Atomic, a new division of General Dynamics that had just been founded in La Jolla, suburb of San Diego."
12 Jonas Salk Archive, Box 369 Folder 2. Letter of Salk to Kahn dated 19 December 1960.
13 See Jonas Salk's extended recollections in Wurman, *What Will Be Has Always Been,* p 296. Salk stated that Kahn's talk was given in September 1959. Kahn's talk was delivered 10 October 1959 and was entitled "Order in Science and Art". Cited in Brownlee and DeLong, *Louis I Kahn In the Realm of Architecture,* p 330. Apparently, there no longer is a record anywhere of this talk.
14 The founding members of the Salk Institute were divided into two groups. The founding resident faculty or fellows were: Jonas Salk, Renato Dulbecco, Melvin Cohn, Edwin Lennox and Jacob Bronowski. The non-resident fellows were: Warren Weaver, Leo Szilard, Jacques Monod and Francis Crick. Cf. Bourgeois, *Genesis of the Salk Institute,* pp xxvii–xxxiv.
15 Contract with the client was not signed until July 1961.
16 Bourgeois, *Genesis of the Salk Institute,* p 69. "On March 9 the local newspapers reported that the city intended to give Lot 1324 to Salk and Revelle delivered a furious letter of protest to the mayor. The conflict became very public and unpleasant. Salk was so popular that Revelle and the university were largely blamed: 'Saying no to Jonas Salk was like saying no to Apple Pie and Motherhood.'"
17 For the Vreeland issue, see: Brownlee and DeLong, *Louis Kahn: In the Realm of Architecture,* p 443. For Scully's characterization of the Meeting House as related to Hadrian's Villa, cf. Wurman, *What Will Be Has Always Been,* p 117: "Actually, somebody else in my office showed me a picture of Hadrian's Villa. He remarked to me with the ins and outs of these two buildings. He showed me how close it was to my own building, something I'd never seen before because I'm unhistorical by nature. Scully, who is an historian, sensed the desire, saw these pictures, and then put things down like that, but it's completely the opposite."
18 McCarter, Robert, *Louis I Kahn,* New York, Phaidon: 2005, p 189.
19 We state this even though we acknowledge that in his earlier model for the 'terraced' Meeting House a serial formation of courtyards already appears.
20 See section 12 in this chapter concerning the 1992 addition.
21 See Bressani's book on Viollet-le-Duc: *Architecture and the Historical Imagination,* Farnham, Surrey, UK, Ashgate Publishing: 2014, p 290, where he references Robert Rogers' essay "Freud and the Semiotics of Repetition", *Poetics Today* 8, nos. 3–4, 1987. Rogers states: "The very act of repeating, whether compulsive or not, may have a capacity of release... Repetition holds representational value, particularly when it is enacted with variations."
22 Wurman, *What Will Be Has Always Been,* p 77.
23 Lobell, John, *Between Silence and Light: Spirit in the Architecture of Louis I Kahn,* Boulder, CO, Shambhala: 1979, p 36.
24 In a conversation with William Whitaker in January 2015 at the Architectural Archives at the University of Pennsylvania he stated that when drawings were pulled from specific project files they lost their historical context. Whitaker is the Director of the Archives, and a Kahn and Venturi scholar in his own right.
25 Scully, Vincent, "Frank Lloyd Wright and the Stuff of Dreams", *Modern Architecture and Other Essays,* Neil Levine ed., Princeton and Oxford, Princeton University Press: 2003.
26 See Merrill, Michael, *Louis Kahn: On the Thoughtful Making of Spaces–The Dominican Motherhouse and a Modern Culture of Space,* Baden, Switzerland, Lars Müller Publisher: 2010.
27 Louis I Kahn had a predilection for ordering based on the ancient Roman quadrata which became the basis of so many cities, from ancient Roman Timgad, to Florence, to Penn's plan for Philadelphia.
28 Cf. Norberg-Schulz, Christian, "Heidegger and the Language of Architecture", *Oppositions 18,* fall 1979.
29 John Summerson once stated that a building could be described as classical if there was some trace of the classical orders evident. See his *The Classical Language of Architecture,* London, Methuen: 1963.
30 Cf. Solomon, Susan G, *Louis Kahn's Trenton Jewish Community Center,* New York, Princeton Architectural Press: 2000.
31 See loose notes from Kahn Archive, file 030.II A.27.33 bottom.
32 Burton mentions the book in Kahn's library, given to him by his daughter Sue Ann, as IES Edwards' *The Pyramids of Egypt* where the pyramid is referred to as a solar stair and the stepped pyramid as the "place of ascension" (by the Pharoah). See Burton, Joseph, "Notes from Volume Zero: Louis Kahn and the Language of God", *Perspecta 20,* Cambridge, MA, MIT Press: 1983, p 78.
33 See Swanson's PhD, *Four Laboratory Designs Considered as Mediative Representation,* University of Pennsylvania, Philadelphia: 1993, p 196. Swanson interviewed Jonas Salk in March 1987. Salk "found it (the Basilica of St. Francis at Assisi) conducive

to meditative thought for a community of men... set the tone for the Institute and resulted in the inclusion of arcades and courtyards in their planning."

34 From a personal conversation with Peter Salk in February 2014.

35 Scully, Vincent, *The Earth, Temple and the Gods.* New Haven, Yale University Press: 1962, pp 206-207. Also, cf. Berve, Helmut, *Greek Temples, Theatres and Shrines,* New York, HN Abrams: 1963.

36 Burton, "Notes from Volume Zero: Louis Kahn and the Language of God", p 73. As part of his interpretation of Kahn's work as a hieroglyphic, Burton mentions the two-dimensional sound figures discovered by EFF Chladni in 1787. These were created by a vibrating bow which struck a fixed plate covered with iron filings. Burton does not state if Kahn was aware of these figures.

37 See Lynn, Greg, "The Talented Mr. Tracer", *Tracing Eisenman*, London, Rizzoli: 2006, p 182.

38 From a personal conversation with Peter Salk in February 2014.

39 See the appendix in this book for Jonas Salk's memorial lecture for Louis I Kahn at the AIA, Philadelphia in 1984. François Jacob (a colleague of Jacques Monod at the Pasteur Institute) saw the development of the concept of life from the time of Kant and his notion of "transcendental field". "The pre-established harmony of the 'Classical Age' was "replaced by the predominance of the faculty of knowing over the objects to be known... It was life itself that served as a reference, a transcendental that allowed consciousness to connect the representations and establish relations, not only between different organisms, but also between the different elements of a single organism. In the study of the living world, the concept of life made it possible to reach *a posteriori* truths and achieve a synthesis." From Jacob, François, *The Logic of Life: A History of Heredity*, Princeton, Pantheon Books: 1973, p 88. Also, Klapwijk defined emergent evolution "as the coming to the fore of a new arrangement of being in such a way that new functions and properties arise, based on the functions and properties that were already present at preceding levels of being but not reducible to them, because they respond to laws of their own." From Klapwijk, Jacob, *Purpose in the Living World?*, Cambridge, UK, Cambridge University Press: 2008, p 104.

40 See Leslie, Thomas, *Louis I Kahn–Building Art, Building Science*, New York, George Braziller: 2005, p 53.

41 Although Fuller's use of tetrahedra was intended for lightweight metal structures Tyng suggested to Kahn that a more radical solution was needed than shallow concrete vaulting for the ceiling/floor structure at the Yale gallery. Kahn's "mis-appropriation" of the tetrahedral system showed just how non-rational his design decision making could be. The expense of forming a pure tetrahedral concrete ceiling was exorbitant and to save the concept more conventional structural beams had to be integrated to lower costs. The incongruity of inserting a tetrahedral/triangular system within a more orthogonal geometry of elements at Yale expressed both difference and an openness to other systems of organization. To that extent Kahn repeated some of the non-orthogonal geometries that Frank Lloyd Wright had utilized.

42 See William Jordy's essay on the Richards Center, "What the building 'wants to be': Louis Kahn's Richards Medical Research Buildings'", *American Buildings and Their Architects, vol. 4,* Garden City, NY, Doubleday: 1970.

43 From a personal conversation with the author at Vincent Scully's Yale office in 1984.

44 In brief, problems included inadequate recognition of the need for secretarial spaces in relation to the labs, the diminution of Kahn's concept of the open lab lofts by partitions that scientists wanted to keep their researches private, the potential for dust collection in the services weaving through the open structure above, the glare through some of the windows and deformation in the corners of some of the labs because of excessive deflection of the cantilevers.

45 Wurman, *What Will Be Has Always Been*, p 127.

46 The double curved lines also resemble the tie markings of a musical score. Kahn often analogized architectural rhythms in light and dark to musical tonalities. He was an excellent pianist and once considered a career in music rather than architecture.

47 Bourgeois, *Genesis of the Salk Institute*, p 115.

48 Vierendeel trusses were used earlier at Kahn's AFL Medical Services building in Philadelphia (1954-1956–later demolished).

49 Anderson, Stanford, "Louis Kahn in the 1960s", special Kahn issue of *Architecture and Urbanism*, 1985.

50 Bourgeois, *Genesis of the Salk Institute*, p 115.

51 In a letter to Kahn, dated 21 March 1963, Jonas Salk indicates that lab construction drawings were complete and there was physical activity at the site. (030.II A107.24) Thomas Leslie indicated that a full architectural/structural package was delivered to the site before 18 January 1963. (See Leslie, Thomas, p 148.)

52 In a letter dated 13 June 1962 Jonas Salk asked that final design be delayed on the layout of the administrative and library wings. (027. II C.37) A letter from Kahn dated 26 July 1962 (027.II C.37) requested his structural engineer August Komendant to begin engineering work for the stairway, service and mechanical rooms. By 8 September 1962 Kahn had just received the program for the scientists' studies. At a meeting in Kahn's office, on 28 August 1962, John MacAllister and Marshall Meyers (site and project architects respectively), Dale L Harvey (owner's rep) and Earl Walls (lab consultant) discussed the programming for the service blocks flanking the north and south sides of the lab wings. These blocks were to include emergency showers and exits for use by the lab workers (minutes of meeting, 027 II C.29). By December 1962 the structural calculations for the labs were completed (027 II C.41) and in August 1963 Kahn's contract was amended to stop work on the Meeting House. In a letter to Komendant dated 28 August 1963 Kahn requested that engineering work be done for an "open" fire stair between the studies and the labs proper.

53 Landscape work for the center plaza was not completed when the scientists left their temporary barracks in early 1966 for the north lab wing. The south wing was not fully utilized for its intended purpose until 1996 and served as temporary space for a variety of functions: seminar rooms, administrative offices, storage rooms, and a recreation area including a small gym. (See Bourgeois, *Genesis of the Salk Institute*, p 116.) Also, Luis Barragán visited the site in February of 1966. This is when he made his famous statement, "I would not put a tree or a blade of grass in this space. This should be a plaza of stone, not a garden... If you make this a plaza, you will gain a façade, a façade to the sky." (See Brownlee and DeLong, *Louis I Kahn: In the Realm of Architecture*, p 100.) In a letter of 19 December 1966 to Salk, Kahn is still considering options for the plaza landscaping including proposals by Lawrence Halprin.

54 Cf. Tafuri, Manfredo, the chapter "Operative Criticism" in his *Theories and History of Architecture.* The "breakthrough" at the Salk courtyard may very well be a "forcing of the future!"

55 Cf. Rowe, Colin, "Classicism and Neo-classicism in Modern Architecture", *The Mathematics of the Ideal Villa and Other Essays*, Cambridge, MA, MIT Press: 1976.

56 McCarter, *Louis I Kahn*, p 98.

57 Susan Solomon has stated this in her book, *Louis Kahn's Trenton Jewish Community Center.* The use of the A-B-A grid at Trenton not only became the basis of Kahn's Kimbell Museum but is an important ordering device for his work at the Indian Institute of Management.

58 See the Banham critique in Chapter Three of this book.

59 Wurman, *What Will Be Has Always Been*, p 138.

60 Ibid, p 150.

61 Peter Gast referred to the oblique piers engaging the courtyard space at Salk as an "oscillation". See Gast, *Louis I Kahn–The Idea of Order*, Basel and Boston, Birkhäuser: 1998. Gast probably appropriated the term oscillation in this context from Gianni Vattimo's essay "Art and Oscillation" in his *Transparent Society*, Oxford, UK, Polity Press: 2005.

62 Swanson is the only scholar to make this observation besides this author. See his PhD dissertation, *Four Laboratory Designs Considered as Mediative Representation*, p 177.

63 Ibid, p 212.

64 McCarter indicates that Jonas Salk wanted this open feeling. He did not want the studies directly opposite the laboratories. McCarter, *Louis I Kahn*, p 203.

65 See Kahn *Complete Works*, 1977 edition, p 31.

66 The gap between the east studies, closer to the garden, is narrower than the gap opening the courtyard to the west.

67 Brownlee and DeLong, *Louis I Kahn: In the Realm of Architecture*, p 100.

68 Wurman, *What Will Be Has Always Been*, p 2: "There must be an order of movement, an order of winds, an order of light."

69 We of course refer to Jonas Salk as leader of the team that discovered the cure for

polio—the same polio that afflicted FDR which he tried to ameliorate on his visits to the pools at Warm Springs, Georgia.

70 Leslie, Thomas, "Things in their best order: technical aspects of the Salk Institute and their role in its design" in *The Journal of Architecture*, Vol. 8, spring 2003. This essay later became a chapter in Leslie's book *Louis I Kahn—Building Art, Building Science*, New York, George Braziller: 2005.

71 This is an expression often attributed to Mies van der Rohe. See the *New York Times* obituary for Mies van der Rohe, 19 August 1969.

72 Wurman, *What Will Be Has Always Been*, p 130. Mesenchyme: loosely organized undifferentiated mostly mesodermal cells that give rise to such structures as connective tissues, blood, lymphatics, bone and cartilage. Also referred to by Bourgeois, in *Genesis of the Salk Institute*, p 118.

73 Quote from Kahn on building with hollow stones. See Wurman, *What Will Be Has Always Been*, p 124.

74 Leslie, *The Journal of Architecture* Vol. 8, spring 2003, p 99.

75 Salk Archive, 397 Folder 2. Jacob Bronowski, a mathematician but specifically a topologist, was originally a British subject. During WWII he headed the statistical unit that analyzed the industrial and economic effects of the RAF's bombing campaign against Germany. He also wrote the report on the atomic bombing of Hiroshima and Nagasaki for the British government. (See Bourgeois, *Genesis of the Salk Institute.*) Bronowski was also a historian of science who had a particular interest in the creative/imaginative dimension of science, which was reflected in his numerous writings (see Bibliography). His work culminated in the multi-part BBC TV series *The Ascent of Man* (1973).

76 See Thomas Leslie's writings in the Bibliography for the documentation concerning the design and fitting out of the laboratory workbenches and coordination of the lighting design by Kahn's office.

77 Crick's comments recorded in a transcript of a meeting in Paris, 25 July 1962, of the resident fellows of the Salk Institute preparing to come to La Jolla. From Salk Institute Files—General Correspondence 1962—Letter to J Salk from WH Glazier, General Manager of the Salk Institute from 1963 onward.

78 Penn Archive letter of 24 September 1963 from Kahn to August Komendant, stating that the Building Department gave approval for the open stair concept desired by Salk and Kahn.

79 Swanson, *Four Laboratory Designs Considered as Mediative Representation*, p 180. "Varied window openings and the dynamic breaking of the western façade introduces a new liveliness and counterpoint to a design overburdened with a symmetry that had dulled the senses." Swanson was still one step away from understanding the formal relationship between the structure of the scientists' studies and the western façade.

80 Venturi, *Iconography and Electronics Upon a Generic Architecture*, Cambridge, MA, MIT Press: 1996, p 91: "Denise [Scott Brown] has written of this issue elsewhere. And I shall note here that Kahn learned from me concerning the elements of layering, holes in walls, and breaking the order described above; his use of inflections in the case of the pavilions in the Salk Center complex derives also from my critique." A fuller treatment of this issue is given in an online thesis: Sam Rodell, *The Influence of Robert Venturi on Louis Kahn*, Washington State University (see Bibliography). On p 13, Rodell makes direct reference to the North Penn Visiting Nurse Association building on the inflections of the Salk Institute.

81 Noted by John Hejduk in a discussion of Venturi's architecture at a Harvard Forum: "Beyond the Modern Movement", *Harvard Architectural Review* Vol. I, spring 1980, p 200.

82 It is difficult to determine which occurred first: vertical segmentation in the Salk office façades or the similar effect in the Richards Biology Towers which were designed and constructed at the same time as the Salk Institute.

83 Bourgeois, *Genesis of the Salk Institute*, p 116.

84 In Brownlee and DeLong's book on Kahn, *In the Realm of Architecture*, it is stated that there was an exhibit of Barragán's work at MoMA. However, what was more likely was that some of Barragán's work was shown as part of a broader exhibit. Barragán had his own first exhibit at MoMA in 1976.

85 McCarter, *Louis I Kahn*, p 204.

86 Ibid, p 204.

87 See letter from Kahn's office to Halprin's office dated 5 January 1967 (014 IA.23.23) where John MacAllister (Salk site architect) reviewed the Halprin office proposal for the entire site. Halprin had already master-planned the famous Sea Ranch housing project on the California coast, north of San Francisco.

88 Theodore Gildred, Sr (1900–1967) was born in Rochester, NY and brought up and educated in Argentina and Ecuador. He was a 1918 New York University graduate in civil engineering and with his brother Phil developed and built the Fox Theater in downtown San Diego (1927). He flew with pioneer aviator Doug Kelly in San Diego and he became the Lindbergh of South America when he pioneered the first long-distance airplane voyage to Quito (1931). He later moved to Mexico and between 1937 and 1965 developed Lindavista—one of the largest subdivisions north of Mexico City. Cf. Theodore Gildred, Sr. Collection on the San Diego Air and Space Museum website: sandiegoairandspace.org.

89 Wurman, *What Will Be Has Always Been*, p 35: "Economy is building the right thing; financing is building the wrong thing."

90 Bourgeois, *Genesis of the Salk Institute*, p 178.

91 Nathaniel Kahn's letter of 25 December 1993 to Lawrence Halprin summarized the attempt to get the project stopped. See 014.I.B.2363 in the Kahn Archive.

92 Wurman, *What Will Be Has Always Been*, pp 29.

CHAPTER TWO

READINGS IN THE LIGHT

THE BUILDINGS OF LOUIS I KAHN 1946–1965 AND THE SALK INSTITUTE

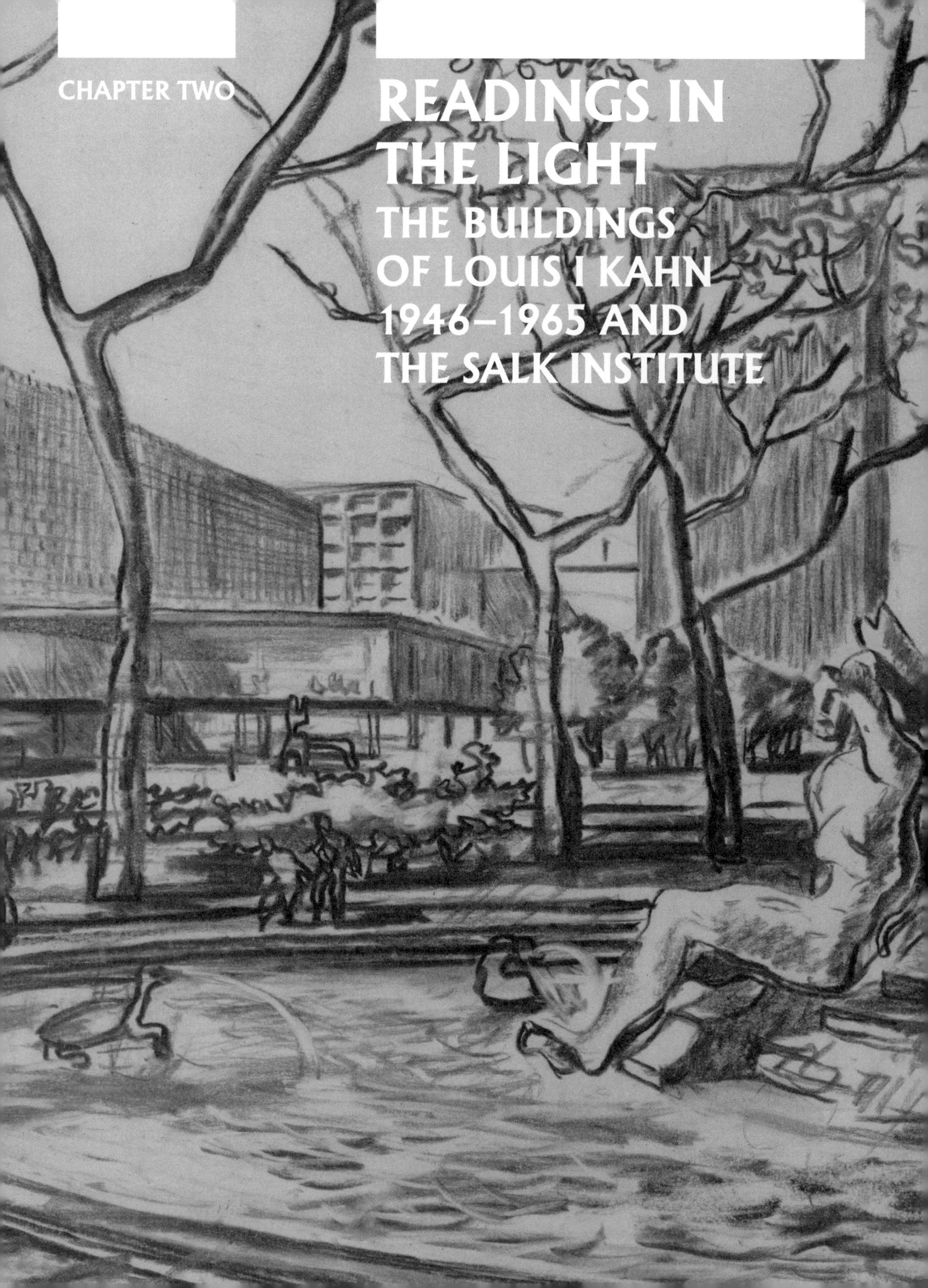

A plan of a building should be read like a harmony of spaces in light. Even a space intended to be dark should have just enough light from some mysterious opening to tell us how dark it really is. Each space must be defined by its structure and the character of its natural light.

Louis I Kahn[1]

FIG.111

As one of the twentieth century's greatest draftsmen Louis I Kahn was sensitive to the varieties of light. Kahn had already mastered the modeling of the human figure in light, shade and shadow by his early twenties, while a student in architecture at the School of Fine Arts at the University of Pennsylvania. The sketches from his 1928-1929 trip to Europe show a remarkable range of effects from pure black, white and gray to art deco abstraction in black and white and in color, to drawings of intense realism that could only have been drawn by a person with a great inner light. **FIG.101** It was historian Vincent Scully's own observation that Kahn himself, his body, emanated a peculiar light.[2] Kahn, in many of his landscape drawings, caught the ambient mood of light caused by varying atmospheric conditions. At the time of his later voyages to Italy, Greece and Egypt, he was a Fellow at the American Academy in Rome (1950-1951), and his drawings reached a new intensity of materiality and abstraction in color, shadow, shade and light.

FIG.112

In 1946 Louis I Kahn and his partner Oscar Stonorov designed a passive solar house for the Libbey-Owen-Ford Company, who commissioned architects in 47 states in a publicity campaign to promote their innovations in glass technology. A year later Kahn began work on the Morton Weiss House, which included vertically sliding wood panels at the windows of the living room and master bedroom suite. **FIG.111** In conjunction with the roof overhangs and an intermediate sunshade these panels modulated the play of light and privacy for the interior. A similar concept was adopted at the double-height space of the Pincus Occupational Therapy Building (1948-1951) at the Philadelphia Psychiatric Hospital. However, at Kahn's three-story Radbill Building (1948-1954) at the same

FIG.111 | Elevations—Morton Weiss House (1948-1949)
FIG.112 | Pincus Therapy Building, Philadelphia (1949-1950)

hospital he experimented with a different approach to roof and sunshade overhangs. At the south- and east-facing façades Kahn pierced the overhangs with small openings lined with tubular terracotta sections, allowing an even serial pattern of small light sparks to penetrate the three levels of shadow over the windows. **FIG.113** Kahn's perspicacious gesture is astonishing, given the context of this dramatic encounter of shadow and light. Kahn's overhangs and their light effect at Radbill were a unique contribution to twentieth-century architecture.[3]

FIG.113

The Yale University Art Gallery, which is Louis I Kahn's first 'significant' work of architecture, was a response to the varieties of light's effects. The origins of the 'blank' brick wall in Kahn's work can be traced back to his first work as a practicing architect: the Ahavath Israel Synagogue in Philadelphia (1935-1939). **FIG.114** However, it is Kahn's drawings and sketches of the late 1940s through 1950 that presage his work at Yale. **FIGS.115-118** These drawings and sketches are of four kinds: perspective renderings for theoretical projects like a Music Hall for the Philadelphia Plan for a Mid-Town City Civic Center (1947-1948), experimental sketches of abstract figures in light, shade and shadow (1948-1950), travel sketches like Kahn's sketch No.2 of the Palazzo Vecchio (1950) and sketches for the Yale project itself, such as the one showing the cast shadow at the entrance opposite Egerton Swartwout's original Yale Gallery (1928). In Kahn's Transparency No.1 experimental sketch there is the play of literal and phenomenal transparency in the hovering of flat planes over converging forms. Optical breaks can be detected. In the Palazzo Vecchio sketch Kahn schematizes the flanking façades of the Uffizi Gallery by eliminating windows and emphasizing the convergence of the cornices and moldings onto the space of the Piazza where the effects of light, shade and shadow are displayed. The latter sketch is particularly important because Kahn emphasized movement toward space—an expression of an architectural intention. At the Yale Art Gallery

FIG.114

FIG.113 | Radbill Psychological Hospital addition (1950-1953)
FIG.114 | Ahavath Israel Synagogue (1935-1939)

FIG.115

FIG.116

FIG.117

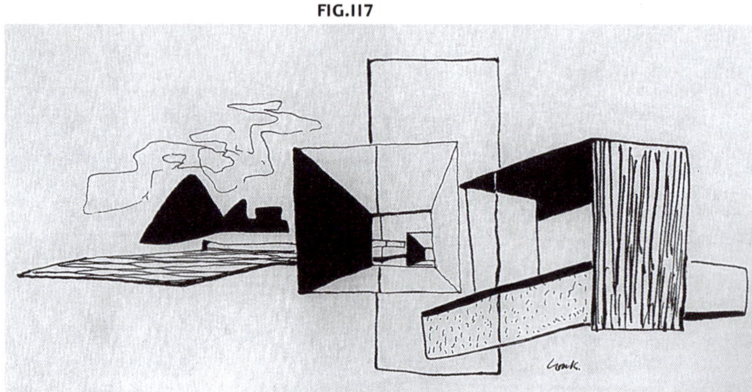

FIG.118

FIG.115 | Music Hall project (1947–1948)
FIG.116 | L Kahn drawing—Yale University Art Gallery (1951)
FIG.117 | L Kahn drawing—Palazzo Vecchio No.2 (1950)
FIG.118 | L Kahn drawing (c. 1949)

Kahn adapted a schema of his historical memory for the purposes of mimicking the movement of traffic along Chapel Street and integrating it with the stack of floor levels defined by the bluestone coursing with their cast shadows. The main wall anchors the overall composition of the Yale University Art Gallery, establishing a boundary, and at the same time is destabilized by the undercutting of the vertical stack of walls by the sidewalk. **FIG.119** The Yale University Art Gallery wall is radically broken off and shifted to create the opening which is the entrance. Four floors are exposed in the gap, and are covered over in curtain wall glazing and translucent white curtains. The displaced wall is dematerialized in the reflection of this double 'curtain' wall which leads us into the virtual condition that is the gallery interior. Both the shift and the dematerialization presage the condition at the Salk courtyard with the shifted disappearance of the study structures toward the sea. One increment of the curtain wall is absent, creating a vestibule which from the exterior is in shadow but from its interior is transparent, opening up views to the gallery on the first floor. The superimposition of shadowed void over the opaque transparency of the curtain wall is uncanny.[4]

FIG.119

FIG.120

FIG.121

FIG.119 | **Pre-2006 entrance at Yale University Art Gallery**
FIG.120 | **Yale University Art Gallery stairwell roof**
FIG.121 | **Yale University Art Gallery main stair**

The tetrahedral ceiling over all the loft levels of the gallery interior allows three lighting conditions. Firstly, gallery lighting can occur below the level of the tetrahedral ribs, meeting the requirements of exhibit lighting. Secondly, the lighting can be mounted deep into the interior apexes of the tetrahedral, creating spot lighting effects at the ceiling level. For the third alternative, the tetrahedra without lights reflects the ambient light of the gallery, expressing its facets in light and shade. For Vincent Scully this was Louis I Kahn's homage to the Egyptian pyramids he had sketched in 1951. At the cylindrical stair core the ceiling/roof structure is an enlarged triangular citation from the tetrahedral field of the gallery spaces, supported by the rim of the cylinder. **FIGS.120,121** The depth of the structural beams determined the height of the gap above the rim and the stair roof slab proper, which is filled with glass blocks. The light diffuses onto the concrete of the stair 'well'. It is reflected off the stainless-steel handrails with their panels of stainless-steel woven wire mesh and absorbed by the black pre-cast terrazzo stair treads and landings. The archaic feel of this space is in the play of light of these contrasting materials—the stair material so reminiscent of ancient Egyptian obsidian. At the rear garden façade of the

Yale University Art Gallery the contrasting effects of the reflective curtain wall, with its shaded entrance vestibule, are repeated in a new way. Here two curtain walls at right angles intersect at the inside corner of the lower terrace in a play of reflections that dissolves any trace of supporting structure. **FIG.122** One exits from the gallery through this reflectivity onto the hard surfaces of the lower garden terrace, from which we ascend to the main garden as if from a crypt via a double run of stairs uncovered by the virtual shift of the upper terrace. **FIG.198** Kahn's sensitive handling of this subterranean condition will be repeated at the design for the 'sunken' basement laboratories at the Salk Institute.

FIG.122

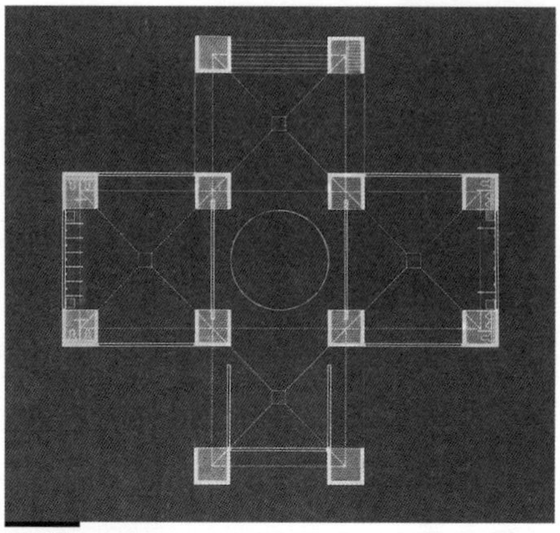

FIG.123

FIG.124

One can only agree with Susan Solomon's comment that the Trenton Bath House was the "seminal" project of Louis I Kahn's career. It was the only building, except for the playground structures, that was realized from the planning for the Jewish Community Center.[5] **FIG.123** The Bath House materialized the intended A-B-A grid planning that had underlain the Jewish Community Center project. As was discussed earlier, the apparent dogmatic tartan grid structuring these works allowed Kahn and his colleague and project architect Anne Tyng to open up the final disposition of the building in unexpected ways.

The bias of the 'Greek' cross planning at the Bath House is countered by the oblique approach to the building entrance and the strong processional axis from the entrance area to the ascending steps leading to the pool. This axis already presages the stream at the Salk courtyard insofar as the latter leads to a pool! All of the planning at Trenton foreshadows the planning at the Salk Laboratory building. The building viewed from the entrance approach also suggests the geometry and elevational form of the future director's house at the Salk Meeting House. In addition, the processional axis is defined by the servant elements that define storage rooms, toilet enclosures and the shaded entrance baffles that lead to the male and female locker areas. The small servant elements embed or interlock the locker room areas to the 'public' corridor. **FIG.124** One disappears into darkness and reappears into the light as one enters transitions through the baffles into the locker areas. The 'earthen' circle at the center of the unroofed pavilion space at the center of the Bath House not only repeats the ancient Roman pattern of the

FIG.122 | Yale University Art Gallery lower garden
FIG.123 | Trenton Bath House plan (1955–1956)
FIG.124 | Trenton Bath House corridor

circle within the square theme but it is literally a 'traffic' circle, helping to organize the circulation pattern while offering a tactile shift underfoot for those crossing it. It acts also as an interruptive element like the wide travertine bench at the entrance to the Salk Institute courtyard. By introducing a geometry of tie-rods to the roof structure of all but the center pavilion Kahn was able to levitate the pyramidal roofs, articulating them from the enclosing walls below. And through these intervening gaps natural light enters the locker areas—but more importantly, the light or the sky itself seems to support the roof structure. **FIG.125**

FIG.125

FIG.126

FIG.125 | **Trenton Bath House male changing room**
FIG.126 | **Richards Research Building corner laboratory view**

As stated earlier, at the University of Pennsylvania Medical Research Building—formerly known as the Alfred Newton Richards Medical Research Building (1957-1965)—Louis I Kahn and his structural engineer developed a new language of architecture based on the 'spacing' of vertical and horizontal elements.[6] This was the first laboratory building with inoperable windows. Glazing covers gaps formed by the complex cantilevered pre-cast, post-tensioned structure which has been analogized to a Chinese puzzle. There is a photo of Richards taken just before the fitting out of the laboratories that indicated the ideal relationship of the lab lofts that Kahn was trying to accomplish within a program on a narrowly constricted site. **FIG.126** The stacking of these laboratory lofts, their transparency and the clustering in towers allowed the scientists to become aware that they were part of a community of fellow explorers and of the university itself. However, the 'excessive' transparency led to an inability to control sunlight which had a negative impact on laboratory activities. The scientists were forced to use ad hoc remedies for sun screening. Kahn had already anticipated the solar light and heat gain problem by provision of interior blinds but these fell victim to the budgetary axe.

The Richards complex was constructed in two phases. **FIG.129** The first phase consisted of the medical research towers (completed 1961), organized pinwheel fashion around a service core which included animal quarters. We enter the building through an absent increment of lab loft just above grade and under the full stack of lofts above, with the open web of supporting structure exposed over our heads. We disappear into the brickwalled-in service core to access elevators to the laboratories proper. On each floor we move back outward through the labs toward natural light.

Meanwhile, the second phase for biological research was based on a linear sequence of three towers with a much simpler cantilever arrangement of structure. However inelegant these later towers may appear they include one of Kahn's most interesting compositional devices. These are the library carrels that define the upper two levels at two of the towers where Kahn famously said, "a man with a book goes to the light". **FIG.128** Each carrel is a fragment of a windowed cube plunged into the tops of these towers. There are two windows on each face of the carrels. The larger window provides light and views to and from the entire floor level. The much smaller window below was planned to serve the reader at his or her desk. On careful examination the windows were formed from notches which protrude beyond normal brick infill walls of the Biology Towers. The protrusions are capped by shallow concrete copings. The notched forms are a theme at the original Richards towers. They can be found at the service door at the tower adjacent to the oblique stair access to the entrance plinth. They reappear in the four half-notches aligned as air intake openings at the four monumental brick shafts, abutting the immense service core at the heart of the complex. **FIG.52** The notch was most prominently displayed at the crown of one of the stair towers. Kahn decapitated the head of the stair tower, reduced and multiplied it into the carrels.[7] **FIGS.127,128** Reyner Banham had criticized the notched form as an ineffective and inappropriate "symbol" for a stair tower, and Kahn replied to Banham.[8] But what Banham missed was that it was not a "symbol" but a 'sign' in a play of 'signs' that we encounter in a number of Kahn works during the period of the Richards design development. Perhaps the most remarkable use of the notch form is to be found in the house for Margaret Esherick (1959-1962):

> **For Kahn, it was the interplay of natural light, the change of mood brought as the sun emerges from the obscurity of clouds, or the nature of light revealed as one season yields to another that gave the Esherick house an 'alive look at all times'.[9]**

One of the interesting revelations in Marcus and Whitaker's book on *The Houses of Louis Kahn* unintentionally sheds light on the plan of the Esherick house. Kahn's colleague and project architect Anne Tyng stated that Kahn had "teased" her about the Harvard bi-nuclear plan, which was the basis of the

FIG.127

FIG.128

FIG.127 | Kahn early sketch—Richards Research Building
FIG.128 | Carrels at later Richards Biology Tower addition

earlier plan for the Morton Weiss house. **FIG.130** This was partly a reference to the bi-nuclear work that Marcel Breuer had developed (1943-1945) in the New England area as well as a jibe at Tyng's Harvard education. The plan of the Yale University Art Gallery could also be construed as part of a bi-nuclear arrangement with the original existing gallery. **FIG.131** But at Yale Kahn undermined this notion by not allowing the linking structural bay of his addition to serve as an entrance to the gallery. One enters the gallery parallel to this linking bay.

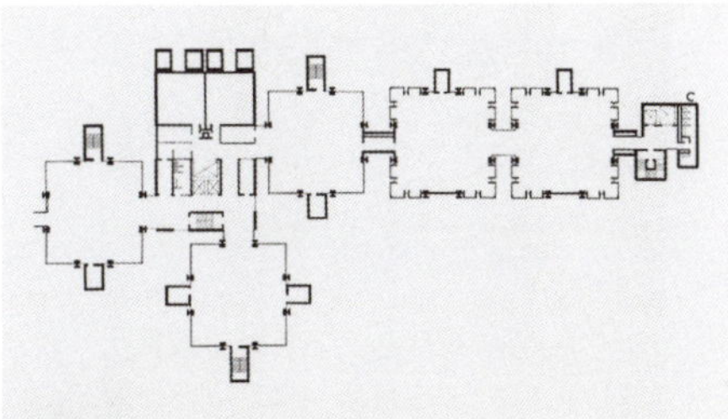

FIG.129

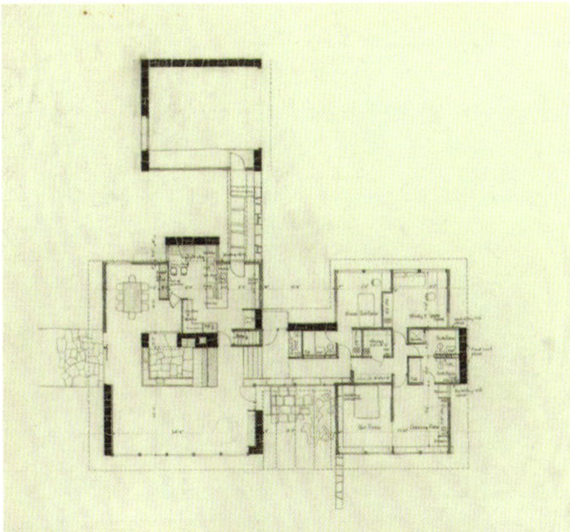

FIG.130

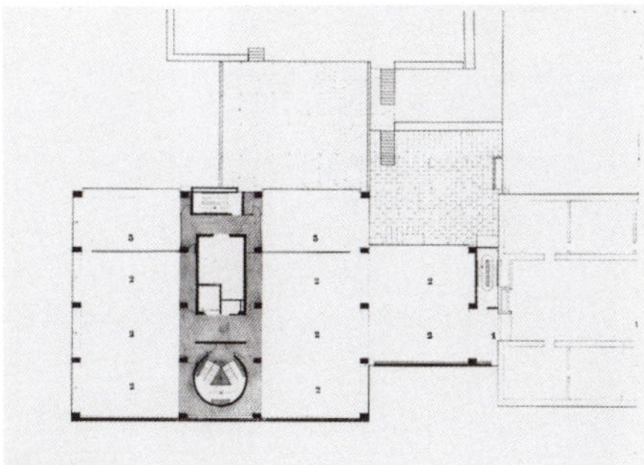

FIG.131

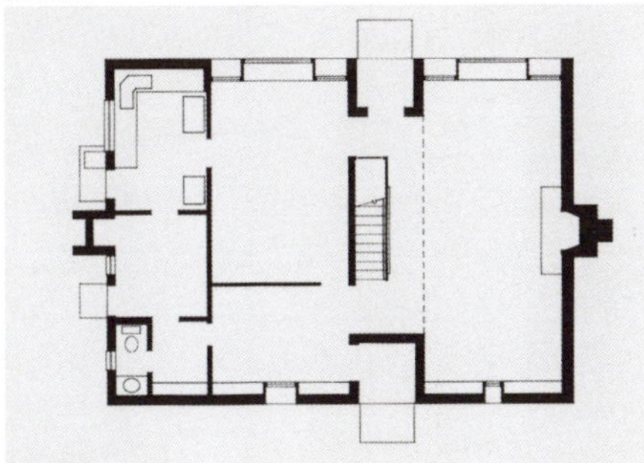

FIG.132

FIG.133

The Esherick House exhibits what Robert Venturi would later call the complexity and contradiction in architecture. **FIG.133** The house is a doubled volume with a flat roof that constrains it into a unitary figure. The two-story deep slot of space divides the house between the living room volume to the west with its double-height space, and the dining/kitchen/service area to the east with the bedroom suite at the second floor. The double-height entrance void is itself split horizontally by a shallow slab that forms a balcony over the entrance. The Esherick House plan exhibits that sense of parallel space or parataxis that was such a defining feature of many of Kahn's projects—especially at the Laboratory building at the Salk Institute. However, another reading of the plan suggests that it is a distorted version of a bi-nuclear composition. **FIG.132** The two-story entrance voids, both at the street and garden façades in plan, are notches. They define the middle zone of the plan, half-occupied by the stair to the upper level, which is essentially a compressed space between the living and dining rooms. Again, Kahn avoids entering a bi-nuclear link by placing the entrance door orthogonally to the house façade. Only at the rear of the house does one exit into the garden frontally. **FIG.134** At the street notched forms dominate the façade. This is certainly one of the most intriguing domestic façades done in the twentieth century.

Marcus and Whitaker end their chapter on the Esherick House with a quote from Vincent Scully: "He zeroed in on the distinctive windows, which, he rhapsodized, 'can fill a volume up to the rim with light, so the house is a cup, high-shouldered to contain air like

FIG.129 | **Richards Research Building plan (1957-1964)**
FIG.130 | **Morton Weiss House plan (1948-1949)**
FIG.131 | **Yale University Art Gallery plan (1951-1953)**
FIG.132 | **Esherick House plan (1959-1961)**
FIG.133 | **Esherick House view from street**

FIG.134

FIG.135

FIG.134 | Esherick House living room view to garden
FIG.135 | Salk Institute intermediate study structures solution

a substance—a brimming chalice of light.'"[10] We are also given biographical information about Margaret Esherick.[11] After leaving college she lived in San Francisco and worked for an antiquarian bookseller. When she returned to Philadelphia she "took over" another bookstore and later moved it around the corner to a house which she renovated with the help of her brother, who was an architect. These biographical details help account for the integration of book shelving as an integral part of the north-facing living room wall at the Esherick House, but they also 'explain' Kahn's insertion of the oak-framed window units and shutters at the level of Margaret Esherick's bedroom suite as a reference to Esherick's bibliophilia. Here Kahn has inserted a variation of the library carrels at the Richards Research Center, "where a man with a book goes to the light", into a large notch level with the second floor and open to the shallow roof fascia above. **FIG.133** The 'residual' spaces flanking the 'carrel' form the floor-to-ceiling voids, glazed in and provided with double wood shutters for privacy.[12] The façade at the living room volume is a higher notch, acting as a clerestory window simply filled with glass above a higher wall which ensures privacy from the street. The asymmetry of the street façade at the Esherick House integrates several light and spatial effects. There is the solitude of the 'carrel' with its glass reflecting the site exterior framed by the deep dark voids. There is the shallow recess of the entrance slot in shade, which is both open and closed. The spatial-volumetric depth of the double-height living room is only hinted at through its clerestory window. In the interior photo of the living room in Marcus and Whitaker's book the light of sunset streams through the tall west window, casting the shadow of the exterior chimney onto the solid wood balustrades of the stairway and balcony. **FIG.134** The light pattern inverts the shadowed deep articulating voids of the street façade.

If the street façade of the Esherick House is indebted to the Richards Research Center the garden façade presages developments at the Salk Institute. The east-to-west walls disappear, opening the volume of the house to the garden and exposing the vertical edges of the north/south walls. The window mullions define curtain walls inset between these edges. **FIG.135** The doubled character of the Esherick House is carried over into the doubled character of the Salk Institute scientists' studies, as well as the play of wood elements against shallow wall and floor slabs. The house for a single woman became the spaces of solitude for the scientists.

The Esherick House was an extremely fertile compositional source for Kahn's ongoing design activity. What Kahn shared with several other master architects was the ability to absorb influences from multiple sources to create an original architecture. At the Unitarian Church in Rochester (1959-1974) Kahn surrounded an almost square sanctuary of 58 feet by 68 feet with an ambulatory, which on three sides is bounded by the school classrooms with bathroom units, meeting rooms and a library. **FIG.136** The fourth side of the sanctuary is open to the foyer entrance hall into the church proper. The folded brick exterior walls of the church are one of Kahn's most powerful accomplishments. **FIG.137** They are the shadowed counterparts to the sanctuary where light is welcomed at the corners of the space through large inward-looking clerestory 'hoods'. **FIG.139** The folded thick walls both make legible, and mask at the building exterior, the difference in height between the sanctuary, which is a 20-foot double-height space, and the two-story surrounding classrooms. These walls integrate several motifs including Kahn's earlier experimental sketches of folded planes in shade and shadow. **FIG.138** His sketches of Carcassonne's crenellations done during his 1959 visit to southern France must be consulted. **FIG.140**

And finally Kahn transformed the 'carrel' elevations of Margaret Esherick's bedroom suite and the reading carrels at the Richards Biology Towers. The smaller lower 'carrel' windows at Esherick and Richards were transposed to become, at the Unitarian Church, the vertical slotted windows at the sides of the brick classroom alcoves. Here Kahn multiplied the Esherick 'carrel' motif to articulate the walls of a school, varying the rhythms as needed: "Where a man (or child) with a book goes to the light." But rhythms are also musical. Kahn was an accomplished pianist. As Joseph Burton indicated, Kahn's mother was a fine musician. The family background can be traced to Felix Mendelssohn, the German Classic-Romantic composer.[13] The rhythmic folded walls of the Unitarian Church evoke the contrasting black and white keys of the piano keyboard. The shadowed voids are the negatives of the black keys.

The importance of the Unitarian Church in the development of Louis I Kahn's career and his architecture cannot be overestimated. It was a project that made up for the loss of another religious commission which was for the Jewish Community Center in Trenton, New Jersey. The Unitarian Church fully embodied Kahn's idea of the plan as a "society of rooms". **FIG.139** It was Kahn's first building with a large interior communal space brought into natural light. The community here is not only the congregants. It is the character of the sanctuary walls, constructed from non-standard square concrete blocks, which highlight the 'unit' or individual nature of the blocks walled up into a 'society' of blocks—a

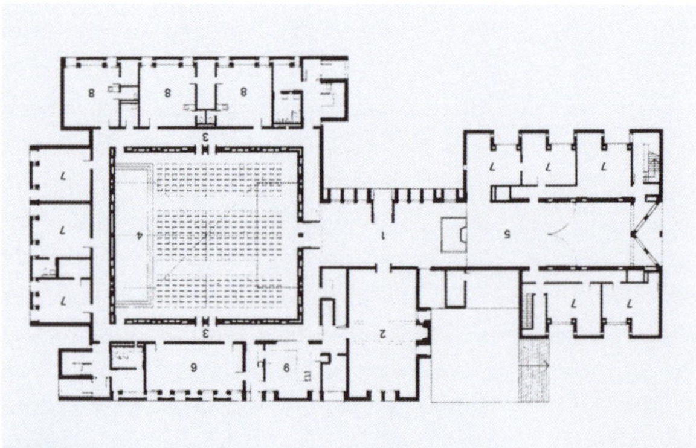

FIG.136

FIG.137

FIG.138

FIG.139

FIG.136 | **Unitarian Church plan (1959–1974)**
FIG.137 | **Unitarian Church, Rochester, NY**
FIG.138 | **Kahn drawing (c. 1949)**
FIG.139 | **Unitarian Church congregation**

mass ornament. The folded plate cruciform ceiling/roof floats over the bounding walls and the congregation. This became possible only because additional structure was inserted into the walls in a prosthetic gesture reminiscent of the projects of Viollet-Le-Duc. FIG.141 Columns support the edge of the roofs at the openings to the light hoods and are tied back horizontally to massive compressed short piers slotted on their face which are at the center of all four walls. These piers are the broken-off solid counterparts of the narrow voids of Kahn's brick order at the exterior of the Unitarian Church. They are upended and articulated from the walls below. The wall hangings designed by Kahn in a spectrum of colors and woven by Jack Larsen bring the proportions of the narrow exterior voids onto the sanctuary walls. The sanctuary of the Unitarian Church is a modulation of grays: from the darker gray of the concrete floor to the lighter gray of the block walls to the formwork vertical imprints of the light hood interiors glowing with light. The sanctuary is one of Kahn's most suspenseful spaces. The highly constricting exterior folded walls conceal a sanctuary space that expands outward to its own enclosing walls. This movement from center to periphery is marked at all four sides by the extension of the buttressing structures above the walls and below the clerestories. The cruciform folded ceiling/roof extends in four directions to an implied infinity.

FIG.140

FIG.141

FIG.140 | Kahn drawing—Carcassonne (1959)
FIG.141 | Viollet-le-Duc design from his *Entretiens* (1863–1872)

Just before one enters the foyer/lobby of the Unitarian Church one almost grazes the north east corner of the building. The classroom wing here extends toward the axial approach to the entry doors. This end wall is an emergency exit cloaked in brick and integrated into the north façade. It has the same profile as the light hoods above the sanctuary. The profile itself also originates from the Esherick House. This can be seen at the street façade at the north east corner wall which hides the laundry room and kitchen. And at the church roof the quadrapartite light hoods on each side slope to a drainage scupper which presages Kahn's solution for uniting the end scientists' studies flanking the courtyard with the intervening raised pool receiving the spillover of water from the courtyard channel. These tactile gestures at the Unitarian Church are intensified at the central hall of the Erdman Dormitories at Bryn Mawr College (1960–1965) in suburban Philadelphia.

Bryn Mawr means "big hill" in Welsh. The Eleanor Donnelly Erdman Hall which was originally a women's dormitory is composed of three 'kissing' cubes clad in predominantly black slate with white stone trim at the piers. It rests over the side of a small hill or ridge acting as a three-story battlement to Morris Avenue. **FIG.142** At the Richards Research Laboratories at Penn the towers are practically up against the neo-Gothic quadrangle along Hamilton Way. Erdman Hall occupies more spacious ground connected by a long path to the portal of another neo-Gothic building: Pembroke Hall. **FIG.143** Erdman Hall is often associated with the Scottish castles that Kahn was familiar with, which practically embodied a served-and-servant concept of space with their large central halls and secondary rooms embedded in the surrounding thick walls. **FIG.144** Wales, incidentally, is home to some of the greatest castles in Britain.

FIG.142

FIG.143

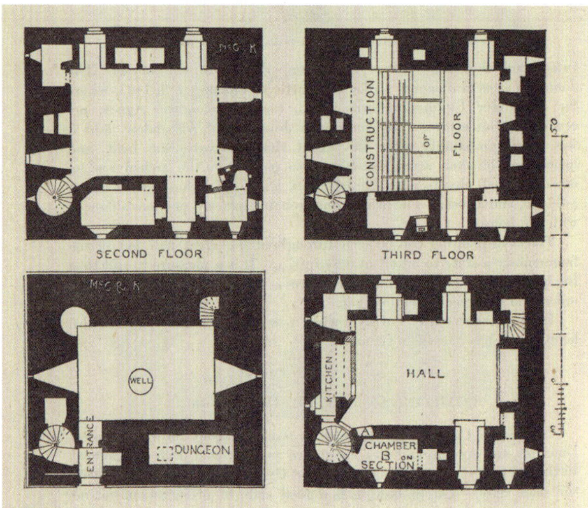

FIG.144

In approaching Erdman Hall the oblique plan geometry is read as an 'oscillation' in the light. Kahn brought the campus path directly into the central hall through a layering of spaces with low ceiling heights that constitutes the middle level of the complex. **FIG.17** First there is the exterior porch incorporated within the two oblique flanks that meet at the building corner. Then there is the transition through the vestibule with its double wood doors with their arched door lights. Next the corner of an ambulatory is encountered that branches off in two oblique directions left and right. Then we pass between two service volumes to the central hall where there is a contained explosion of space in the light. We discover that Kahn has broken the double cubes of the Esherick House and turned them face-to-face with their notches, now reduced in size, in alignment. **FIG.145** As at Rich-

FIG.142 | Erdman Hall street view
FIG.143 | Erdman Hall campus view showing entrance
FIG.144 | Scottish castle plans fromMacGibbon +Ross

ards, Kahn placed stairs in these notched enclosures. The abstract gesture of the notched stair tower at Richards, however, becomes at Erdman Hall a true tactile experience. The notches, hip-height at the landings within the cubes, are above our heads from within the central hall. **FIG.145** It is as if Kahn was invoking a child's sense of space with these overscaled blocks inaccessible directly from the central hall. This brings to mind Kahn's comment on the availabilities of the city: "A city is a place where a small boy, as he walks through it, may see something that will tell him what he wants to do his whole life."[14] Jonas Salk made parallel comments concerning the potential of the child.[15] At any time this evocative statement could be applied to the student inhabitants of the dormitory. The stair cubes match the plan proportions of the dormitory rooms themselves.

FIG.145

FIG.146

The routes within Erdman Hall are labyrinthine. In our initial experience of the building we lose orientation within the oblique corridors serving the dorm rooms because all 12 corridors are identical and are isolated from external reference or natural light. We regain orientation only at the connecting corners of the diamond formations where a visual axis penetrates the center of the complex through the layering of notched stair cubes, doorways and central halls. The drama of the three halls at Erdman—but especially at the central hall—is enhanced by the 12 clerestory structures positioned over the stair landings or interior balconies. A clear light diffuses through the clerestories with the occasional shaft of intense sunlight marking the floors and walls of the halls. The perimeter's interlocking

FIG.145 | Erdman Hall central hall
FIG.146 | Kahn drawing—Carcassonne (1959)

nature of the dormitory rooms in plan is transformed at the central hall. The broken-off notched stair cubes engage the void of the central hall in a tactile manner. Framing the main axis they link the flanking dormitory volumes to the central hall. The stair cube notches are the bottom sections of doors aligned with the doors below the clerestories. The oblique walls of the hall unfold from the stair cubes. At the ceiling line, slots (return air vents) which suggest the bottom sections of doors also appear—doors which remain inaccessible to us. At the Salk Institute terraces Kahn constructs different doors which frame the interrupted passages between the scientists' study structures—the architect's threshold conditions.

At Erdman Hall one of the interesting material contrasts is between the Pennsylvania slate cladding and the interior silvery-gray concrete work, which is very similar to the refined quality of work at the Salk Institute. At Bryn Mawr a further contrast is found in the relatively light stone cladding on the structural piers which bracket the slate cladding. The building seems to absorb light. The client refused to accept from Kahn a building whose exterior was concrete.[16] Therefore, the exposed concrete block infill walls defining the exterior of the dormitory rooms were clad with the slate.

FIG.147

Kahn considered using slate for the pavements as a contrast to the concrete at the Salk Institute but, given the climatic differences between La Jolla and the Philadelphia area, it was decided to use travertine for the pavements. Also, early on, the decision to use sandstone as infill/cladding for the Meeting House walls probably influenced his decision to use the more durable travertine at the courtyard/plaza.[17] Travertine is a form of limestone formed from geothermal springs and contains the remains of micro-organisms.[18] The major source of travertine is from the quarries at Tivoli, which provided stone for Hadrian's nearby villa (AD 120-140) and numerous buildings in nearby Rome including a number by Michelangelo and Bernini. Early in the design process Kahn had discarded the Hadrian-inspired composition of scientists' studies. Yet 'Tivoli' returned underfoot in the pavement framing the spring-like channel of water.

FIG.147 | Salk Institute courtyard view toward original garden

A question had arisen as to why travertine could not be used to clad the entire laboratory building, since this material was used at the recently completed Lincoln Center in New York City. But at the Salk Institute any cladding of the concrete would have negated one of Kahn's greatest expressions of pure wall as structure. The oblique piers rest on the courtyard/plaza with the directness of the ancient Greek Doric columns resting on their stylobates.

It was Jonas Salk and his client representative Dale Harvey who asked Louis I Kahn to examine the

FIG.148

concrete work at IM Pei's recently completed Kips Bay apartment blocks in New York City to determine a standard for concrete work at the Salk Institute.[19] In the final concrete mix Kahn decided to add red pozzolana (volcanic ash). Material resonates with light. Varying atmospheric conditions produce varying effects. Among the subtle effects at the Salk Institute courtyard are the reflections from the oblique piers onto adjacent concrete surfaces. This creates an alternating pattern of warm and cool toned concrete. Sometimes the

FIG.148 | **Salk Institute courtyard view toward ocean**

concrete will exhibit a flat silvery-gray tone on foggy days. Much of the time, because of the bright blue skies of La Jolla's Mediterranean climate, the southern arc of the sun will cast deep shadows from the south line of the scientist studies onto the courtyard/plaza, putting these studies into shade as well with the north flank of the studies bathed in direct sunlight. **FIGS.66,147**. Deep shadows are overlain with ghostly reflections from the scientist study structures and sparks/slits of light from the gaps in Kahn's architecture. On clear days at sunset the courtyard stream can seem like a river of fire in the glow of the red pozzolana walls. **FIG.148**

READINGS IN THE LIGHT: THE BUILDINGS OF LOUIS I KAHN 1946–1965 AND THE SALK INSTITUTE ENDNOTES

1 Wurman, *What Will Be Has Always Been*, pp 55, 89, 128.

2 There is the story as well of how "Kahn at the age of three shoveled burning coals onto the apron of his pinafore. The flames severely burned Kahn's face and hands, scarring him for life." McCarter, *Louis I Kahn*, p 14.

3 The only comparable detail existed at the Imperial Hotel in Tokyo, but the light play from the overhangs on the variegated fenestration of Frank Lloyd Wright's building was more diffused.

4 Louis I Kahn's work at Yale was indebted to the uncanny reflective effects of Mies van der Rohe's architecture. There was a major retrospective of Mies van der Rohe's architecture at the Museum of Modern Art in New York in 1947–1948. For a study on the uncanny in Mies see Robin Evans, "Mies van der Rohe's Paradoxical Symmetries", *AA Files*, no. 19, spring 1990.

5 Solomon, Susan G, *Louis Kahn's Trenton Jewish Community Center.*

6 Alfred Newton Richards (1876–1966) was chairman of the University of Pennsylvania School of Medicine's Department of Pharmacology (1910–1946) and the university's Vice-President of Medical Affairs (1939–1948). Richards also served the government as an expert on medical research under both Franklin D Roosevelt and Harry Truman. He headed the National Academy of Sciences until 1950 and was a director at Merck + Co.

7 In a conversation about an earlier version of the brick servant vent/duct towers Kahn proposed a hollowed column with a capital-like head. Kahn's structural engineer August Komendant said to the architect, "But sir, do you remember, you were claiming these stacks to be servants. Servants are commonly considered not too bright because of their small heads but yours are the contrary." Kahn answered: "You are right, let us change them to brainless." From August Komendant, *18 Years with Architect Louis I Kahn*, Englewood, NJ, Aloray: 1975, p 9.

8 Banham, Reyner, "The Buttery Hatch Aesthetic", *Architectural Review*, March 1962. For Kahn's reply to Banham, see Alessandra Latour ed., *Louis I Kahn–l'uomo, il maestro*, p 415: "The critic should tell what he sees, realizing he is not in his realm, and inspire the architect to make the next building better."

9 Marcus, George H, and William Whitaker, *The Houses of Louis Kahn*, New Haven, Yale University Press: 2013, p 177.

10 Ibid, p 191.

11 Ibid, p 173.

12 Marcus and Whitaker indicate that Kahn's use of the shutters was influenced by the ventilating shutters/doors of Le Corbusier's La Tourette, which Kahn had seen after his Otterloo visit for CIAM in 1959.

13 Burton, "Notes from Volume Zero...", *Perspecta 20*, p 75.

14 Wurman, *What Will Be Has Always Been*, p 164. Architect Denise Scott Brown stated that: "You can interpret the women's dorms as a set of row houses, each room a little row house, interlocked the way row houses look as if they do. And the form–the public sector is created by how the buildings are put together. And so there are three public spaces in the middle, three public squares with houses all around. He [Kahn] is being very urbanistic." From an interview conducted by Sam Rodell with Denise Scott Brown and Robert Venturi, and featured in his Master of Architecture thesis, *The Influence of Robert Venturi on Louis Kahn*, 2008, p 60.

15 "It is clear that the course of human evolution will be determined, in large part, by the degree to which freedom exists for experimenting with the ways for achieving the fullest expression of the child's potential." From an undated typed manuscript commemorating Jonas Salk's first visit to the state of Israel. Salk Archive, Box 350 Folder 5.

16 Cf. Brownlee and DeLong, *Louis I Kahn: In the Realm Of Architecture*, essay by Michael Lewis on Erdman Hall, p 356. A campus committee was totally against the use of concrete as the major material in the project. However, Katharine McBride, the President of the school, supported Kahn and a compromise was reached allowing concrete at the interior with the exterior slate cladding.

17 See note 8, p 30 on the Salk essay, in Kent Larson, *Unbuilt Masterworks*, New York, Monacelli Press: 2000. Vincent Scully thought that sandstone contained fossil remains of "crustaceans and more"; ambiguous biological forms. We believe this is an error. Sandstone is composed of purely lithic materials. Limestone contains the microbiological forms that Scully mentions. Travertine is a form of limestone. The section drawing in Larson's book does not indicate which stone was to be used.

18 Goldhagen refers to a book in Kahn's library by Robert Impey Murchison: *Siluria–The History of the Oldest Fossiliferous Rocks and Their Foundations*, London: 1859.

19 Salk and Harvey inspected the Kips Bay apartments in person. See Kahn Archive: Harvey Letter to Kahn's office dated 25 October 1962. Kahn Archive, Box/Folder 030. IIA107.36

CHAPTER THREE

CRITICAL INTERLUDE

BRUTALISM, THE CUT AND TRANSCENDENTALISM

In the early 1950s (Colin) Rowe's earliest intimations of modern architecture's polemical contradictions emerged—that late Victorian marriage of French rationalism and German metaphysics that provided the intellectual basis of modernism's rapid postwar ascension in Europe and America.

Alexander Caragonne[1]

What did Kahn share with some of the other major architects of the twentieth century, and where did he differ on issues that transcended the national boundaries separating these architects? Kahn shared with Mies van der Rohe, Le Corbusier and Frank Lloyd Wright the utopian impulse to bring a new rigor and enhanced architecture to the masses. This is the central reason why these architects were concerned with the reform of housing settlements and the rebuilding of cities. In Kahn's case, this meant the design of new housing in and around Philadelphia during the 1930s and 1940s, and urban design experiments for that city in the 1950s.[2] But this book has focused more on the individual buildings of Kahn's later career, where he established his own version of architectural monumentality in the post-World War II period.

Kahn's architecture of incrementalism or iteration and the emphasis on the solid wall differentiates his work from that of Mies van der Rohe, whose architecture of 'almost nothing' is a minimalism of skeletal structure and membranous glass walls. Although there is a neo-Gothic aspect to Kahn's early experiments with skeletal structure, the overwhelming sense of his architecture is the aggregation of the massive volumes whose hollowness is made evident by negating wall slots and joints. What separated Kahn's work from Le Corbusier's was his inability to use Corbu's notion of the free plan as Colin Rowe had hoped or wished for. And the rigor of Kahn's work in concrete lacked the plastic element of Le Corbusier's work in the same material. This plastic element, which was already evident in the earliest paintings of Le Corbusier's Purist period and would permeate his architecture from his first works of the 1920s, found its greatest expression in his Unité d'habitation apartment block in Marseille (1947-1952), a building Kahn had visited while it was under construction. This building, with its oversized 'archaic' pilotis in rough concrete, was essentially the origin of what Reyner Banham later termed 'Brutalism' in architecture.

Reyner Banham anglicized the origins of the term 'Brutalism'. He was fully aware of this word's origins in the art brut movement (Dubuffet and Paolozzi) and in the 'béton brut' treatment of concrete in Le Corbusier's work from the late 1930s to his late 1940s project at the Unité d'habitation at Marseille. **FIG.149** Banham, whose book was titled *The New Brutalism—Ethic or Aesthetic?*, considered 'The New Brutalism' to be a parody term of the New Humanism espoused by contemporary British architects, who under the influence of Swedish domestic architecture sought a return to nineteenth-century brick building traditions. However, Banham's critical use of the term was rather vague. He considered the first Brutalist building to be Peter Smithson's Hunstanton School, which clearly expressed the unadorned structural steel frame and exposed mechanical services.[3] A coarser brick infill than what Mies would have used insured that the Hunstanton School met Brutalist criteria.

To Banham, Mies van der Rohe's use of steel, brick and glass in works like the campus buildings at the Illinois Institute of Technology, or the 860/880 Lake Shore Drive apartment buildings, was too refined and 'purist'. The steel work at both projects was encased in concrete for fire proofing with additional steel plate and I-sections applied as expressive 'decoration'. William Jordy's Mies essay had dealt with the symbolic meaning of these construction issues.[4] However, Brutalism as a totalizing effect does not reach its full expressive potential unless there is an effective contrast of materials and/or services—between what is 'Brutalist' and what is more 'refined'. What could be more Brutalist than Mies van der Rohe's cut-off W-sections supporting the raised entry plinth contrasted with the extreme refinement of the rest of the Farnsworth House? **FIG.150** What could be more Brutalist than not only the 'béton brut' of Le Corbusier's Unité d'habitation in Marseille but also the disjunctive nature of the oversized columns supporting the Modulor-ordered apartment units above? Banham applied similar criteria to Kahn's Yale University Art Gallery. He found so much there to be "muddled" or "too arty".[5] Banham did not mention Kahn's seminal Trenton Bath House which, with its exposed wood-framed pyramidal roofs, would have perfectly met Brutalist criteria. But alas, this subtle building was too indebted to Beaux-Arts practice. Banham's criticism was unfair because he applied too 'pure' criteria in his demand that architecture be a direct

FIG.149

FIG.150

FIG.149 | Hervé photo of Le Corbusier's Unité d'habitation, Marseille. ©J Paul Getty Trust. Getty Research Institute. Los Angeles (2002 R.41)
FIG.150 | From Mies van der Rohe's Farnsworth House, Plano, IL (1951)

utilitarian expression of structure, services and material.[6] He could not deal with the inherent "incongruities" in Kahn's work at Yale and elsewhere. Alan Colquhoun criticized Banham's stance, evident in his earlier *Theory and Design in the First Machine*:

> If, as Dr. Banham shows, academic systems of thought persisted even in those works which laid claim to the most extreme functionalism, it would seem to indicate that they were the necessary ingredient of practice which could not be assimilated into the rationale. In the writings of Le Corbusier we see two attitudes lying side by side—on the one hand, the unitary view in which form and function are presented as identical; on the other, the idealist view that function is preceded by form. But Le Corbusier made no claims to be writing a systematic treatise (*Towards a New Architecture*), and it could be that the contradictions in the argument represent a necessary conflict of ideas which can only be resolved in the works themselves—a dialectical sequence the third term of which can only be introduced at the level of symbolic representation.[7]

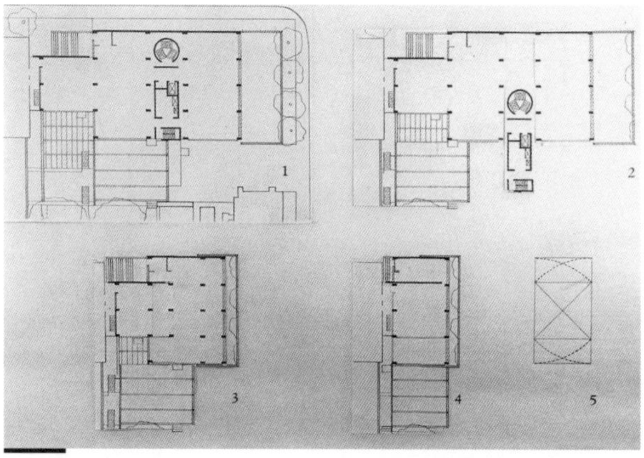

FIG.151

FIG.152

FIG.151 | Author's Yale University Art Gallery analysis drawing
FIG.152 | Richards Research Building entrance

Peter Eisenman had referred to Kahn's work as an architecture of "extrusion". Another term with a less material connotation is that Kahn's architecture often expressed a pure Cartesian "extension" of matter (material) but... cut off. Kahn "existentialized" his architecture of extensions by emphasizing the contrasts between up and down, forward and back, the frontal and the oblique, center and periphery and plan and elevation. At the Yale Art Gallery there is the hidden Brutalism of how Kahn plunged the conventional beams into the tetrahedral ceiling/floor system. **FIG.55** There is the exposed Brutalism in how Kahn broke off the three-and-a-half story south wall and recessed part of it to create the entrance condition to the gallery. This breaking off is enhanced by the horizontal blue stone coursing expressing the hidden floor levels behind. The south wall is an 'effacement' of memory and evokes any one of a number of Italian precedents from the Uffizi Gallery to the great wall at Hadrian's Villa. At the Richards Medical Research Center what could be more Brutalist than Kahn's decapitation of the notched crown of the entry stair tower using it to form the library carrels that are plunged into the upper levels of the biology tower in a hydra-headed formation of blocks–the multiplicity of knowledge?

All extensions in Kahn's architecture are conceptually collapsible. This includes the Yale University Art Gallery back to the face of the existing Gallery that it was appended to. **FIG.151** This includes the stacked lab lofts at Richards hovering ominously over our heads at the entrance. **FIG.152** When Kahn brought the cantilevered structural floors of the lab lofts just directly above grade he allowed light penetration into the basement labs through the complex interweaving elements. **FIG.56** But it also suggested that the stack of lab lofts could collapse back into the ground. At the Salk Institute the courtyard could be considered a street cut off from the garden behind. The series of scientists' study structures with their oblique piers are also conceptually collapsible back to the singular study structures at the east end of the courtyard. The gaps between the study structures are spatial temporal interruptions that are nihilistic in character. The view through the enfilade of scientists' studies end in blind walls. **FIG.153** These cuts or disjunctions of architecture are set within the 'type' frames of Kahn's work. There is the 'clumsiness'—the almost Brutalist, primitive (what Vincent Scully called the "primitive power" of Kahn's work) or childish way that Kahn fitted both the mechanical functions and the administrative offices into the corner end blocks of the Salk Institute. Then there are the oblique piers themselves. Are they merely wall segments suggesting the possibility of infinite building above and beyond, or are they finite elements cut off from transcendence? Brutalism in Kahn's work is not surface texture (eg Paul Rudolph) but compositional tactility.[8] It is evident in how the figure/ground plan of the scientists' studies and lightwells interlock with or grasp the center void. **FIG.70** The Salk Institute is a tempus—a cut in space and time.[9] In its structures it embodies the constructive/destructive aspect of time. In its austerity and repetition it embodies the monastic ideal raised to the level of the modernist conception of the city as envisioned in the 1920s, which was a nihilism fulfilled. **FIG.154**

FIG.153

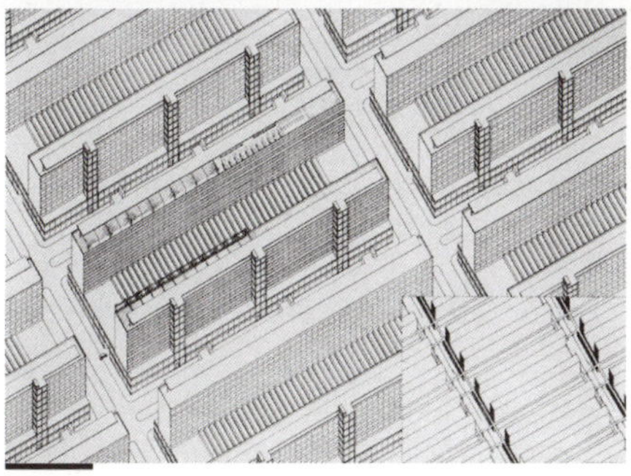

FIG.154

In a pragmatic, technologically oriented and commodified society, Kahn's poetic aphorisms, what some called his sermonizing, would have been forgotten without the realization of his buildings. His numerous transcendental musings on "silence and light", on what the building wants 'to be' etc, reflect not only his concern for the phenomenal aspect of architecture and the 'environment' but his expression of values. To that extent, he is a radical as Frank Lloyd Wright defined it: from the root. Louis I Kahn's architectural activity is linked to the transcendentalist tradition in American thought, which found its greatest physical

FIG.153 | **Salk Institute view at terrace**
FIG.154 | **Hilbersheimer Proposal for a High-Rise City (1927)**

expression in the work of Wright. Transcendentalism in nineteenth-century America had two major aspects: the theoretical tradition is found in the writings of Emerson, Thoreau and others. Transcendentalism was a critique of the rationalist biases of the Enlightenment, of American puritanical Calvinism and the corruptions of the new industrial order. Although transcendentalism promoted a mysticism of nature, it was not anti-urban, per se. Parallel to the theory was the rise of religiously based utopian communities, such as those founded by the Mormons, Shakers and other sects, often sited in the 'wilderness'.[10] Kahn's buildings, like these cities, were founding gestures.[11] As he said, "I love beginnings." And like Frank Lloyd Wright in his Unity Temple (1905-1908), Kahn designed his comparably monumental Unitarian Church (1959-1969). Unitarianism, like transcendentalism, originated from the 'progressive' Protestant congregations of early-nineteenth-century New England. It is important to note that Kahn's first 'prestigious' commission, the Yale University Art Gallery, is sited in one of these New England centers (New Haven—think of the place name!). And his greatest advocate, Yale professor Vincent Scully, continued the transcendentalist tradition.[12]

Ultimately, Frank Lloyd Wright aspired to the Asian (specifically Japanese) artistic and poetic interpretation of nature. However, transcendentalism originated not only with the Anglo-American nature poets and philosophers but with the poetry of Goethe, which influenced Wright through the German intellectual currents that existed in Chicago in the late nineteenth century.[13] There was also a Germanic influence on Kahn even though his parentage was Russian. His mother was a student of Goethe and Nietzsche, and there was a Jewish mystical element in his family history.[14] We will explore these elements of Kahn's work in the next chapter.

CRITICAL INTERLUDE: BRUTALISM, THE CUT AND TRANSCENDENTALISM ENDNOTES

1 Cf. *As I Was Saying–Recollections and miscellaneous Essays/Colin Rowe–Vol I*, Alexander Caragonne ed., p xi.

2 Cf. Brownlee and DeLong, *Louis I Kahn: In the Realm of Architecture*, Chapter 1, "Adventures of Unexplored Places".

3 Banham alludes to the fact that in college Peter Smithson's nickname was Brutus because of his alleged resemblance to ancient Roman busts. See Banham, *The New Brutalism: Ethic or Aesthetic?*, New York, Architectural Press: 1966, p 10.

4 Jordy, William, "The Laconic Splendor of the Metal Frame: Ludwig Mies van der Rohe's 860 Lake Shore Apartments and His Seagram Building", *American Buildings and Their Architects*–Vol. 4, p 243: "Esthetically, they [the I-beams] provide an element of depth, and hence the animation resulting from their louver-like opening and closing as we circle the towers. They also give a discreet play of light and shadow to the elevation... If the I-beams are left unclosed and self-contained elements, abruptly severed top and bottom, much as the black lines of a Mondrian canvas—not ended by a closed composition, but severed by a limited field. Their qualities of openness, and discreteness permit the I-beams to characterize the modern idea of harmony arrived at through an equilibrium of tensions symbolically, finally, the I-beams not only record the technology, but celebrate it."

5 Whitely, Nigel, "Banham and Otherness: Reyner Banham and the Quest for an Architecture Autre", *Architectural History* Vol. 33, 1990, p 201.

6 This unfairness was also recognized by Thomas Leslie in his writings on Kahn.

7 Colquhoun, Alan, "The Modern Movement in Architecture", *Collected Essays in Architectural Criticism*, first published in *The British Journal of Aesthetics*, January 1962. We propose that Banham's entire writing career may be a detailed response to the various chapters and implications of Le Corbusier's *Towards a New Architecture.*

8 Refer to Kahn's statement "Touch, Sight" in Lobell, *Between Silence and Light...* p 8: "...From touch there is a striving to touch, not just touch and from this developed what could be sight. When sight came, the first moment of sight was the realization of beauty..."

9 The physical cuts or breaks may reflect the notion of the epistemological break as Dominique LeCourt described it in *Marxism and Epistemology*: "Scientific activity is a divergence from the 'spontaneous' interests of life. The scientist, however, never succeeds in being the pure agent of scientific practice. Obstacles from within science and from its social-cultural context have a breaking effect on science itself." (pp 14-15)

10 Concerning transcendentalism and religious utopianism in the development of the nineteenth-century American city consult Dal Co, Francesco, "From Parks to the Region: Progressive Ideology and the Reform of the American City", *The American City–From the Civil War to the New Deal*, pp 144-154 and Miller, Perry, *The American transcendentalists their prose and their poetry*, Garden City, New York, Doubleday: 1957.

11 Tafuri, *Theories and History of Architecture*, p 7: "The gap between Louis Kahn's myth of Order, with his hermetic delving into the material offered by history so as to de-historify, to the extreme, architectural planning; and the neo-plastic mysticism tending to resolve oppositions and contrasts in a messianic appeasement, is not as crucial as it may first appear, when we compare works like the Salk laboratories and the Schröder house."

12 Cf. Scully, *Louis I. Kahn*, which is the first important book on Kahn. Also, see Scully, *Architecture: the Natural and the Manmade.*

13 Smith, Norris Kelly, *Frank Lloyd Wright: A Study in Architectural Content*: Smith lists all the cultural and literary influences on Wright including Beethoven, Goethe and Wagner. Frampton in his opening remarks of "Frank Lloyd Wright and the Textile-Tile Tectonic", in his *Studies in Tectonic Culture*, refers to the Germans who formed one-third of the population of Chicago in the 1890s. Wright referred to Louis Sullivan as his Lieber Meister. One of the major works by Adler and Sullivan, in Chicago, was the Schiller Theater. Frampton traces Wright's Textile-Tile Tectonic back to the German theoretician Gottfried Semper.

14 Burton, "Notes from Volume Zero: Louis Kahn and the Language of God", *Perspecta 20.*

L
L

CHAPTER FOUR

HERMETICISM AND UTOPIANISM IN THE ARCHITECTURE OF LOUIS I KAHN

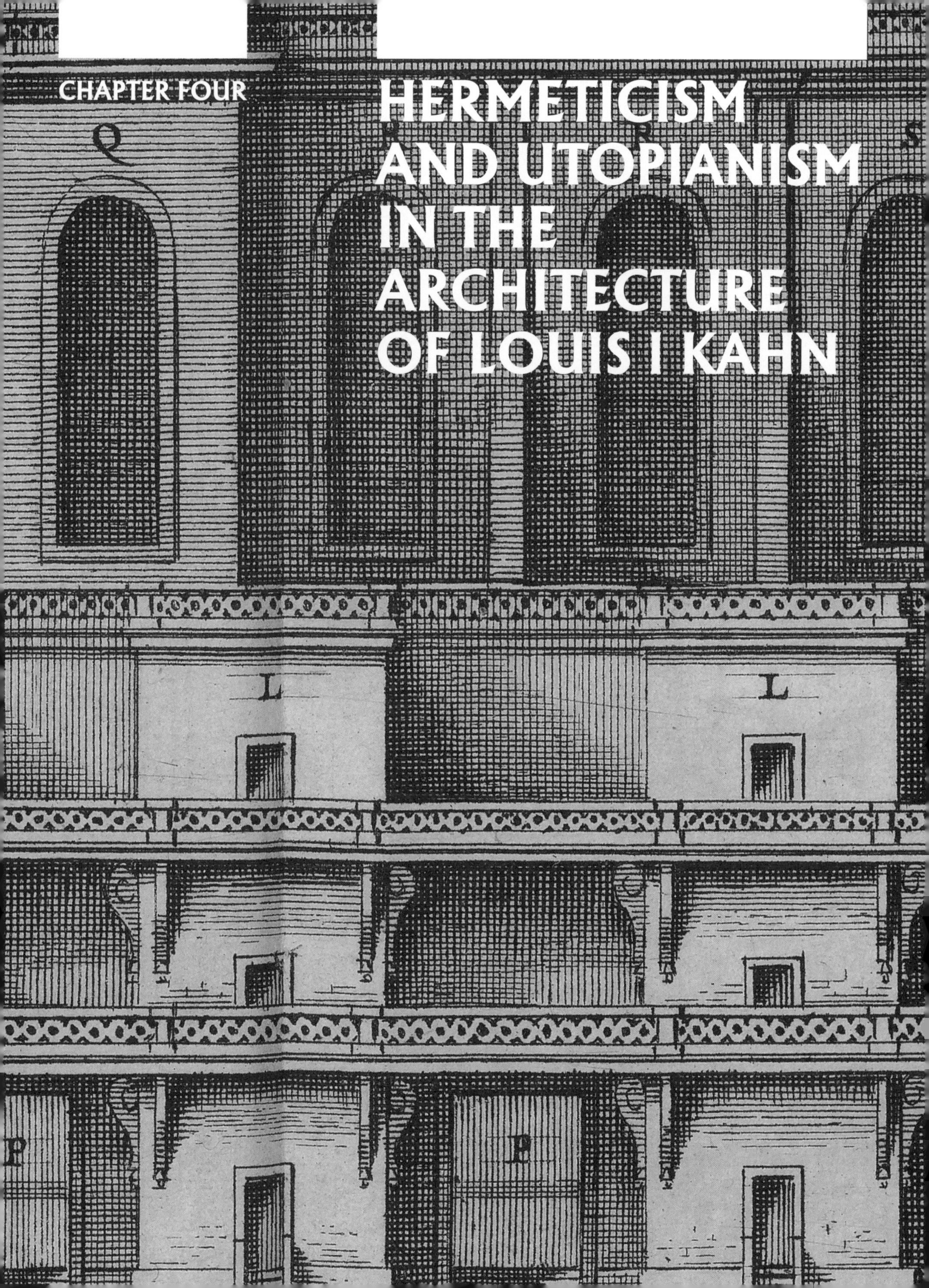

All material is spent light.

Louis I Kahn[1]

In the late 1970s the architectural historian Joseph Burton catalogued Louis I Kahn's personal library and in the 1980s and 1990s published two fundamental essays: one on Kahn's language of architecture as a "language of God" and one on Kahn's early education.[2] In the earlier essay Burton traces the place of light in Kahn's work as part of the hermetic tradition from the ancient Egyptians, through Plato to Neoplatonism and Kabbalah in the Renaissance. Burton identified late-eighteenth- and early-nineteenth-century Romanticism with this complex hermetic tradition. One of the key figures that emerged from this tradition was the great German poet, natural scientist and diplomat Johann Wolfgang von Goethe (1749-1832), whose monumental *Faust* is the most important work of literature in the German canon.[3] Goethe and Friedrich Schiller were the favorite authors of Louis I Kahn's mother Bertha Mendelssohn Kahn. Esther Kahn, Louis' wife, stated that Bertha was an expert 'upon' Goethe. As a teenager Louis I Kahn struggled to read *Faust*, as he later recalled:

> I'm only reading Goethe now because I have a great reverence for a person who loved Goethe, and because I love this person I had to read it. Before this I struggled to read *Faust* page by page. I met *Faust* for the first time and discovered a wonderful thing: that Gretchen was more soul than body, that Faust was a balance between body and soul, and Mephistopheles was really all body, the body of man. He had no soul. Two people can't have the same sense of soul. The singularity is a soul and a body, though I believe that soul is a prevalence and that soul is the same in all, no different in anyone. The only difference is the instrument, our body, through which we express desire, love, hate, integrity, all the measurable qualities of soul.[4]

That a reader of *Faust* should be the architect of the Salk Institute of Biological Science is one of those marvelous coincidences that Kahn himself referred to as the play between accident and circumstance.[5] And in another coincidence a book was published on Frank Lloyd Wright which occurred the year the Salk Institute was completed in construction, a book which stressed the romantic and Goethean background of that architect.[6] Who was Faust? The character who sold his soul to Mephistopheles to obtain a mystical transcendence beyond the limitations of earthly human knowledge. The extraordinary effort that Kahn made to resolve the relationship between the scientists' studies and what was to become the central void of the Salk courtyard/plaza with the Pacific Ocean ahead and the garden behind may have been the conscious response to the unconscious influence of *Faust.* Faust was dissatisfied with the life of the study. He wanted to leave his study to embrace the world in every sense. Kahn aligned the stream at the Laboratory courtyard/plaza directly with the sun's setting at the horizon. Faust's speech in response to the setting sun (Part I, lines 1077-1099) has been described as the central programmatic poetic text for European romanticism:[7]

> The silent Earth beneath my feet, forever,
> The heights on fire, each valley quiet
> While silver streams flow to a golden river.
> The wild peaks with their deep clefts,
> Would cease to bar my godlike way,
> Already the sea with its warm depths,
> Opens to my astonished gaze.
> At last the weary god sinks down to night:
> But in me a newer yearning wakes,
> I hasten on, drinking his endless light:
> The dark behind me: and ahead the day.
> Heaven above me: and the waves below,
> A lovely dream, although it vanishes.
> Ah! Wings of the mind, so weightless
> No bodily wings could ever be so.
> Yet it's natural in every spirit, too,
> That feeling drives us, up and on,
> When over us, lost in the vault of blue,
> The lark sings his piercing song,
> When over the steep pine-filled peaks,
> The eagle widely soars,
> And across the plains and seas,
> The cranes seek their home shores.

There is further material in Part II (lines 11587-11603) in which Mephistopheles reflects on Faust's life:

> *Mephistopheles:*
> No bliss satisfied him, no enjoyment,
> And so he tried to catch at shifting forms:
> The last, the worst, the emptiest of moments,
> He wished to hold at last in his arms.
> Though against me he tried to stand,
> Time is master: age lies on the sand.
> The clock stands still –
>
> *Chorus:*
> Stands still! As midnight: silent
> The hand moves.
>
> *Mephistopheles:*
> It falls, and all is spent.
>
> *Chorus:*
> It's past.

> *Mephistopheles:*
> Past! A stupid word.
> Then, why?
> Past, and pure nothing, complete monotony!
> What use is this eternal creation!
> Creating, to achieve annihilation!
> 'There, it's past!' What's to read in it?
> It's just the same as if it never lived,
> Yet chases round in circles, as if it did.
> I'd prefer to have the everlasting void.

The Salk Institute frames nature: the garden behind, the sky above and the sea ahead which is the soup of creation. The scientists' studies, which are the decomposed versions of the service blocks at the north and south flanks of the building, are still part of a space that flows through the courtyard/plaza. They disappear at the end of the courtyard/plaza. The oblique piers at the Salk Institute are actualizations of the virtual about the mirror axis that is the stream at the courtyard/plaza. In the look back toward the garden the Salk Institute is an 'infinite' regression—Kahn's recessions of the mind. The Salk Institute courtyard/plaza is not only an opening out and up in the light, a Heideggerian clearing, but it is an abyss, a mise en abyme—a recursive space in its delayed movement toward an illusory horizon.[8]

In Joseph Burton's essay on Kahn's architecture as a "language of God" he mentioned, right after the long passages on the German romantic and Goethean family influences on Kahn, another important facet of the architect's background: his Jewish inheritance. The Kahn family name was originally 'Schmuilowsky' and Kahn began with the name 'Leiser-itze'.[9] It is worth repeating some of Burton's description:

> In addition to the strong German cultural current running through Kahn's background, a form of Jewish mysticism, most likely kabbalah, appears to have come from this same maternal source. According to a story that Kahn told William Huff, his maternal grandfather, Abraham Mendelssohn, was a 'famous,' well beloved Jewish mystic and spiritual healer in Riga. Kahn reported that the entire city of Riga, Christian and Jew alike, had expressed their esteem for his mystic grandfather by burning candles in their windows on the evening of his death. He also told Huff, as well as Anne Griswold Tyng, that in Philadelphia his mother was considered the neighborhood counselor and 'wise woman,'...[10]

In light of this passage one can begin to imagine that the windows of the library carrels at the Biology Towers of the Richards Research Building, where Kahn said "a man with a book goes to the light", might in a night time view look like 'burning candles'.

In 1963 the young architect Richard Meier organized an exhibition at the Jewish Museum in New

York entitled *Recent American Synagogue Architecture.*[11] The exhibition included work by architects Pietro Belluschi, Marcel Breuer, Philip Johnson, Erich Mendelsohn, Frank Lloyd Wright and the artist Barnett Newman, and Louis I Kahn submitted his project for the Mikveh Synagogue which he began work on in 1961. The original Mikveh congregation was founded in Philadelphia in 1740 and meetings were conducted in various homes. Its first building was dedicated in 1782. The congregation changed locations

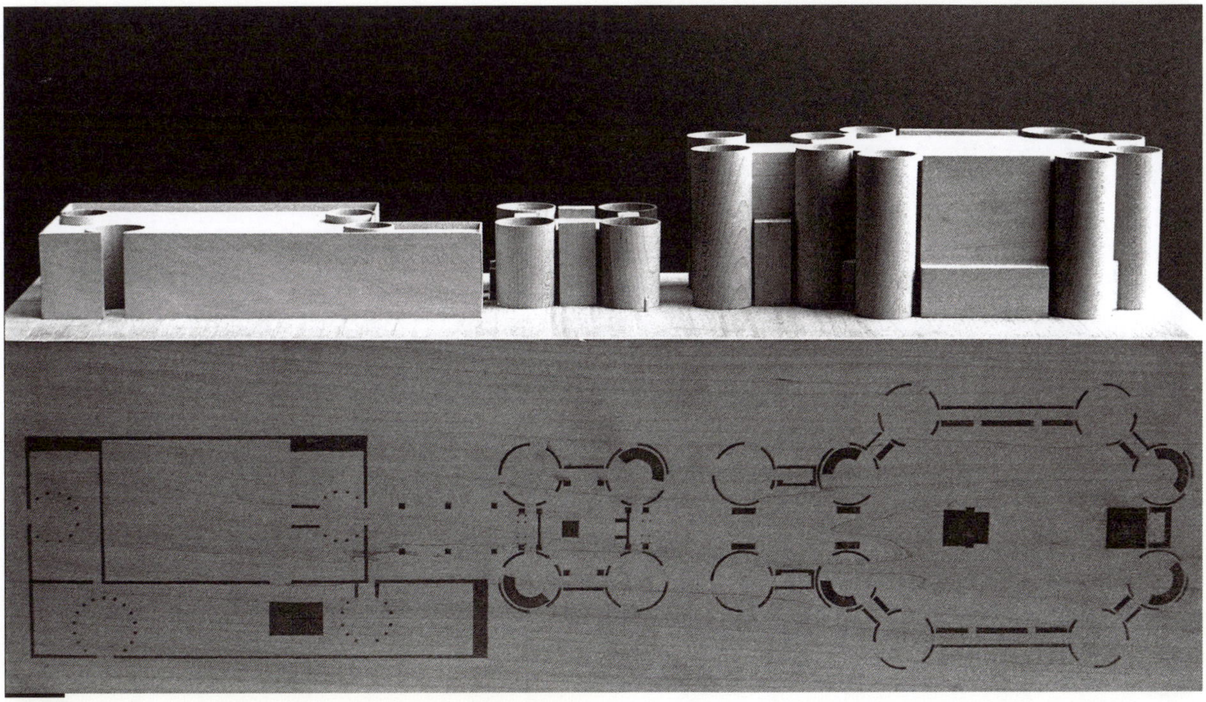

FIG.155

FIG.156

several times through the nineteenth century. In the first book on Kahn, Vincent Scully had mentioned one of its early congregants, Haym Salomon, who bankrupted himself financing the American Revolution.[12] In 1961 the congregation decided to move to a site to the south of the Christ Church burial ground (where Benjamin Franklin is buried) and to the east of Independence Mall. Because of budget limitations Kahn's final scheme (dated 29 October 1963) could not be constructed. **FIGS.155,156** As Kent Larson indicated there was a conference at the Jewish Museum 23 years after the synagogue exhibition attended by Richard Meier, Paul Goldberger and Vincent Scully, who all concluded that the Mikveh Synagogue was the greatest synagogue conceived in the twentieth century.[13]

In 1979, while preparing a lecture on Kahn to be delivered at the University of the Andes in Bogotá, Colombia, this author perused Thomas Hess's book on the artist Barnett Newman. This book, published in 1971, was in Kahn's personal library. Hess described the Kabbalistic background of Newman's work especially

FIG.155 | Mikveh Synagogue (1961–1970)—model photo with plan
FIG.156 | Section showing diaphragm roof over Mikveh congregation

through the writings of Gershom Scholem.[14] In this book an illustration appeared which showed the Jewish mystic contemplating the Tree of the Sephiroth–the divine emanations of God. Although this book was published after the development period of the Mikveh Synagogue and the Salk Institute, it only confirmed Kahn's interest not just in Newman's work but in the Kabbalah. My discovery was shared with Joseph Burton who was writing his essay on Kahn's "Language of God" at the time.[15] Burton's essay also confirmed that Victor Rivera, a member of Kahn's office, had in 1963 seen a book with a cover illustration of the Jewish mystic contemplating the Tree of the Sephiroth.[16] **FIG.157** This was a book by Scholem on *The Zohar*–the Kabbalistic book of splendor. The comparison between the final plan of the Mikveh Synagogue and the Tree of the Sephiroth is striking. The main congregation would have been lighted indirectly through the arches cut into the exterior and interior brick-enclosed cylinders whose architectural inspiration also stemmed from Kahn's visits to southern French sites: the brick cathedral at Albi (1282–1480) and the thirteenth-century fortress at Carcassonne.[17] **FIG.158** These lightwells were designed while work on the great cut out cylinders at the library of the Salk Institute was ongoing. But perhaps more remarkably, a fragment of the Tree of the Sephiroth may have already been the basis of Kahn's quadrapartite circular site platforms defining the Laboratory complex as presented to the San Diego City Council in 1960.

FIG.157

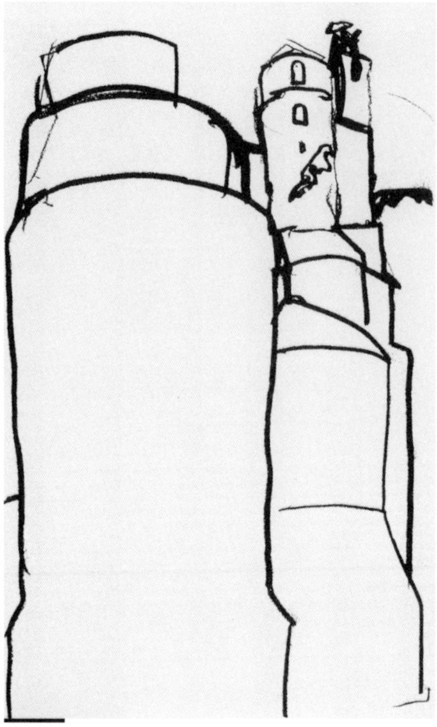

FIG.158

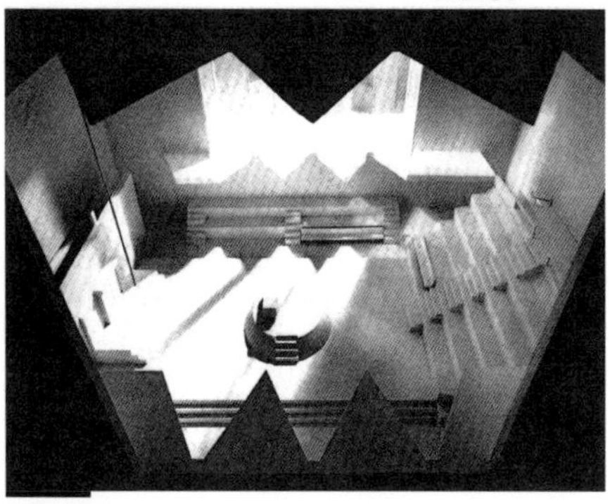

FIG.159

Barnett Newman's synagogue scheme was the only one at the Jewish Museum exhibit to rival Kahn's project. **FIG.159** It too remained unbuilt. Newman's use of the zigzag glass walls, flanking the congregation from above, was his representation of the Kabbalistic Tzim-Tzum or withdrawal of God in the initial act of cosmic creation.[18] The stream at the Salk Institute courtyard/plaza is like one of the zips in Newman's paintings. **FIG.160** It is duration in an 'event' space. It is presence within an absence.[19] The withdrawal of God prepared the place of science that is the void of the courtyard/plaza at the Salk Institute.

FIG.157 | Cover of book once in Kahn's office
FIG.158 | Kahn drawing–Albi Cathedral (1959)
FIG.159 | Newman's synagogue model (1963)

OPPOSITE
FIG.160 | Newman's *Onement I* (1949)

In 1627 Sir Francis Bacon, one of the early pioneers of modern science, published his utopian novel *The New Atlantis*. "The novel depicts a mythical island, Bensalem, which is discovered by the crew of a European ship after they are lost in the Pacific Ocean somewhere west of Peru. The minimal plot serves the gradual unfolding of the island, its customs, but most

FIG. 161

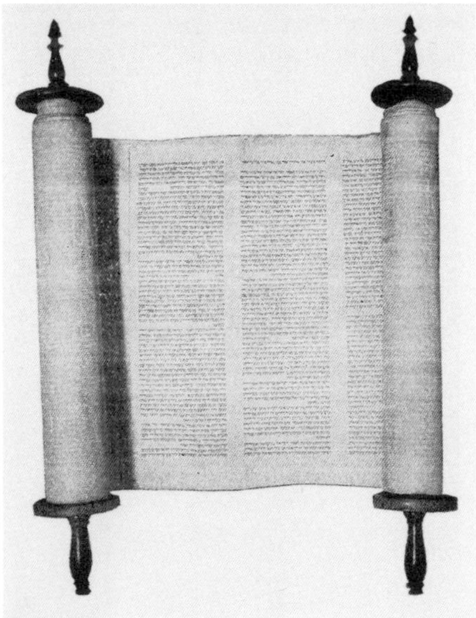

FIG.162

importantly, its state-sponsored scientific institution, Salomon's House, 'which house or college... is the very eye of this kingdom.'"[20] Salomon's House is a variation of Solomon's Temple whose theoretical reconstruction was part of a long tradition in the West.[21] Claude Perrault, physician, anatomist and natural scientist, designer of the east front of the Louvre (1665-1680), envisioned a reconstruction in 1683 only one year after the founding of Philadelphia by William Penn. **FIGS.6,161** He continued, in France, the Renaissance obsession with the measurement of ancient monuments. It was also an attempt to define a universal religion in an age of continuing religious strife on the European continent. The north and south enfilade of service volumes at the Salk Institute, inverted enlarged versions of the Erdman Dormitory notched stair cubes, are highly reminiscent of the elevations of Perrault's reconstruction of Solomon's Temple. And the plan of the Salk Institute is not only the adaptation of a permutation by Durand; it is also the image of the Torah which in Judaism is considered a living thing. **FIG.162** The Salk Institute for Biological Studies is also the fulfillment of Bacon's utopian vision for scientists.[22]

FIG.161 | Reconstruction of Solomon's Temple—C Perrault (1678)
FIG.162 | Jewish Torah—to evolve comes from Latin *ēvolūtiō*, to unroll a scroll

HERMETICISM AND UTOPIANISM IN THE ARCHITECTURE OF LOUIS I KAHN ENDNOTES

1 Wurman, *What Will Be Has Always Been*, p 150.
2 Burton's essays are indicated in the bibliography. It is a curious fact of Burton's essay on "Kahn and the Language of God" that the illuministe architects of the late-eighteenth and early-nineteenth centuries—Boullée, Ledoux and Lequeu—are not mentioned. Kahn wrote an introduction to a book on their work which he extolled.
3 Walter Kaufman, in his *Goethe, Kant and Hegel—Discovering the Mind*, Vol. I, offered a severe critique of Kant and Hegel compared to Goethe's literary and poetic achievements.
4 Burton, "Notes from Volume Zero...", p 75.
5 In the film *My Architect* (2003), directed by Nathaniel Kahn, his father is quoted as saying "When I went to high school I had a teacher, in the arts, who was head of the department of Central High, William Grey, and he gave a course in Architecture, the only course in any high school I am sure, in Greek, Roman, Renaissance, Egyptian, and Gothic Architecture, and at that point two of my colleagues and myself realized that only Architecture was to be my life. How accidental our existences are really, and how full of influence by circumstance."
6 This was Norris Kelly Smith's *Frank Lloyd Wright: A Study in Architectural Content*. Englewood Cliffs, NJ: 1966, p 45: "Goethe who developed polarity as the general principle at work in the universe... active and passive, male and female, plus and minus, atomistic and dynamic, centripetal and centrifugal, analysis and synthesis and summing up all the rest, systole and diastole—that basic principle of contraction and expansion, attraction and repulsion, which, as he saw it, permeates the order of the universe."
7 See *Faust*—Goethe Norton Critical Edition, Cyrus Hamilton ed., p 357 (interpretative notes). Text in this essay taken from online: Translated by AS Kline.
8 The 'scene' of the courtyard/plaza evokes several terms: Hegelian sublation (the *Aufhebung*), Heideggerian 'releasement', Bergsonian and modernist simultaneity. Concerning the latter term, the contractions and expansions, the spacings of Kahn's architecture touch on the time problem, as adumbrated in Bergson's debate with Einstein, and Bergson's insistence that time not be spatialized and that duration is a form of multiplicity. As Gilles Deleuze stated in *Bergsonism*, New York, Zone Books: 1988, p 43: "In reality duration divides up and does so constantly: that is why it is a multiplicity. But it does not divide up without changing in kind, it changes in kind in the process of dividing up: this is why it is a non-numerical multiplicity... where we can speak of 'indivisibles' at each stage of division."
9 Wiseman, Carter, *Louis I Kahn: Beyond Time and Style—A Life in Architecture*, New York, WW Norton: 2007, p 12.
10 Burton, "Notes from Volume Zero: Louis Kahn and the Language of God", *Perspecta 20*, p 75.
11 Held 6 October 1963 through 8 December 1963.
12 Scully, *Louis I Kahn*, p 42.
13 Larson, *Unbuilt Masterworks*, p 81.
14 Scholem's writings include *Major Trends in Jewish Mysticism* (1941) and *On Kabbalah and Its Symbolism* (1965). Scholem was a friend of Walter Benjamin, Theodor Adorno and Leo Strauss.
15 Kahn's original family name was Schmuilowsky as Carter Wiseman indicated in his biography of Louis I Kahn. Burton, "Notes from Volume Zero", p 75, states: "According to a story that Kahn told William Huff, his maternal grandfather, Abraham Mendelssohn, was a 'famous', well beloved Jewish mystic and spiritual healer in Riga."
16 Burton, "Notes from Volume Zero", p 81. This was probably the original version of this book published in 1949.
17 Both Albi and Carcassonne are part of the Languedoc region in France and the sites in the thirteenth century of the Albigensian revolt against the Roman Catholic Church, which was overcome by the Inquisition.
18 The word zigzag was first applied as a reference to the alternating directed walls of fortifications. One thinks of the bastions of numerous sixteenth-century fortifications in Europe. See *The Oxford Dictionary of English Etymology*.
19 Cf. Lyotard, Jean-François, "Newman: The Instant", *The Lyotard Reader*, Oxford, UK and Cambridge, MA, B Blackwell: 1989, pp 240–249.
20 Dubos, *The Dreams of Reason—Science and Utopias*, p 28, and the Wikipedia entry on the *New Atlantis*. In Swanson's PhD, *Four Laboratory Designs* of Louis Kahn, p 58, he stated that "Bacon's New Atlantis did not present a centralized place of inquiry, but disbursed laboratories above, below and throughout the island."
21 See Rykwert, Joseph, *On Adams House in Paradise*, New York, Museum of Modern Art: 1972, and Rosenau, Helen, *Vision of the Temple*, London, Oresko Books: 1979.
22 The utopian dimension of the Salk Institute is part of that tradition of utopias founded in America by the various religion sects: the Mormons, the Shakers, etc. See Dal Co, "From Parks to the Region: Progressive Ideology and the Reform of the American City", *The American City—From the Civil War to the New Deal*, pp 144–154.

CHAPTER FIVE

THE SALK INSTITUTE AND FOUR LATER KAHN WORKS

Kahn's explorations and discoveries during the Salk commission would be adapted and transformed for different client, programmatic and site regimes in the Chemistry Building at the University of Virginia, the Indian Institute of Management at Ahmedabad, the capital complex at Dhaka, Bangladesh and the FDR Four Freedoms Memorial in New York City. At the University of Virginia, Kahn adopts, almost wholesale, the parti or schema of the Salk Institute Laboratory building, including a variation of the discarded box beam interstitial structure from Salk. In India at the Institute of Management Kahn reworks elements of the plan of the Salk laboratories in response to the asymmetries of a more complex site/institutional arrangement. For the Dhaka capital complex variations of some of the spatial aspects of the Salk Laboratory building appear in some of the residential units, and the unbuilt Meeting House at Salk becomes an important prototype for the Dhaka Assembly building. Finally, at the FDR Four Freedoms Memorial, Kahn's last project (finished many years after his death), both at the level of form and historical content, invokes memories of the Salk Institute courtyard space and the importance of President Franklin Delano Roosevelt's Presidency to Kahn's early career–indeed to the careers of many architects during the Depression and World War II years in the United States. For the most part we will not focus on the design development of these projects, preferring instead to examine them as built, in relation to the Salk Institute.

UNIVERSITY OF VIRGINIA CHEMISTRY BUILDING (1960–1963)

In November 1960 Louis I Kahn was contacted by the University of Virginia for a commission for a new chemistry building at that campus. Between 21 March 1961 and 19 April 1963 Kahn developed five schemes for this project.[1] FIGS.163A,B,C The major feature of all of the schemes was the repetition of the Salk Institute laboratory parti. Two extended lab wings, two stories high, with scientists' studies flanked in inner courtyard oriented north/south. Small incremental service

FIG.163A

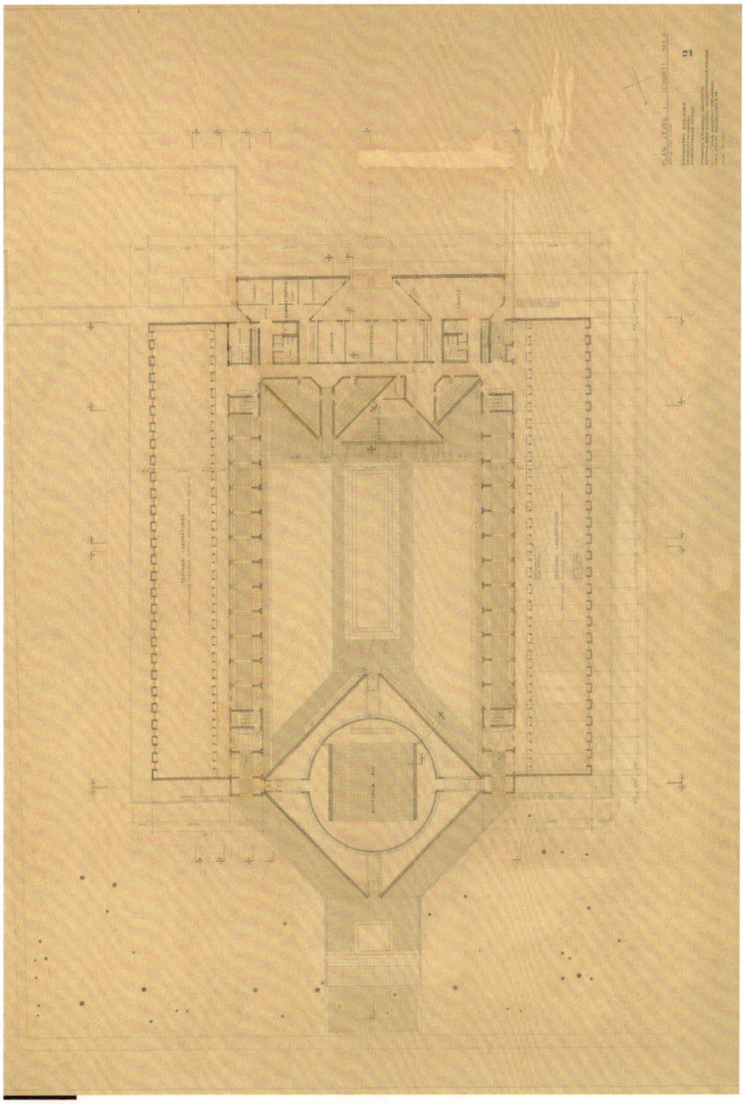

FIG.163B

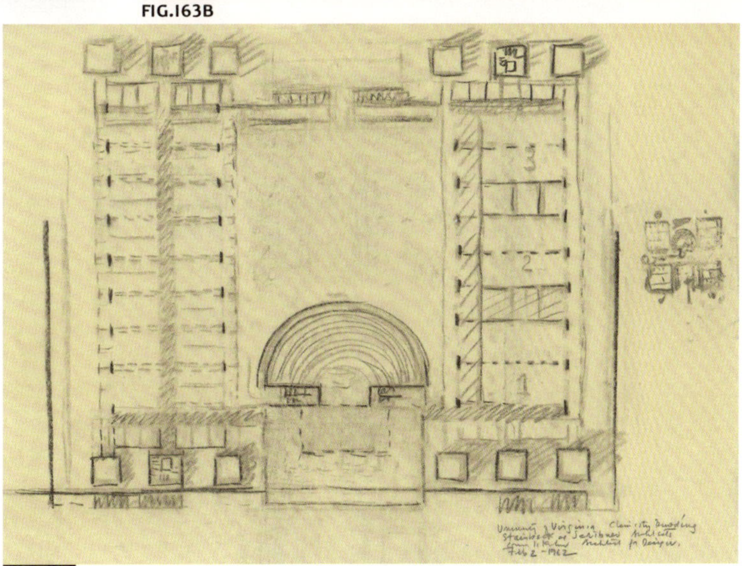

FIG.163C

FIG.163A | University of Virginia Chemistry Building project intermediate model (1963)
FIG.163B | UVA Intermediate scheme
FIG.163C | UVA original scheme

shafts engaged the east and west perimeters of the labs in continuous series. Kahn reintroduced the folded plate mechanical interstitial spaces over the labs which were discarded at the Salk Institute. **FIG.164** In scheme one Kahn closed the south end of the project with an auditorium, with the courtyard space slightly elevated, open to the campus on the north side. It was this scheme that was closest in character to the laboratory building at the Salk Institute and which most clearly resembled Jefferson's original campus at the University of Virginia. **FIG.165** In scheme two the auditorium was removed from the courtyard to a position to the north forming a bi-nuclear arrangement with the rest of the building. In all the later schemes the auditorium was brought back into the courtyard, either closing the south end or positioned more centrally

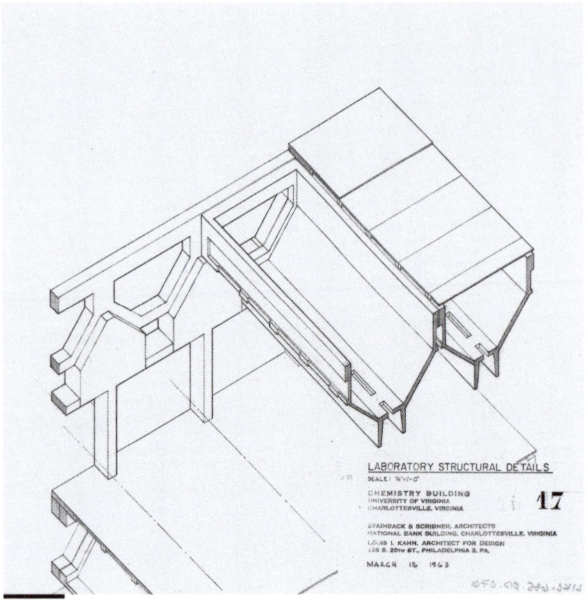

FIG.164

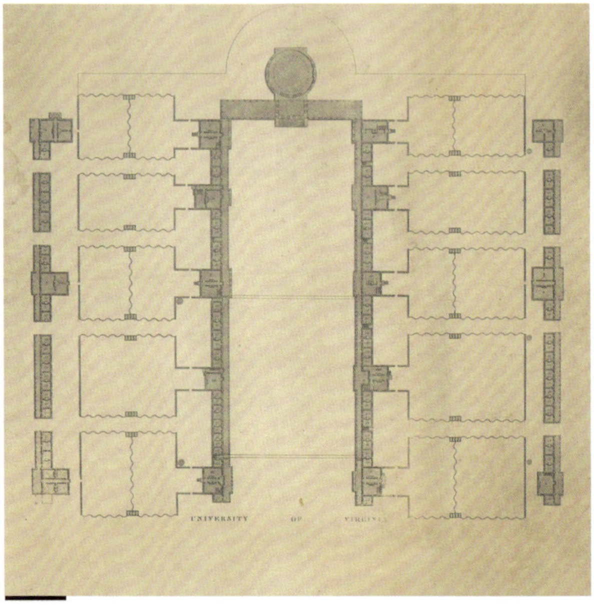

FIG.165

in the courtyard. In these schemes the north end of the courtyard was closed off by lecture halls, offices and conference rooms. When Kahn adapted a Mikveh Synagogue-like enclosure for the auditorium in the centrally located scheme, this 'imagery' had a negative impact on the building committee whose members desired a more future-oriented technological vision for a chemistry building. Unlike at the Salk Institute, where Kahn had a singular client and advocate in Dr. Jonas Salk, at Virginia he had a difficult relationship with the building committee. This situation repeated his experience from years earlier with the building committee at the Trenton Jewish Community Center.[2] Kahn lost both the Trenton and Virginia commissions.

FIG.164 | Isometric drawing of UVA interstitial structure for final scheme
FIG.165 | Original UVA campus plan–Thomas Jefferson (1825)

THE INDIAN INSTITUTE OF MANAGEMENT (1962–1974)

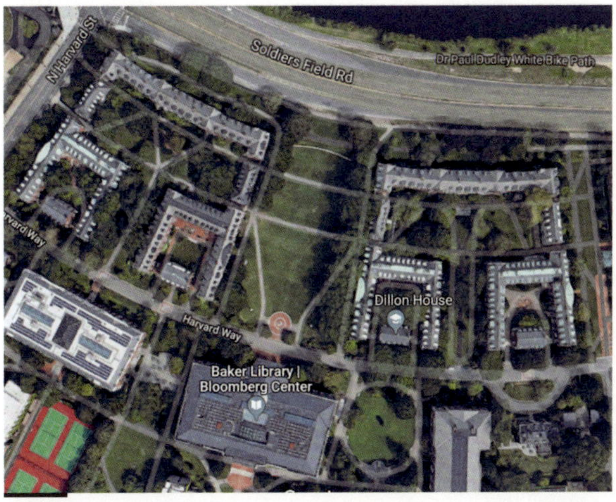

FIG.166

FIG.167

The Indian Institute of Management, in Ahmedabad, India, was organized in 1962 as a business school run by the government of India and the western Indian State of Gujarat. It was modeled on the Harvard Business School. FIG.166 The center of the Harvard Business School is the Baker Library designed by McKim, Meade and White and dedicated in 1927. The building, with its classical pediment entrance and cupola, terminates a green flanked by the Neoclassical dormitories of the school axially oriented to the north toward the Charles River. FIG.166 The other buildings of the business school are located around adjacent yards. The focal point of Kahn's Indian Institute of Management is also a library building. FIG.167

The Indian Institute of Management (IIM) is the greatest example in Kahn's work of an architecture based on the 'layering' of space. FIG.169 This layering defines not one building but a complex of programmatic elements responding to multiple factors reflecting Kahn's served-and-servant concept of architecture. One of the prime ordering devices at IIM is the tower at the north west corner of the site supplying all the water needed by the complex in a hierarchically organized distribution network. The servant bathroom stacks, in diamond plan formation to the served dormitory units, are part of this hierarchy. The water tower acts as an axis mundi or vertical axis about which the entire complex is obliquely related. The second axis organizing the Institute is the horizontal axis established by the library on the

FIG.166 | Harvard Business School focused on Baker Library
FIG.167 | Courtyard at IIM focused on Business Library

east, the four-story administrative wing to the north and the three-story classrooms to the south which form the open-ended courtyard facing the setting sun.

Another key organizing element of the site was to be the artificial lake, which was eliminated because of fear of mosquito infestation. The outer layer of four-story student dormitories were to be oriented towards the lake and the south west breezes. Embedded into the southern and eastern edges that was to be the lake are the ends of the L-shaped disposition of two-story faculty housing, again obliquely oriented, which form deep pockets of space eventually filled with lush shading vegetation. These pockets of space appear earlier at the unbuilt Trenton Jewish Community Center, where landscaping instead of housing defined outdoor rooms reminiscent of the secluded gardens of, for example, the Tuileries in Paris. **FIG.168**

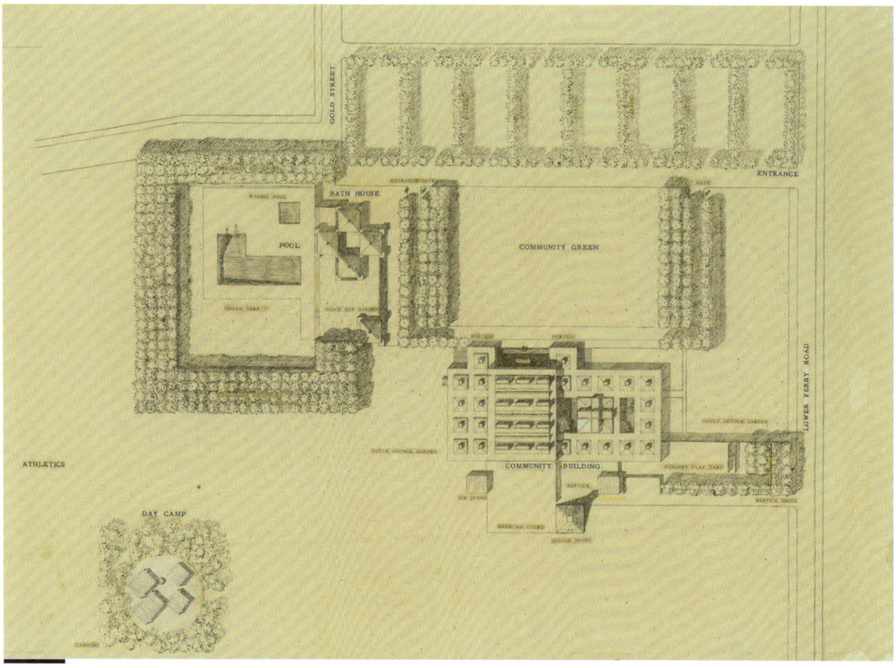

FIG.168

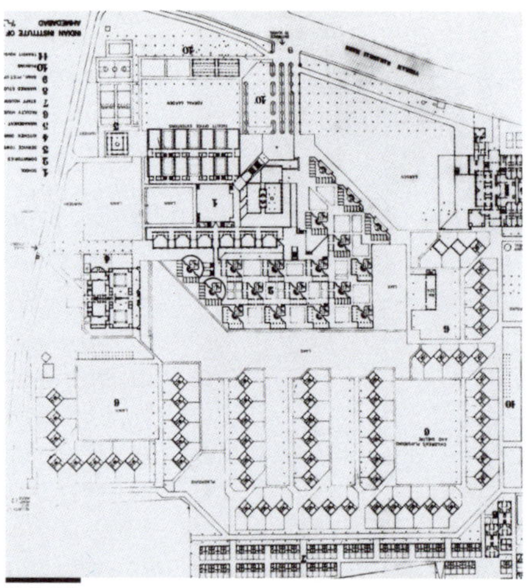

FIG.169

Kahn's enormous effort at IIM was to define the inner courtyard, the inner sanctum, as one of these deep spatial pockets. It was to be a courtyard or outdoor room. In earlier schemes the library, an outdoor auditorium and a kitchen/dining complex occupied the courtyard.[3] The library became part of a folded wall bounding the central space united to the administrative wing but disarticulated from the classroom wing to the south. If the Baker Library at the Harvard Business School was the initial model for IIM then surely at the courtyard Kahn also evoked the memory of Jefferson's library at the University of Virginia, substituting the hard surfaces of one of his beloved Italian piazzas for Jefferson's lawn.

The student dormitories organized around courtyard spaces are cross-axially related structures, enlarged versions of the Trenton Bath House, but they are also organized as three L-shaped layers hugging the inner sanctum of IIM and repeating the ordering of the faculty housing. **FIG.169** The student dormitories are orga-

FIG.168 | Trenton Jewish Community Center site plan
FIG.169 | IIM site plan

nized in an A-B-A grid plan, inspired by Kahn's earlier plan for the Trenton Jewish Community Center. FIG.168 The minor B bays define cross-axial passages under the dormitories which provide those shaded passageways and define courtyards which become those "spaces of no obligation", those outdoor classrooms, "founded on the causal meetings of students".[4] The under passages are extended developments of the under passages at the Salk Institute office blocks. The brick buttresses reinforce the under passages by resisting the loads of the dormitory floors above and in their repetition mark the trace of the passages behind the blind first-floor walls of these structures.[5]

At the approach road to the Indian Institute of Management we first become aware of the triple façades of the four-story married student housing. FIGS.170,171 Kahn merged the Mughal architecture of a work like the Darwza or Lofty Gate (1576) of Fatehpur Sikri with his own conception of an architectural brick order. But instead of allowing entrance to a precinct the dorms are blockages only defining the edge of the site. Around the north west corner of the third married student dormitory one is led to a drop-off at a grove of trees, from which we proceed to a monumental stair to the entrance area between the administrative wing and the library, and to a long ramp bringing us to the dormitories on the other side.

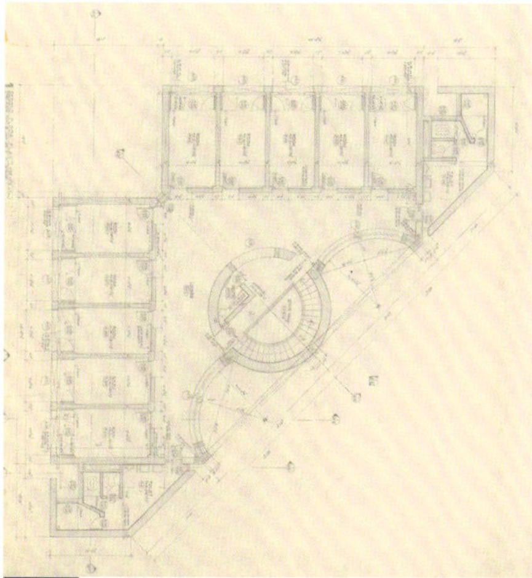

FIG.170

FIG.171

The façades of the married student dormitories are variations of several of Kahn's works. First the stair cylinder of the Yale University Art Gallery is essentially exposed in the façade, but in brick form, bringing to mind the brick cylinders of the Albi cathedral which Kahn had sketched in 1959. In plan the cylinder is tangential to the outside diagonal defining the building and the organization of dormitory rooms is reminiscent of the spatial ordering at Bryn Mawr. The cylinder establishes the stable vertical anchor for the dormitory. Kahn generated an interior/exterior spatial tension through the brick diaphragm-like

FIG.170 | IIM plan of married student housing block
FIG.171 | IIM view at approach to main entrance

walls flanking the cylinder. Here he was finally able to construct the diaphragm structure he experimented with at the Salk Laboratory building and at the Unitarian Church and Mikveh Synagogue roofs. The 'diaphragms' are peeled away from the stair cylinder and 'hinged' inward. As at the double cylinders of the Salk Meeting House library, Kahn cuts into these diaphragm walls a series of eye-like arches. Kahn introduced his composite order of structure based on the extended interior reinforced concrete tie beams of his Unitarian Church to unite the areas flanking the cylinder. Tangential to the exterior face of the brick cylinder the structure reinforces the double 'brow' arches above. The rising character of the eye-like arches below the double brows mimics the rising sun from the east. They also ventilate the interior of the dormitory structures. The double curvatures of the arches within their diaphragm walls act as if they respond to Kahn's 'order of winds'. It is important to note that for Kahn's later Kimbell Art Museum (1966–1972) he enlivened the vaulting structure by using cycloid-like sections inspired by his earlier experiments with diaphragms. The vaults there are uplifted and seem to billow within their restraining structure. At IIM an architectural beat runs across the three dormitory façades in the contrast between the contractive brick stair cylinders and the lateral extension of the double-brow shallow arches which express the unity of the married 'couple' in another Kahnian variation of the prosthetic architecture of Viollet-le-Duc.[6]

FIG.172

It is in the administrative offices and the library at IIM that the influence of the Salk Institute becomes most evident. The conjunction of the administrative block with the library is a 'Brutalist' juxtaposition. Kahn has transformed the outer service blocks of the Salk Institute Laboratory building–five in number–into the four administrative blocks at IIM. Whereas the Salk blocks are primarily closed figures in concrete, mute sentinels at the north and south flanks there, at IIM the side brick walls are perforated for window openings. The perforations are in the form of deep-set waffle patterns acting as brise-soleils to protect the windows from sunlight from the east and west. This fenestration pattern is also used on the east-facing wall of the multi-level book stack area of the library. The administrative blocks are appended to four levels of corridor overlooking the courtyard where the façade is clearly indebted to the architecture of Hadrian's Villa.[7] FIG.172 This façade merges with the diagonal corner of the courtyard space which

FIG.172 | Elevation at Hadrian's Villa (second century AD)

in plan is one side of a square in 'diamond' orientation. The square contains the entrance lobby and, above, the IIM director's office. The lobby opens to the courtyard under the composite arch that is a continuing theme in Kahn's architectural language at IIM. FIG.167 Above the lobby 'exit' is the IIM director's office with its private balcony framed by a more 'conventional' arched wall opening. The disjunction between the plan and the façade in this area is an example of Robert Venturi's complexity and contradiction in architecture. In plan the 'diamond' lobby and

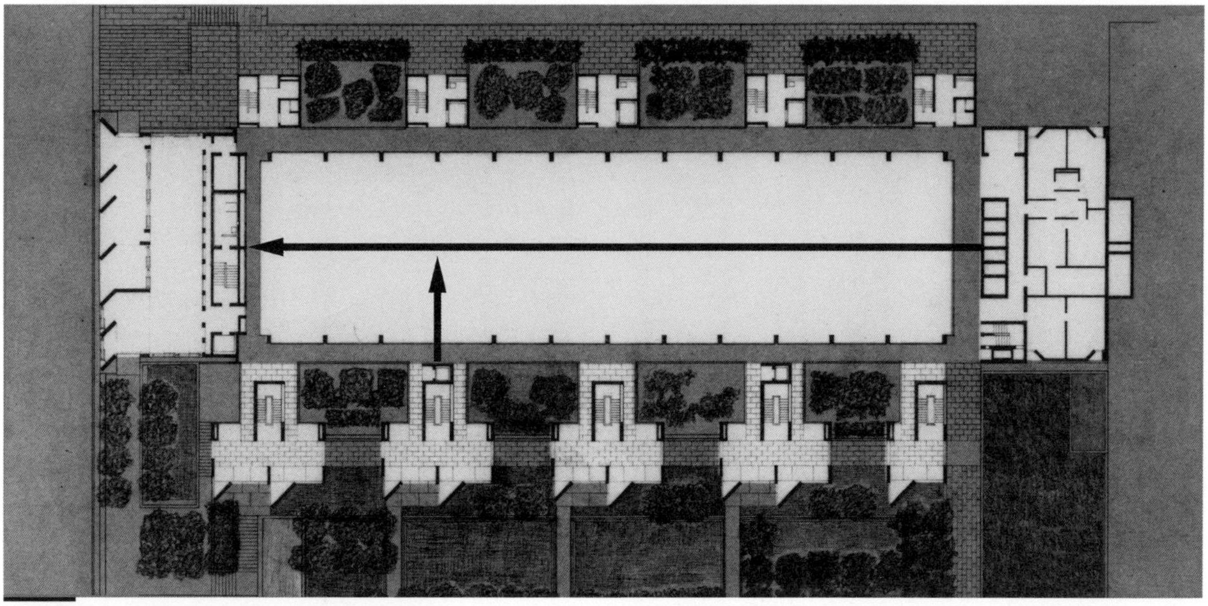

FIG.173A

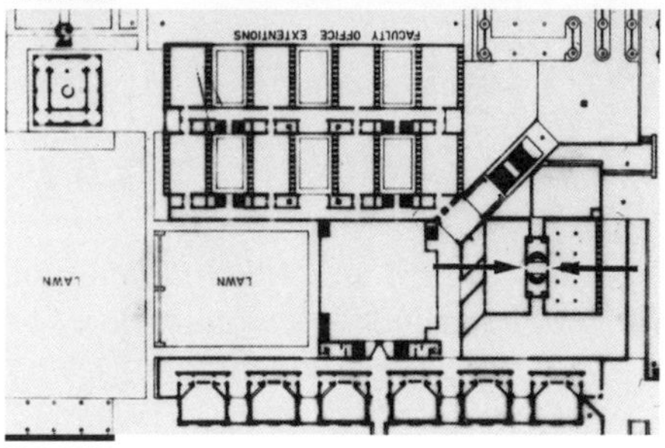

FIG.173B

FIGS.173A,B | Salk plan compared to IIM plan

director's office mediates between the administrative wing and the library, maintaining their individuality, but in the façade the oblique wall is part of the library wing.

The composition of the IIM library is a 'Brutalist' variation of one of the complete flanks of the Salk Institute Laboratory building. If we collapse one of the Salk end mechanical blocks to the back face of the aligning Salk administrative block, eliminating the intervening laboratory space, and conjoin these blocks with one of the stairs servicing the Salk studies, we have the basic parti for the IIM library. FIGS.173A,B The oblique walls of the IIM library are exaggerations of the oblique piers of the Salk office blocks. The deep vertical void, facing the IIM library and acting as a sun baffle for the multi-height reading space behind, is a variation of the deep voids that gash the Salk office blocks. One can pass from the entrance lobby through the library oblique walls to the lecture hall wing at the south side of the courtyard. An alternative covered passage from the north to the south side is also offered below the raised courtyard platform fronting the library. These 'under passages' are variations of the under passages at the Salk Institute.

Louis I Kahn's radical act of architecture is inscribed on the face of the in-folding diagonal wall of the IIM library, which is essentially a giant door. In cutting a circular opening onto the face of the diagonal brick wall he violated the 'purity' of structure that defined the diagonal walls of the scientists' studies at the Salk Institute. The entire architectural vocabulary utilized in the dormitory structures at IIM is presaged in this singular in-folding wall, creating the deep vertical void capped by the shallow composite brick arch. It is also an intense variation of the folded wall within the mechanical blocks of the Salk Institute. In plan the folded wall around the courtyard terminates at the library in a single oblique pier pointing to the face of the lecture hall wing to the south. This architectural 'gesture', as well as the in-folding wall, is the climax of the entire spiraling movement of space that moves from the site periphery into the open-ended courtyard. The conjunction of the administrative wing to the library at IIM is a form of architectural detritus. At Dhaka, Kahn would re-assemble and integrate the discarded remains of his prior architectural schemes to fashion a new capital for East Pakistan—Sher-e-Bangla Nagar, the City of the Bengal Tiger.

THE CAPITAL COMPLEX AT DHAKA (1962–1983)

As Robert McCarter stated Louis I Kahn's master plan and buildings for the capital complex for Dhaka, East Pakistan (now Bangladesh) was the architect's magnum opus.[8] FIG.174 It is one of the notable examples of new capital complexes constructed in the twentieth century at sites such as Canberra (Australia), New Delhi (India), Chandigarh (India), Islamabad (West Pakistan, now Pakistan) and Brasília (Brazil). Like at New Delhi the new capital complex for Dhaka was master planned in relation to an existing urban center. The original 1,000 acres allocated to the project by the Pakistan Department of Public Works was to include not only official government buildings but a hospital, library, mosque, museum, schools, clubs, markets, offices, recreation areas, a special diplomatic enclave and low- and high-income housing. Although this was a large, ambitious project for East Pakistan it did not rival in scale the projects at New Delhi or Brasília. Kahn eventually master planned the entire 1,000 acres, but the initial focus of his activities was on the 200 acres for the government buildings which included an Assembly Building (now called the National Parliament Building) for 300 representatives, with a prayer hall, hostels for the parliament members, ministers and secretaries, and the surrounding landscaping which included gardens and a lake framing the assembly building. The project was significantly divided between what Kahn called the Citadel of Assembly and the Citadel of Institutions. The latter area was transformed in Kahn's final master plan into an enormous nine-story wall building over two thousand feet long for the secretariat, which was to be located about fifteen hundred feet from the north entrance to the Assembly Building.

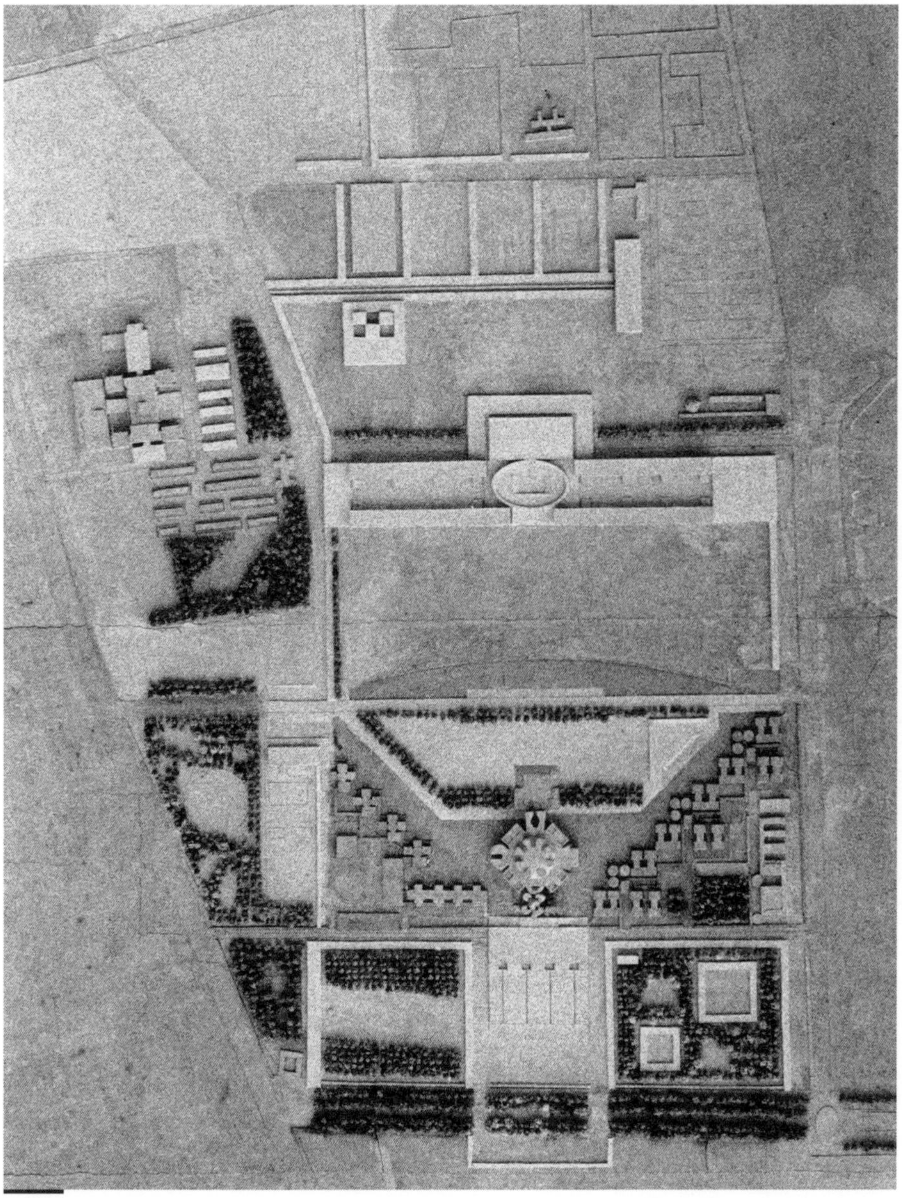

FIG.174

Sarah Williams Goldhagen compared Kahn's planning at Dhaka to the plan of Versailles. There is a graphic similarity between these two plans, and Kahn, in the Presidential Plaza platform to the north of the Assembly Building and in the immense ramp to the south, evoked the terrace levels of Versailles. However, that is where the resemblance ends. The approach to Versailles is a convergence onto the palace entrance that does not exist at Dhaka. Also, at Versailles the primary relationship to the landscape is one that penetrates a forest, suggesting an axial relationship to the gardens beyond and to infinite space.

FIG.174 | Capital master plan–Dhaka, Bangladesh (1962–1974)

The south approach at Dhaka is a blockage and a divergence of space around the Assembly Building organized by the splay formation of the lake. **FIG.174** We enter the building via a narrow-arched bridge from the ramp area. On exiting onto the Presidential Plaza on the north side of the building we descend to an expansive wide space defined by the subtle arc of the Crescent or Lunar Lake along the access road. The views north would have been blocked by the immense wall of the secretariat building. If anything resembles the splayed planning at Dhaka, it would be the diamond formation of a baseball field.

As an island formation, the Assembly Building evokes the lake palaces of cities in India such as Udaipur and Jaipur. Kahn on one of his score of trips to India had visited Jaipur. It is astonishing to think that the Assembly Building which is one of Louis I Kahn's last works–completed nearly ten years after his death–should also evoke another building surrounded by water: the fourteenth-century Bishop's Castle at Kuressaare (Kahn's birthplace) on the Baltic island of Saaremaa, Estonia.[9] This small castle is sited within a precinct defined by Baroque defensive walls and a moat connected to the mainland by a bridge. **FIG.175**

FIG.175

The design development of the Assembly Building at Dhaka was clearly based on the typological precedent of the initial scheme for the Unitarian Church and on the intermediate and final schemes for the Salk Meeting House. **FIGS.176A,B** Kahn converted the dodecagonal (twelve-sided) congregation area with its ambulatory at the Unitarian Church into the hexadecagonal (sixteen-sided figure) Assembly Hall with its seven-story 85-foot-high ambulatory. The split cubic nature of peripheral programmatic elements at Dhaka with their wall cut outs for the offices set back from the corners, the east-facing cafeteria and the north entrance volume are all indebted to the forms of the Salk Meeting House. The north entrance volume is a multi-height foyer flanked each side by the folded double cut out walls supporting and sandwiching stair runs in

FIG.175 | **Bishop's Castle-Kuressaare, Saaremaa, Estonia (fourteenth century)**

Kahn's version of Piranesi's visionary *Carceri* ('Prisons') etchings. FIGS.177, 178 The under passages at the Salk Institute Laboratory building–below the head of the courtyard, the scientists' studies and the office blocks–are extended and amplified at Dhaka in the vehicular access ways below the arch-supported monumental south ramp/platform, and the passage from there into the south foyer, which is below the prayer hall. The quadrapartite lightwell formation, embedded in the cubic form of the prayer hall over the entrance, is based on a discarded scheme from the Salk Meeting House library. This form also served as the basis for the chapel and entrance foyer to sanctuary at the

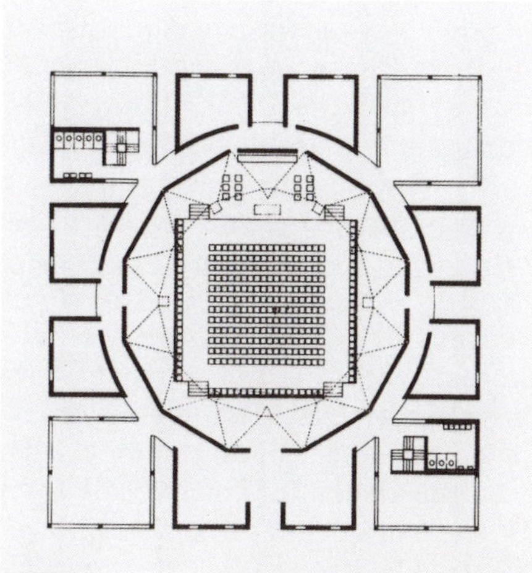

FIG. 176A

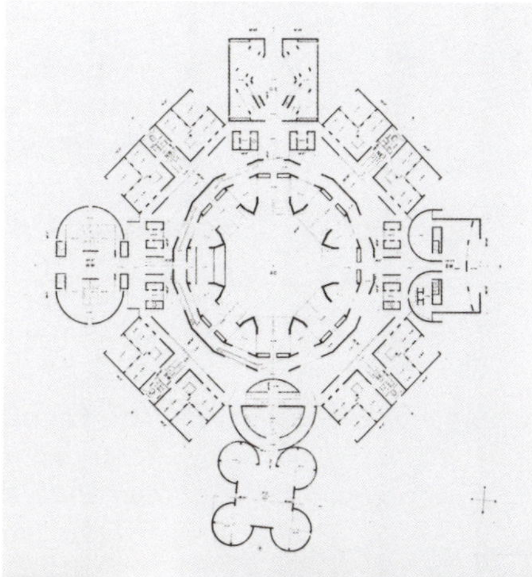

FIG. 176B

FIG.177

FIG.178

Mikveh Synagogue. At Dhaka the cylinders reach their purest form in the way their centers are aligned with the block corners. Kahn's use of this form was honorific. It was adapted for a library, a synagogue and a Muslim prayer hall. The unhing-

FIGS.176A,B | Unitarian Church original scheme compared to Dhaka Assembly Building
FIG.177 | Piranesi–one of his *Carceri* (prison) etchings (1750)
FIG.178 | Assembly Building north hall

ing of the assembly hall at the Salk Institute Meeting House is repeated in the skewing of the prayer hall toward Mecca.

The splayed lake is the urban amplification of the oblique geometry organizing the Erdman Dormitory at Bryn Mawr College. Each arm of the lake is bordered along the west edge by the two-story hostels for ministers and secretaries and at the east edge by the two-story hostels for parliament members. These units are designated as hostels because they were primarily intended for government members active during legislative sessions only. The west hostels are a series of hybrid buildings formed of four block units cross-linked through a center entrance/stair hall. This hybridity is generated by the three two-story housing blocks with roof terraces based on the cross-wall housing pattern from the faculty housing at IIM, linked to a cross-wall-ordered service/pantry/lounge block with veranda that is reminiscent of the overall volumetric form of the Yale University Art Gallery. Kahn here repeats the cross-axial form which linked multiple dormitories at IIM but, instead of being embedded in a chessboard pattern, the hybrid clusters are exposed along the lake edge. The west hostels are organized as four clusters in an A-A-A-A pattern with an additional linear run of hostels just to the south.

The plans of the parliament members' east hostels are adaptations from two areas at the Salk Institute: from a discarded courtyard scheme for the unbuilt Visiting Fellows housing, whose ordering was in turn indebted to the interlocking solid/void relationships of scientists' studies to laboratory wings. The east parliament members' hostels are organized in three clusters of three pairs of units with intervening kitchen/dining structures in an A-B-A-A-B-A-A-B-A pattern. The triple dining structures in each cluster are clearly indebted to the cylindrical dining halls at the Salk Institute Meeting House. **FIG.179** But here Kahn eliminated the screening fragmented walls at Salk and exposed pure cylindrical forms in brick which shield the interior from the sun. The dining 'salons' are on two levels set back from the face of the cylinder and provided with glass fenestration. The salons are air-conditioned. The setback is marked by a ceiling/roof opening over an intervening garden within the cylinders. The curved facing brick wall is doubled, sandwiching ramps to the upper level. Views over the lake are provided along the ramp through arched openings. From the exterior these arched openings are actually upper segments of two-story circular openings bricked in below, suggesting veiled figures. The triple dining cylinders share a common vestibule which ties them to the kitchen/service block. Together they form a cluster of elements inserted in between the hostels and terminating the road approach to the kitchen/service block. The formations of east and west hostels erode a series of grids along the edge of the lake. These grids order the gardens, and the pedestrian and vehicular access on the approach sides to the hostels. The pedestrian approaches are in the form of arcaded sidewalks with runs of

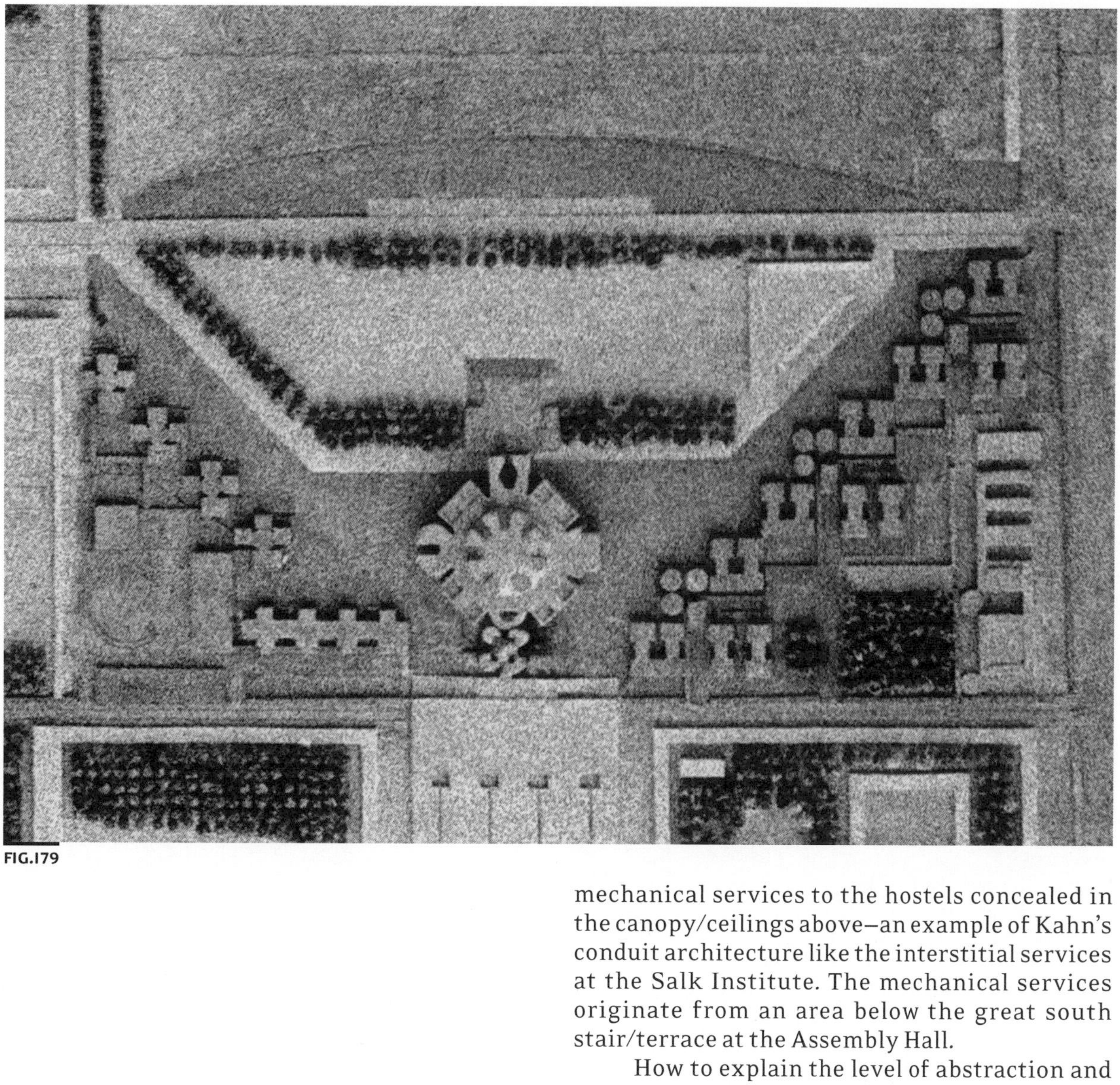

FIG.179

mechanical services to the hostels concealed in the canopy/ceilings above—an example of Kahn's conduit architecture like the interstitial services at the Salk Institute. The mechanical services originate from an area below the great south stair/terrace at the Assembly Hall.

How to explain the level of abstraction and haunted quality of these brick blocks, the hostels with their holed apertures? Kahn's use of the circular openings in series was both childlike and unparalleled in the history of architecture, East or West. Was this not a touch of Kahnian humor?

FIG.179 | **Model—ministers' and secretaries residence (left) and parliament members' residence (right)**

Insofar as the parliament members are only temporary residents are these blocks not reminiscent of bird houses with their holed openings?[10]

The Assembly Chamber of the National Parliament building at Dhaka is one of the great architectural spaces of the twentieth century. FIG.180 As Kahn stated: "A house of legislation is a religious place. No matter how much of a rogue you are as a legislator, when you enter the assembly, there is something transcendent about your view..."[11] Perhaps Kahn not only had legislators in mind when he made this statement but also the ultimate client for this project: Ayub Khan, former chief of the army, who came to power in a coup in 1958. Kahn not only transcended the client but the building project survived the Civil War of 1971-1972 which led to the birth of Bangladesh from East Pakistan.

Robert McCarter has emphasized that the planning of the Assembly Chamber owes much to the centralized planning of Renaissance churches.[12] We would like to shift the interpretation to yield a more suggestive set of relationships uniting an ancient with a modern symbol and in turn relate this to the Salk Institute. We enter the Assembly Chamber from the west through a series of layered zones. In other words we move toward the direction of the rising sun even though light comes from above and outside of the chamber. We pass through the chamber's own ambulatory, then through a passage to a dais/lectern which diverts the procession down stairs to either side where we descend to the floor of the chamber from which all seating is accessible. The chamber is octagonal. Behind each of the seating areas are raised visitors' galleries with their own rear connecting passages to the ambulatories. In plan these gallery/passages abut the sides of the octagon and form spokes in a wheel, with the residual spaces in between forming the lower ends of lightwells extending up to clerestory roof monitors.[13] Islam is an aniconic religion and has a very limited symbolism, preferring to express itself visually in calligraphic script. Yet Kahn adapts the symbolism of the more ancient religions of the sub-Continent in the Hindu-Buddhist Wheel of the Law.

It is said that the Wheel cannot survive without practicing the eight virtues.[14] But the eight spokes also represent the mid-points between seasons as well as the equinoxes and solstices—the wheel is a solar wheel.[15] An eight-wheeled formation appears in a work of Piranesi: the Collegio of 1750, and it is possible that Kahn knew this work. FIG.181 In the modern era wheels are found in electrical dynamos and radial

FIG.181

OPPOSITE
FIG.180 | The Assembly Chamber
FIG.181 | Piranesi–plan of a Collegio (1750)

engines. At the Assembly Chamber Kahn unites the symbolism of the political wheel of fortune to power and the engine of a society. This was not the first time that a symbolic 'device' was used to express democratic aspirations on the sub-Continent; Le Corbusier had formed the Assembly Chamber at Chandigarh from the hyperboloid structures used in nuclear power station cooling towers. FIG.183 Kahn's reliance on cylindrical forms, inspired by the medieval architecture of southern France in places like Albi and Carcassonne, is negated by the industrial character of these forms at Dhaka. This industrial character results from the use of cast-in-place concrete as the main building material, ironically enough placed by a multitude of manual laborers and from the superimposition of a marble-filled modernist grid over the architecture used to mark the five-foot vertical daily limit of pour stops.

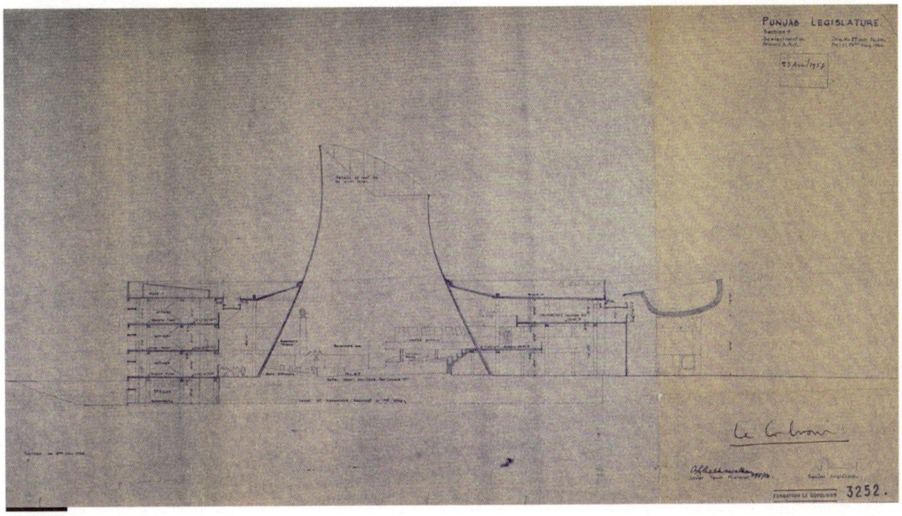

FIG.183

Like at the courtyard of the unbuilt Meeting House at the Salk Institute, finalizing the roof structure at the Assembly Hall became problematic. Kahn's original intent was to have overdetermined beams with circular cut-outs in the solar wheel formation hovering over the Assembly Chamber. FIG.182 However, the loads from these beams exceeded the structural capacity of the building. It was only at the Exeter Library (1967-1972) when Kahn was able to build his overdetermined X-formation of roof beams.[16] Kahn must have keenly felt the loss of his original roof design for the Assembly Chamber. The solution to the roof problem at Dhaka was finally resolved after the end of the Civil War two years before Kahn's death. A lighter-weight 'umbrella' shell structure was adapted and, although this too was an appropriate symbol for Bangladesh, it literally did not have the symbolic 'weight' of Kahn's original intention.

There is a rhythmic beat that governs the entire plan of the Assembly Building at Dhaka. The building acts like an architectural 'alternator'.[17] There are two main cross axes superimposed on each other. The primary one is formed from the north, south, east and west axes which

OPPOSITE
FIG.182 | Assembly Chamber—original roof concept
FIG.183 | Assembly Building section—Chandigarh, India—Le Corbusier (1951-1965)

are terminated by processional, honorific and servant spaces. These spaces comprise the entrance hall from the Presidential Plaza, the prayer hall, the cafeteria area and the ministers' lounge. Forty-five degrees to this cross axis are the servant axes of identical office blocks. This difference between the identical office blocks and the varying forms of the main cross axis expresses this architectural rotational beat. The energy for this ordering comes from the solar wheel. The triple cut out wall openings at the corners of the office blocks, supposedly for sun 'control' for the fully fenestrated offices set back from the corners, are less a nod to Mughal architecture than consistent with Kahn's long-term involvement with the solar theme. The steep equilateral triangular cut outs above rectangular cut outs are negative abstractions and magnifications of the crowns of the ancient Egyptian obelisks which solidify the vertical axial descent of light to the Earth. FIG.184 They can also be read as the negative versions of a tholos, such as that found in the burial chamber of the Treasury of Atreus, or from the Lion Gate with its massive relieving triangle. FIGS.185,186 The tholos was a shrine for demigods or heroes which, in its later evolution, became a shrine for monarchs and later a ritual place of assembly. At the Salk Institute and at Dhaka, Louis I Kahn created symbols of what Lewis Mumford called the mega-machine. Both buildings are places of assembly empowered by the sun and Kahn's attempt to enlighten human institutions.

FIG.184

FIG.185

FIG.186

FIG.184 | Assembly Building north view
FIG.185 | Tomb of Agamemnon (1250 BC)
FIG.186 | Kahn drawing (1951)— Lion's Gate, Mycenae, Greece

THE FDR FOUR FREEDOMS MEMORIAL (1973–2012)

Louis I Kahn signed a contract with the New York State Urban Development Corporation (UDC) on 1 January 1973, to design the Franklin Delano Roosevelt (FDR) Four Freedoms Memorial on Roosevelt Island in the East River off Midtown Manhattan. Nearly all aspects of the project were finalized in design just before Kahn died in March 1974. Kahn's concept began with his notion of a room and a garden **FIG.188**:

FIG.187

> I had this thought that a memorial should be a room and a garden. That's all I had. Why did I want a room and a garden? I just chose it to be a point of departure. The garden is somehow a personal nature, a personal kind of control of nature, a gathering of nature. And the room was the beginning of architecture. I had this sense, you see, and the room wasn't just architecture, but was an extension of self.[18]

FIG.188

FIG.189

The overall length of the FDR Memorial is 767 feet. The south end of this extent is the memorial room proper, which has an outside perimeter of 72 x 72 feet. There are a series of thresholds including a garden strip with five copper-beech trees, before one ascends the broad flight of stairs to the elevated garden which slopes subtly toward the memorial room.[19] Harriet Pattison was the landscape architect in Kahn's office who was associated with this project. One can approach 'the room' either on the elongated, trapezoidal-shaped grass area, or from the flanking granite-paved paths with their double allées of little-leaf linden trees. **FIG.187** One is not aware of the monumentality of FDR's portrait head (by Jo Davidson, sculpted in 1933) until one is practically upon it. **FIG.189** The 'floating' head is positioned exactly at the 'neck' of the scheme, separating the room from the garden, and is the focal point of the converging access paths. This is as radical a gesture—albeit more perverse—as Kahn's truncation of forms that are the library carrels at the Richards Biology Towers. The protective thick walls to either side

FIG.187 | FDR Four Freedoms Memorial—view south
FIG.188 | Memorial model photo
FIG.189 | FDR portrait head by Jo Davidson (1933)

of the 'head' also seem to insulate its ears from the noise of the surrounding urban environment—or is it to preserve the memory of FDR from the contradictions and depredations of capitalism as represented by Manhattan? FDR's portrait head is forever linked to his Four Freedoms speech, inscribed on the rear face of the massive granite blocks within which it is set.

At the FDR Memorial Kahn transformed the stepped Presidential Plaza at Dhaka into the elongated plinth of the garden and substituted for the Assembly Chamber an outdoor room dedi-

FIG.190

cated to the memory of a singular political leader. FIG.188 The paved sloped edges of the garden flanks bring to mind the mounded geometrical forms of Kahn and Noguchi's unbuilt Levy Memorial Playground in Riverside Park, New York (1961-1965). The outdoor room formed at each flank by 14 massive granite blocks—referred to as columns—which are each 12 feet high x 6 feet x 6 feet, weighing 36 tons each and set one inch apart. FIG.190 These blocks or columns are variations of the massive transparent/translucent glass blocks of Kahn's earlier Jewish Martyrs' Memo-

FIG.190 | View south through memorial room

rial (1964-1972) that was to be built at Battery Park in New York City.[20] But they are also reminiscent of the large crenellation blocks at the director's apartment at the unbuilt Salk Meeting House. FIG.191

The memorial room is formally the reversal and expansion of the contracted blocks of granite defining the niche for FDR's portrait head. Within the room Kahn placed to the east and west two massive seating slabs whose inner faces align with the indented walls flanking the entrance and which force visitors up against the massive walls when traversing the room. FIG.190 At the south end of the memorial room Kahn placed double steps as seating before a recessed floor closed off by a low parapet wall separating the visitors from the East River. Both the seating slabs and the double steps are variations of the flanking courtyard benches and the recessed seating area before the west pool at the Salk Institute courtyard. There the stream bisects the seating areas as it enters the pool. The Salk Institute is a space 'eroded' from within by its channel stream, whereas the FDR Memorial as a whole is impacted by its position within the flows of the East River. Its riff-raff perimeter was designed to resist the river's tidal flows.

FIG.191

FIG.191 | Detail model photo–Salk Meeting House director's residence

The massive granite 'columns' of the FDR Memorial, each placed one inch apart, are intense confirmations of Kahn's notion of architecture as the relationship of the 'measurable to the immeasurable'. The Memorial is also in plan an exclamation point on an island devoted to government-initiated housing, which was an important part of Kahn's early career. Twenty-three years before Kahn worked on this memorial, he had done a sketch of the Palazzo Vecchio in Florence (1950). In its perspective convergence can be found the parti for the FDR Four Freedoms Memorial on Roosevelt Island. FIG.117

It was fitting that Kahn had been selected to be the architect for this project, since his early architectural career in the 1930s and 1940s was aligned with the progressive housing policies of FDR's New Deal, and the development of the Salk Institute is forever linked to the National Foundation for Infantile Paralysis–an organization inspired by FDR and headed by his former law partner Basil O'Connor.[21] So at the level of form and historical content the Four Freedoms Memorial is intimately linked to the development of the Salk Institute for Biological Studies. The work of an architect such as Louis I Kahn is a concatenation of meanings giving shape to seemingly random events in a life or history. As Kahn stated: "How accidental are our existences really and how full of influence by circumstance."

At the time that the Salk Institute was under construction on the West Coast, the great Beaux-Arts Pennsylvania Railroad terminal was being demolished in New York City. **FIGS.192,193** Capitalist values gave us the original Penn Station monument, a product of the City Beautiful movement in America, and capitalist values took it away. The existing terminal was retained below street level, accessed via a passageway lined with numerous shops. Vincent Scully lamented the changes to Penn Station: "...Through it one entered the city like a god. Perhaps, it was really too much. One scuttles in now like a rat." Added to the site was a nondescript office building and the cylindrical building for the new Madison Square Garden.

In March 1974 Kahn died of a heart attack in the men's room of the 'new' Penn Station. He had just come back from a grueling trip to the sub-Continent where he was supervising

FIG.192

FIG.193

work at the Indian Institute of Management and at Dhaka. The architect, then 73 and under the immense strains of his practice, must have wondered about the destruction of McKim, Meade and White's original Penn Station, whose monumental entrance hall was patterned on the ancient Roman Baths of Caracalla (AD 192–235), the plans of which Kahn had sketched over as a student...

FIG.192 | Memorial service for L Szilard (13 June 1964)
FIG.193 | Demolition of Penn Station, NY, NY (1962–1964)

THE SALK INSTITUTE AND FOUR LATER KAHN WORKS ENDNOTES

1 Swanson, *Four Laboratory Designs*, p 227.
2 Solomon, *Louis Kahn's Trenton Jewish Community Center*, pp 128–134.
3 Ultimately, the programmatic requirements for the auditorium and the dining/kitchen facilities could not be contained within the space of the courtyard. The current location of the dining/kitchen facilities designed by Kahn's office was more effectively positioned between the 'inner sanctum' and the student and faculty housing.
4 Brownlee and DeLong, *Louis I Kahn: In the Realm of Architecture*, p 104.
5 See Scully, Vincent, "Louis Kahn and the Ruins of Rome", in which Scully mentions the ancient Roman basis of these passages in Trajan's market. This would be another Western 'foundation' for an Indian school of management. Kahn also seems to have merged the exterior openings of Trajan's market with some of the pavilion structures at Fatehpur Sikri.
There is also a possibility that the oblique planning of the student dormitories is indebted to Ledoux's
Hotel de Montmorency. Geoffrey de Montmorency, whose genealogy is contested between Irish and claimed French sides of the family in the nineteenth century, was a civil administrator during the development of New Delhi and later governor of Punjab.
6 The 'coupling' at the IIM married student housing perhaps is even more strongly expressed at the Erdman Dormitories at Bryn Mawr College. Isn't the juxtaposition of the notched stair cubes a face-to-face relationship? As memory fragments of Carcassonne aren't they defensive elements in a confrontational relationship? Don't they axially link through their notches the two adjacent women's dorm units to a central unit/hall? How did Kahn regard this building given who the program was for and his relationship at the time to two women: his wife Esther, and Anne Tyng? Are we limited to the meaning of the work as a resolution of the complexities and contradictions of architecture only?
7 As are the façades of the lecture halls at the opposite wing.
8 McCarter, *Louis I Kahn*, p 258.
9 August Komendant, for many years Kahn's structural consultant, was also born in Estonia.
10 This brings to mind William Jordy's comments on representational metaphor in his discussion of the Guggenheim Museum in his *American Buildings and Their Architects* Vol.4, p 344: "Critics, as well as the casual observer, have variously ridiculed the museum as a spaceship, an ice cream freezer, a cereal bowl, and so on. Tedious such taunts may be; yet, even when made with a degree of affection, they suggest the form does not express its conceptual metaphor in the fully architectonic sense of the chapel at Ronchamp or for that matter, of Fallingwater. Instead the architectural metaphor is always threatened by interference from representational metaphor of a trivializing or incongruous sort."
11 Hubert, Bruno J, "Kahn's Epilog", *Progressive Architecture*, December 1984. See Goldhagen, *Louis Kahn's Situated Modernism*, for comments on Kahn's relationship to the military dictator of Pakistan.
12 McCarter, *Louis I Kahn*, p 268.
13 We surmise that each 'spoke' represents one of the seven administrative regions of Bangladesh: Rangpur, Rajshahi, Khulna, Dhaka, Barisal, Chittagong and Sylhet. The eighth section is for the dais/lectern area.
14 1. Abstain from causing harm and taking life (both human and non-human). 2. Abstain from taking what is not given (for example stealing). 3. Abstain from sexual activity. 4. Abstain from wrong speech: telling lies, deceiving others, manipulating others, using hurtful words. 5. Abstain from using intoxicating drinks and drugs. 6. Abstain from eating at the wrong time (the right time is after sunrise, before noon). 7. Abstain from singing, dancing, playing music, attending entertainment performances, wearing perfume, and using cosmetics and garlands. 8. Abstain from luxurious places for sitting or sleeping, and overindulging in sleep.
15 Morin. *The Nature of Nature*, pp 158–160: "Stars, suns are machine beings... The most archaic of motors, the most archaic of regulatory systems. They remain the greatest known distributors of energy, the most advanced of all nuclear reactors, the greatest transmuting ovens known."
16 At the Exeter Library the overdetermined deep X-beams also become negative symbols of the library (of knowledge). X as the unknown as in Nietzsche's statement in book I of his *Will to Power*: "Since Copernicus man has been rolling from the center toward X." The circular cutouts at the unrealized Dhaka Assembly roof beams are displaced to the position of the giant circular openings of the Exeter interior cube where they frame the 'servant' book stack areas. They are symbols of illumination where, as Kahn said, "a man with a book goes to the light".
17 Alternators convert mechanical to electrical energy.
18 See *Coming to Light—The Louis I Kahn Monument to Franklin D Roosevelt for New York City*, Steven Hillyer and Gina Pollara eds, New York, Cooper Union: 2005. See table of contents page.
19 Ibid, p 32. The mound of the elevated garden was established years ago from material at the site left over from a subway station excavation.
20 The most detailed aesthetic analysis of this project is given in Mark Godfrey's *Abstraction and the Holocaust*, New Haven and London, Yale University Press: 2007.
21 See Bourgeois, *Genesis of the Salk Institute*, for numerous comments on Basil O'Connor.

APPENDICES

ARCHITECTURE OF REALITY

Jonas Salk

The Salk Institute for Biological Studies
Post Office Box 85800
San Diego, California 92138

Louis Kahn Memorial Lecture
American Institute of Architects
Philadelphia, Pennsylvania

5 April 1984

KAHN LECTURE
Proof Copy 4/19/84

When invited to give the Louis Kahn Commemorative Lecture this year I was told that I could speak on any subject of my choosing. Quite spontaneously I suggested "Architecture of Reality." However, as I began to reflect on this singular opportunity to pay fitting tribute to Louis Kahn, I recalled, once again, what I have long realized: meeting and getting to know him was one of the most unexpected and significant experiences of my life. I now understand the nature of the forces that led me to him and I am beginning to recognize that one gives meaning to chance encounters by what one chooses to do with such opportunities and by the effect that chance, in this sense, then has on one's life. In some instances the effect is transforming, leaving us permanently altered, never again able to revert to be as we were before.

* * * * *

The relationship with Louis Kahn had such an effect upon me and, I dare say, that I may also have had the same impact upon him. It was instantaneous--like love at first sight. While I went to see him merely to learn from him how one chooses an architect, the question was never answered and I discovered that it could have been answered in no other way than through the experience of our meeting. The effect is seen not only in what has thus far been constructed of the Institute in San Diego but in the master plan itself which reflects in an architectural statement the spirit of the conversation at our first encounter.

-2-

It was for me like the Big Bang--the moment when the process of evolution began--filled with promise, filled with potentiality and filled with purpose. The purpose, in this instance, was to serve and to celebrate the process of creativity; to form a crucible for creativity not only in the life sciences, but in the arts, the humanities and in philosophy. It was intended to be a place that would be concerned with evolving human values and human knowledge. It was to house a special library containing a collection of books reflecting the evolution of man's view of himself; it was to be a living library, a place of work for those who, in deciphering the scriptures of nature, were also contributing to the scriptures of man and to the merging of the epistemology of science and of human experience. It was to be a place for exploring the laws of nature--of life and of human life--and the laws of evolution as revealed in nature and in man. It was to be a place for contemplation and of work, a place to observe and to study the workings of the mind and to guide the workings of the hands, a place of meeting and of interaction in the same discipline and between different disciplines. It was to be a place of cross-fertilization and of hybridization for the emergence of new species of thought, of concepts and of ideas, a place that would illuminate from deep introspection and deep understanding. It was to be a place where all could bring out the best in each other.

This is what Lou Kahn and I did for each other--each from different disciplines and both joined together in a creative act. We were inseparable in our thoughts from the moment we met. And out of that relationship emerged a work of art to serve the work of science. It surged out of an intentional joining of artist and scientist to create something latent in both of us, and was made possible by the generosity of the benefactors who offered the resources and the land where all came together--perceptions, plans and people.

How improbable were the events that led to our meeting! It defies rational explanation and yet it all happened as if it were meant to happen, as if somehow intended. The existence of the Institute is now taken for granted as if as a natural occurrence, awaiting only the propitious moment to become manifest, to unfold.

Whatever emerges in the course of evolution makes explicit what was previously implicit. Potentiality and intentionality arise from the concatenations of circumstances that evoke the possibility that awaits to be expressed at the moment of need. So our minds must have been prepared by our earlier experiences--personal and of the world at large--and by the need that was felt and wanted to be satisfied.

And so it is when all of the necessary elements come together in one place--potentiality, need, intention, plan, and resources! This is what occurred when we met and when the master plan began to unfold. This may well be what its completion awaits--a propitious moment for the coming together of perceptions, plans, resources and people.

In the more than two decades since the Institute began its work, it has fulfilled its promise for creativity and excellence. It has justified itself in a great many different ways and has revealed to me--and I hope to others as well--the importance of architecture, the importance of art, and the value of an aesthetically pleasing ambience for the evocation of creativity. This is not to say that human imagination can express itself only under certain specific conditions; it is merely to say that works of art and works of science are nutured mutually, and in similar ways, and it is not coincidental that each form of creativity enhances the expression of the other. This may well be one of the rare experiments of nature--through the collaboration between artist and scientist--to establish a place for discovery, and in the many ways in which discovery is made in science, in art, in literature, in philosophy.

The Institute was conceived to be such a place, conducive to enhancing the quality of its work; for this, appropriate structures and spaces were needed and were created. It was to be a living entity, responsive to the living beings who would occupy it, capable of adapting and even of evolving as necessary. It was to be responsive to change, to small and rapid changes over the short term, and to more gradual and greater changes over the long term. It was designed to allow the functional parts to be easily arranged and to be replaced at such time as use required renewal. It was designed to evoke a feeling of permanence as well as flexibility; it was planned to outlive many generations into the future. There is something perpetual in it as a living and functional entity, as if to say that it is concerned with, and is the guardian of, the future and of the evolutionary process itself.

It was built with an evolutionary plan in mind; the capacity to adapt and to change is an integral part of the structure itself. It was not only built with a concern for its own evolution in mind, but it was also to be concerned with evolution itself, with human evolution, as a subject of interest and, in time, with universal evolution as a central and unifying theme. In evidence of this the Institute has itself evolved to become concerned with systems of greater and greater complexity; at the beginning it focused on the sciences of molecular-cellular biology, on genetics and immunology, now with work in the neurosciences. It has developed new capacities, new functions and new purposes. My own special interest and concern with evolution continues; I see evolution not only as a process but as a way of life, as a philosophy and as a way of seeing ourselves in the world and in the cosmos.

I see reflected in the Institute--in its structure, in its relationships and in its interactions, and even in my interactive relationship with Lou Kahn--the essence of the fundamental relationship of which all of reality is composed. I have come to see, in the course of time and in the course of many different experiences in my life, the nature or the architecture of reality. What I have learned about the nature of relationship in the universe, the nature of order, and of the unity that I see in all of its diversity, has all become apparent to me since I met Lou Kahn and since the Institute was born.

I now see the structure of the universe as binary, as made up of two elements, of networks of two elements integrally related to each other at all levels of complexity, thus creating the unity by which the whole becomes greater than the sum of its parts. I would like to show how this concept emerged, what it may mean for the way we see ourselves and what it may portend for the future. Consciousness of this fundamental relationship must exist within us, within our minds, and is seen at all levels and in all realms of reality. It reveals, in many different ways, our consciousness of the nature of order, as is reflected in organized perceptions emanating from the human mind. It is expressed in the architecture of the Institute as well as in the architecture of reality. It is evident in symbols created in the human mind, for human creativity expresses itself in many forms of art and was expressed even before the art of science was born.

The full meaning for me of the experience of working with Lou Kahn, and its significance, remains still to be recognized; I will, in due course, have further insights as to the value of this experience in my own evolution. As a way of paying tribute to his genius, I will try to explain what I mean by the "Architecture of Reality," which I would have like to have been able to discuss with him. I shall do so with you, inspired by his spirit which now fills this hall.

* * * * *

Again, I see in these diagrams a reflection of the binary nature of reality and I was struck when I noticed this also reflected in the design of the Institute in San Diego. I show in the next figures photographs of the north and south elements of a binary pair joined by a court; at one end they are also joined underground. When seen from the east or from the west the two distinct elements are seen in relationship to each other. This is clearly evident, also, in the relationship of the studies to the laboratories, and of the dry laboratories of the west wing to the wet laboratories and to the studies.

It is of interest to observe the difference in the intended function of the studies and of the laboratories: in the studies, a place for reflection, for thought; and in the laboratories, a place for thinking and working with one's hands. Again we see the relationship between a place for the workings of intuition and a place for the workings of reason; a place for imagining, for speculating and theorizing, and a place for establishing validity and proof. The separation and balancing of these structures and functions must have meaning in the workings of minds that occupy and work in buildings shaped this way. We see asymmetry not only between studies and laboratories but in the work of the North Building in molecular-cellular biology and in the South Building in the neurosciences, and the effects of the interaction between the two in encounters across the court, each nourishing and enriching the other.

I would now like to show you the master plan and the placement of the Meeting Center and the Residences for Visitors. The place of meeting was to be concerned with the humanistic and human values aspect of the Institute's work. And in it was to be located the special library containing works that would reveal the evolution of man's view of himself. There was also planned the Residences for Visitors, for those coming to work for a period of time in the Meeting Center, or in the laboratories or in the studies. Again we see the separation of function in each of the different elements. In their relationship to each other, I see the binary plan--the network of binary relationships--reflected in this orderly arrangement.

I come now to the last figure to show how this plan evolved from an earlier one in which there were to be four structures with two courts. This was the first plan, for the construction of which a contract was signed with a managing builder. On that day I experienced some discomfort that I did not understand. I went to the site alone and after awakening the following morning I realized that we would have to start over again; I said that to Lou Kahn (on the place on the way to San Francisco): rather than the four structures, I sketched two in relation to each other essentially as was later designed and constructed. Many of the elements conceived for the first set of plans were not used, but eventually appeared in the design of Lou Kahn's later buildings. In their place emerged new ideas, new plans, new designs, responsive--as always--to the urge toward perfection, as if the second set of plans wanted to emerge out of the first for reasons that can be described as aesthetic, as if one court felt more unifying than two. What was intended to be distributed in four structures then had to be contained in two; this was approximated without increasing height by building one-third of the structure below grade, enveloped in embracing courts.

I was struck by the unconscious expression of the unit of order, relationships which I describe as dynamic, interactive, asymmetric and binary, and, through the tension that exists in the asymmetry, this has brought forth the human mind and the human institutions to serve the process of human evolution.

It is through the tension in the asymmetry of function between pairs of structures that the process of evolution advances. Out of these observations has emerged the concept of universal order and universal evolution, and the evolution of evolution itself, with the emergence of the human mind and human consciousness, both of which are now undergoing evolution. Through the evolution of consciousness, and the consciousness of evolution, humankind--as a product of the process of evolution--is now entering a phase when we can become consciously engaged in guiding and ordering our own evolution. In this way will emerge evolutionary man, thinking and acting as if guiding and acting as part of the process of evolution--our own evolution.

This, it seems to me, is the meaning of the Institute. This is what has emerged from its intention. What this portends for the future is suggested by the recognition of the phenomenon of emergence in all relationships in the cosmos as seen in the orderly matrices that suggest that we must now begin to learn as much about the realm of the mind, the realm of metabiological evolution, as we have about the biological realm of the cell and the prebiological realm of the atom. The time will come when we will understand intuition as well as we understand genes and particles in the nucleus of the atom, and when we understand reason as well as we understand the expressive elements of the cell and the electrons of the atom. We will understand metabiological creativity as we understand biological procreation and prebiological interaction. We will need to acquire the wisdom to choose as wisely as in the process of natural selection in choosing that which has the greatest probabilities for survival and for evolution.

These are the thoughts that occurred to me, as I related myself to the ideas that my mind projects, as if ideas were structures in which our minds can live, can wander as we do in the labyrinths of a building, in the relationship between the abstract and the concrete, between the imagined and the real, and in the realms out of which reality is made.

Someone once said to me on approaching the Institute while still under construction, "How does it feel to be able to put your hand on a dream?" Later, Lou Kahn said to me that of all of the buildings in which he was involved this is the only one that in its execution exceeded his expectations. My encounter with Lou Kahn, in its effects upon me, far exceeded my expectations. We miss him but his spirit lives in the structures he designed. His presence in the building he created enabled me to reveal these thoughts and feelings about our relationship and about the experience that emerged in the labor of love in which we were united.

The Louis I. Kahn Preservation Group
1649 Stearns Drive
Los Angeles, California 90035-4515

25 December 1993

Lawrence Halprin
444 Brannan
San Francisco, CA 94107

Mrs. Louis I. Kahn

Sue Ann Kahn

Nathaniel Kahn

Stuart Emmons, AIA

Susan Stevens Emmons

Kirk Pawlowski

Nils C. Finne, AIA

Liv Svendsen Finne, Esq.

Pat Apperson

Re: Salk Addition

Dear Larry:

Please accept our late thanks for signing the May 10, 1993 letter to the Salk Board regarding the addition to their Institute. The letter played a key part in getting this tragedy onto the National front burner. Numerous articles concerning the addition appeared in newspapers in New York, Los Angeles, Chicago, San Diego, Philadelphia, and other cities. In addition, all of the major national architectural magazines have featured stories - with the most extensive coverage having just come out in the October issue of *Progressive Architecture*. Currently, many international magazines are preparing to release articles about the Salk.

As you know, the Salk Institute refused a meeting to discuss the addition requested in the May 10 letter. The meeting continued to be turned down despite a follow up May 14 letter from prominent San Diego architects and the full support from the State of California and the national preservation community. Dr. Salk personally promised AIA President Susan Maxman a meeting at the Chicago AIA convention to avoid bringing the addition issue onto the floor only to renege after the convention was over.

From latest report, the subterranean level of the Salk Institute addition is almost completely poured and construction is proceeding.

We would like to give you a brief summary of related events over the last year:

The international letter writing campaign in May 1993 directed to Dr. Brian Henderson (the recently appointed President of the Institute) resulted in hundreds of letters going to the Salk Institute. We believed that influential people at the Institute other than Dr. Salk were not fully aware of the architectural value of the building they worked in - or the damage that the addition was going to cause.

The May 10 letter, in addition to another letter that we wrote with background information, was sent to all Board members and major Donors for the addition. A number of Donors and Board members privately contacted the Salk Institute to request a review of the addition and at least one major donor withdrew funding for the project.

Telephone: (213) 939-1431 Facsimile: (213) 939-7108

Halprin
25 December 1993
Page 2

When plans were submitted to the local and State regulatory agencies for review in 1991, The Salk Institute and their architects implied that the eucalyptus grove in large part would be preserved. After the grove was leveled, in obvious contradiction to the Salk's agreement with these agencies, the agencies were contacted and urged to rereview. In addition to the grove issue, letters were sent to the agencies to make them aware of the architectural and historical importance of the site as well as the building.

There was strong criticism of the project in speeches at the San Diego AIA Design Awards ceremony on May 22. The Los Angeles AIA President issued a letter at this gathering from the chapter's Board of Directors urging reconsideration of the project.

From the beginning the National Trust for Historic Preservation has been very concerned about the addition. On July 12, Richard Moe, President of the Trust, wrote a strongly worded letter to Secretary Donna Shalala urging, "the National Institutes of Health *(NIH)* in the strongest possible terms to call for a halt to preliminary construction activities at the Salk Institute, and to conduct a full investigation of the relationship between the facility expansion and federal financial assistance..."

The National Trust urged the NIH to call for a National Historic Preservation Act Section 106 review. Briefly, any project that is a "federal undertaking" that impacts a property eligible for the National Register of Historic Places is required to be reviewed to minimize harm on the landmark. The Trust strongly believes that the Salk is eligible for such a review.

The President's Advisory Council on Historic Preservation voted to call for a review. The California State Historic Preservation Office was also very active in trying to halt the construction, or should we say, the destruction.

We have recently learned that the NIH was notified in May 1992 by the Institute that Federal funds were being used for the addition. We are still pursuing this matter.

It has been an uphill struggle since 1991. Salk Institute officials laid the groundwork for a successful project very carefully. A few examples: San Diego Historic Site wording (coincidentally written just a few months prior to Planning Department review in 1991) was custom tailored such that it would have been possible to construct a "U" shaped 30' high structure on the East, North, and South of the Kahn buildings without impacting the historical significance of the buildings! Support in the San Diego community was well planned and the regulatory process was masterfully handled by

Halprin
25 December 1993
Page 3

seasoned regulatory specialists and attorneys. In addition, Dr. Salk cajoled scores of architects across the country mostly in private or small meetings.

It is ironic that those that stated that the Kahn building was a "marriage of science and art" heard but did not listen to the profound concerns of the architectural and preservation communities. We hope that the experience garnered in the effort to save the Salk from an inappropriate and senseless act can serve as a catalyst for future efforts to preserve masterpieces of Modern American Architecture.

Again, thank you for your support.

Sincerely,

Nathaniel

Nathaniel Kahn

Stuart Emmons

Attached: May 10, 1993 letter

VENTURI, SCOTT BROWN AND ASSOCIATES, INC.
4236 MAIN STREET, PHILADELPHIA, PA 19127-1696

215 487-0400 FAX: 215 487-2520

Robert Venturi FAIA
Denise Scott Brown RIBA
Steven Izenour
David M. Vaughan

David W. Marohn
Daniel K. McCoubrey
Ann Trowbridge

May 10, 1993

Members of the Board
The Salk Institute
10010 N. Torrey Pines Road
La Jolla, CA 92037

Members of the Board:

We urge you to meet with us to discuss our concerns over the current construction plans for the new buildings at the Salk Institute.

We feel that such a meeting will allow us to chart a course which will be mutually beneficial to both the needs of the Institute and the legacy of great architecture.

Sincerely,

Robert Venturi

Frank O. Gehry

Denise Scott Brown

Philip Johnson

Kevin Roche

Robert A.M. Stern

Lawrence Halprin

David G. De Long

Richard Meier

Richard Koshalek
Director, MOCA

James Ingo Freed

Vincent Scully
Trustee, National Trust
for Historic Preservation

Antoine Predock

Barton Myers

Richard Moe
President, National Trust
for Historic Preservation

SALK INSTITUTE ENGINEERS, CONSULTANTS, ARCHITECT AND CONTRACTOR

August Komendant
Structural Engineer–New York City

Keast and Hood
Associated Engineers–Philadelphia

Ferver-Dorland and Associates
Supervising Structural Engineers–San Diego

Fred S Dubin Associates
Mechanical Engineers–Boston

Rick Engineering Company
Civil Engineers–San Diego

Roland Hoyt
Landscape Architect–San Diego

Lawrence Halprin
Landscape Architect–San Francisco

Earl Walls
Laboratory Consultant–San Diego

Louis I Kahn, Fred Langford, John MacAllister, Marshall Meyers, David Rinehart, Galen Schlosser, Carles Vallhonrat, Thomas Vreeland, David Wisdom
FAIA–Philadelphia Architects and designers in Kahn's office

(Note: It was not determinable from office records if any other persons in Kahn's office worked on the Salk Institute project.)

George Fuller
General Construction Contractor

SALK INSTITUTE COST ESTIMATE

From the Jonas Salk Archive Box 359 Mss. 14:

Letter from Charles Wilson (Salk Institute General Manager) to Louis I Kahn dated 5 March 1962.

(Figures in parentheses are 2015 estimates based on doubling the cost of construction every 10 years.)

Labs (double garden)
$10,193,000 ($424,028,800)

Meeting House
$2,300,000 ($95,680,000)

Fellows' Housing
$985,000 ($40,977,300)

Site Work
$450,000 (including utilities and service tunnels) ($18,720,000)

Additional Costs
Profit, OH, supervision, anticipated construction cost increases = $1,884,000 ($78,374,400)

Total cost
$15,812,000 ($657,780,500)

From the Salk Institute General Correspondence file 1962 Box 350 Mss. 1, 8 December 1961:

Letter from Basil O'Connor to the NFIP Board of Trustees–equipment costs were estimated at $2,500,000 ($104,000,000).

From Daniel Friedman's essay on the Salk Institute in *In the Realm of Architecture*, p 336:

It is stated that by July 1965 construction cost of the laboratory building totaled $14,500,000 million ($603,200,000).

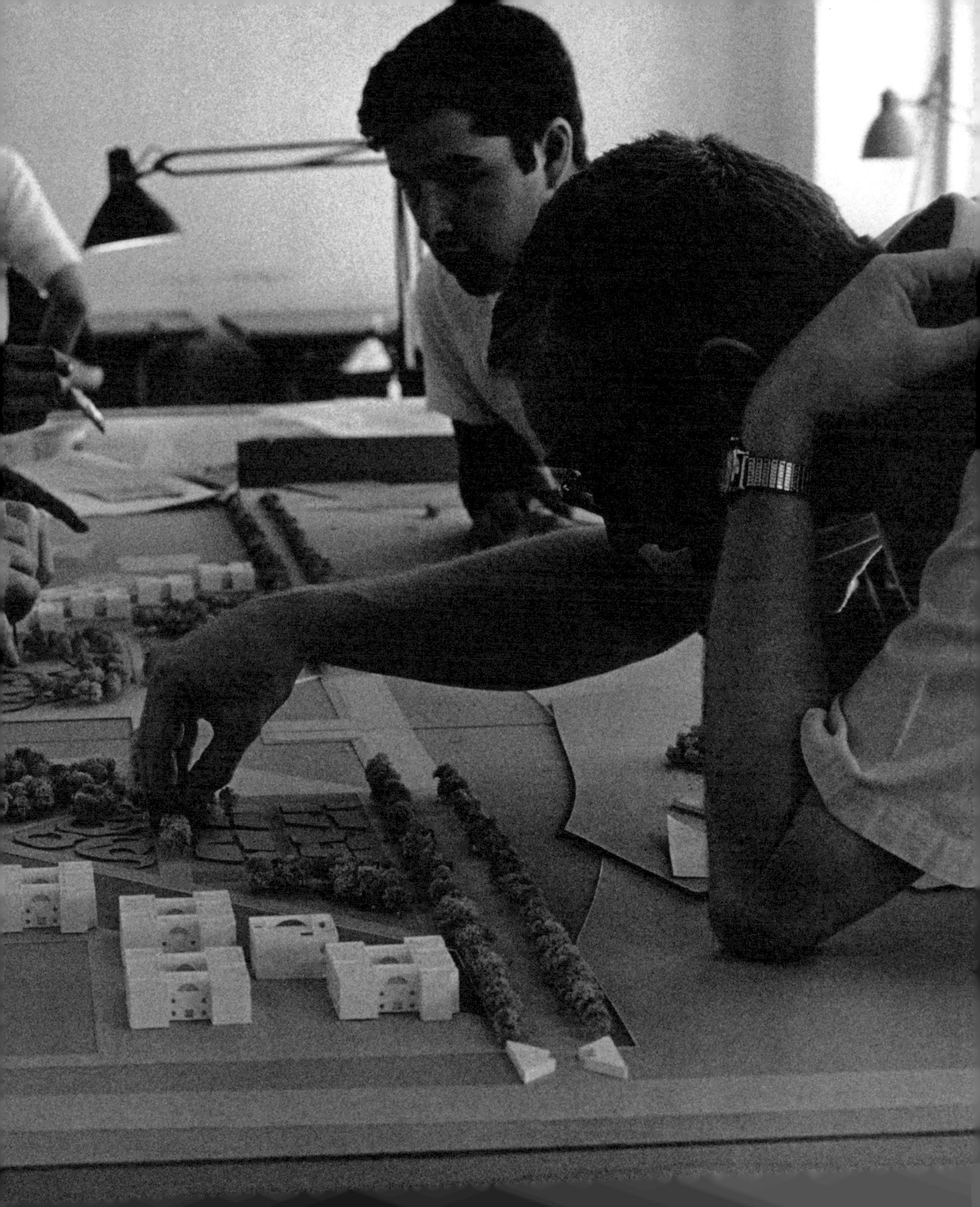

BIBLIOGRAPHY

Anderson, Stanford, "Louis Kahn in the 1960s", *Architecture and Urbanism*, special issue, 1985.

Banham, Reyner, *The Architecture of the Well-tempered Environment*, Chicago, University of Chicago Press: 1984.
—"The Buttery Hatch Aesthetic", *Architectural Review*, Vol. 249-252, March 1962.
—*The New Brutalism: Ethic or Aesthetic?,* New York, Architectural Press: 1966.
—*Theory and Design in the First Machine Age.* Cambridge, MA, MIT Press: 1980.

Benedict, Michael, *Deconstructing the Kimbell–An Essay on Meaning and Architecture*, New York, SITES/Lumen Books: 1991.

Berman, Marshall, *All That's Solid Melts in Air*, New York, Simon and Schuster: 1982.

Berve, Helmut, *Greek Temples, Theatres and Shrines*, New York, HN Abrams: 1963.

Boethius, Axel and JB Ward-Perkins, *Etruscan and Roman Architecture*, Harmondsworth, Penguin Books: 1970.

Bonnefoi, Christian, "Louis Kahn and Minimalism", *Oppositions 24,* spring 1981.

Bourgeois, Suzanne, *Genesis of the Salk Institute: The Epic of Its Founders*, Berkeley and Los Angeles, University of California Press: 2013.

Bressani, Martin, *Architecture and the Historical Imagination: Eugène-Emmanuel Viollet-le-Duc, 1814-1879,* Farnham, Surrey, UK, Ashgate Publishing: 2014.

Bronowski, Jacob, *The Ascent of Man*, London: 1973.
—*The Origins of Knowledge and Imagination*, New Haven, Yale University Press: 1978.
—*Science and Human Values*, New York, Harper and Row: 1965.
—*William Blake and the Age of Revolution*, New York, Routledge and Kegan Paul: 1965.

Brownlee, David, and David G DeLong, *Louis I. Kahn: In the Realm of Architecture*, New York, Rizzoli: 1991.

Burton, Joseph, "Notes from Volume Zero: Louis Kahn and the Language of God", *Perspecta 20*, Cambridge, MA, MIT Press: 1983.
—"The Aesthetic Education of Louis I Kahn", *Perspecta 28,* Cambridge, MA, MIT Press: 1997.

Cacciari, Massimo, *Architecture and Nihilism: On the Philosophy of Modern Architecture*, New Haven, Yale University Press: 1993.

Colquhoun, Alan, *Collected Essays in Architectural Criticism*, London, Black Dog Publishing: 2009.

Crick, Francis, *Of Molecules and Men*, New York, Prometheus Books: 2004.

Dal Co, Francesco, "From Parks to the Region: Progressive Ideology and the Reform of the American City", *The American City–From the Civil War to the New Deal*, Cambridge, MA, MIT Press: 1979.

Deleuze, Gilles, *Bergsonism*, New York, Zone Books: 1988.

Dubos, René, *The Dreams of Reason –Science and Utopias*, New York, Columbia University Press: 1961.
—*The Professor, the Institute and DNA*, New York, Rockefeller University Press: 1976.

Eigen, Edward. Between Stations and Habitations: *The Architecture of French Science at the Shore 1830-1910*, MIT PhD, Cambridge, MA: 2000.
—"The Place of Distribution in Architecture and the Sciences", *Architecture and the Sciences Exchanging Metaphors*, New York, Princeton Architectural Press: 2003.

Ellis, Russell and Dana Cuff eds., *Architects' People*, New York, Oxford University Press: 1989.

Evans, Robin, "Mies van der Rohe's Paradoxical Symmetries", *AA Files*, No. 19, Spring 1990.

Fleming, Steven, *The Bed Maker's Model: A Thematic Study of Louis I. Kahn's 1961 Article "Form and Design" in terms of Plato's Theory of Forms as treated in the Republic*, Saarbrücken, Germany, VDM Verlag Dr. Müller: 2009.

Frampton, Kenneth, "Louis Kahn and the French Connection", *Oppositions 22*, Fall 1980.
—"Louis Kahn and Modernization and the New Monumentality, 1944-1972", *Studies in Tectonic Culture*, Cambridge, MA, MIT Press: 1995.

Giurgola, Romaldo, and Jaimini Mehta, *Louis I. Kahn*, Boulder, CO, Westview Press: 1975.

Gallison, Peter, and Emily Thompson (eds), *The Architecture of Science*, Cambridge, MA, MIT Press: 1999.

Gast, Peter, *Louis I. Kahn—The Idea of Order*, Basel and Boston, Birkhäuser: 1998.

Godfrey, Mark, *Abstraction and the Holocaust*, New Haven and London, Yale University Press: 2007.

Goethe, Johann Wolfgang von, *Faust*, Norton Critical Edition, Walter Arndt trans. Cyrus Hamilton ed., New York: 2001.

Goldhagen, Sarah Williams, *Louis Kahn's Situated Modernism*, New Haven and London, Yale University Press: 2001.

Green, Wilder, *Louis I. Kahn Architect, Richards Medical Research Building*, New York, Museum of Modern Art: 1961.

Grosz, Elizabeth A, *Architecture from the Outside*, Cambridge, MA, MIT Press: 2001.

Gubler, Jacques, "Is the Bay a Type?", *Casabella* 509/510, January-February 1985.

Hejduk, John, "Beyond the Modern Movement", *Harvard Architectural Review*, Vol. I, Spring 1980.

Hess, Thomas, *Barnett Newman*, New York/Greenwich, Conn., Museum of Modern Art/New York Graphic Society: 1971.

Heyer, Paul, *Architects on Architecture—New Directions in America*. New York, Van Nostrand Reinhold: 1993.

Hillyer, Steven, and Gina Pollara (curators for the exhibition catalog), *Coming to Light—The Louis I. Kahn Monument to Franklin D Roosevelt for New York City*, New York, Cooper Union: 2005.

Hochstim, Jan, *The Paintings and Sketches of Louis I. Kahn*, New York, Rizzoli: 1991.

Hubert, Bruno, "Kahn's Epilog", *Progressive Architecture*, December 1984.

Jacob, François, *The Logic of Life: A History of Heredity*, Princeton, Pantheon Books: 1973.

Jordy, William, "What the Building 'Wants to Be': Louis Kahn's Richards Medical Research Buildings", *American Buildings and Their Architects Vol. 4*, Garden City, NY, Doubleday: 1970.

Kaufman, Walter, *Goethe, Kant and Hegel: Discovering the Mind*, Vol. I, New Brunswick, NJ, Transaction: 1980.

Kieffer, Jeffry, "A Reading of Louis Kahn's Salk Institute Laboratories", *Architecture and Urbanism*, Vol. 4, No. 271, April 1993.
—*Readings from the Architecture of Louis I Kahn*, Philadelphia, Xlibris Corp.: 2001.

Kimball, Roger, "'The Two Cultures' Today", *New Criterion*, Vol. 12, February 1994.

Klapwijk, Jacob, *Purpose in the Living World? Creation and Emergent Evolution*, Cambridge, UK, Cambridge University Press: 2008.

Kluger, Jeffrey, *Splendid Solution: Jonas Salk and the Conquest of Polio*, New York, GP Putnam's Sons: 2004.

Komendant, August E, *18 Years with Architect Louis I. Kahn*, Englewood, NJ, Aloray: 1975.

Lanouette, William, *Genius in the Shadows—The Man Behind the Bomb: A Biography of Leo Szilard*, Chicago, University of Chicago Press: 1994.

Larson, Kent, *Louis I. Kahn: Unbuilt Masterworks*, New York, Monacelli Press: 2000.

Latour, Alessandra ed., *Louis I. Kahn: L'uomo, il maestro*, Rome, Edizioni Kappa: 1986.

Latour, Bruno, and Steve Woolgar, *Laboratory Life: The Construction of Scientific Facts,* Princeton, Princeton University Press: 1986.

Leavis, FR, *Two Cultures? The Significance of C.P. Snow—Being the Richmond Lecture*, Cambridge, UK, Cambridge University Press: 1962.

Lecourt, Dominique, *Marxism and Epistemology—Bachelard, Canguilhem and Foucault*, London, NLB-Atlantic Highlands Humanities Press: 1975.

Leslie, Thomas, *Louis I. Kahn: Building Art, Building Science*, New York, George Braziller: 2005.
—"Things in their best order: technical aspects of the Salk Institute and their role in its design", *The Journal of Architecture*, Vol. 8, Spring 2003.

Lobell, John, *Between Silence and Light: Spirit in the Architecture of Louis I. Kahn*, Boulder, CO, Shambhala: 1979.

Loud, Patricia Cummings, *The Art Museums of Louis I. Kahn,* Durham, NC and London, Duke University Museum of Art: 1989.

The Louis I. Kahn Archive: Personal Drawings, seven vols., New York, Garland Press: 1987.

Lucan, Jacques, *Composition, Non-Composition: Architecture and Theory in the Nineteenth and Twentieth Centuries*, Lausanne, Switzerland, Presses polytechniques et universitaires romandes: 2009.

Lukacher, Ned, *Time-Fetishes*, Durham, NC, Duke University Press: 1998.

Lynn, Greg, "The Talented Mr. Tracer", *Tracing Eisenman*, London, Rizzoli: 2006.

Lyotard, Jean-François, "Newman: The Instant", *The Lyotard Reader*, Oxford, UK and Cambridge, MA, B Blackwell: 1989.

MacGibbon, David and Ross, Thomas, *The Castellated and Domestic Architecture of Scotland from the Twelfth to the Eighteenth Century*, Edinburgh, D Douglas, 1887-1892

Marcus, George H, and William Whitaker, *The Houses of Louis Kahn*, New Haven, Yale University Press: 2013.

Marton, Kati, *The Great Escape: Nine Jews Who Fled Hitler and Changed the World*, New York, Simon and Schuster: 2006.

McCarter, Robert, *Louis I. Kahn*, New York, Phaidon: 2005.

Meier, Richard, *Recent American Synagogue Architecture*, New York, The Jewish Museum: 1963.

Merrill, Michael, *Louis Kahn: On the Thoughtful Making of Spaces—The Dominican Motherhouse and a Modern Culture of Space,* Baden, Switzerland, Lars Müller Publishers: 2010.

Miller, Perry, *The American Transcendentalists: Their Prose and Their Poetry*, Garden City, New York, Doubleday: 1957.

Morin, Edgar, *The Nature of Nature*, New York, P Lang: 1992.

Nietzsche, Friedrich, On *the Genealogy of Morals*, New York, Vintage Books: 1989.

Norberg-Schulz, Christian, "Heidegger and the Language of Architecture", *Oppositions 18,* Fall 1979.

Ortolano, Guy, *The Two Cultures Controversy: Science, Literature and Cultural Politics in Postwar Britain*, Cambridge, UK, Cambridge University Press: 2009.

Popper, Karl, *The Logic of Scientific Discovery*, London, Hutchinson: 1959.

Reed, Peter Shedd, *Toward Form: Louis I. Kahn's Urban Designs for Philadelphia, 1939-1962*, U Penn PhD: 1989.

Rodell, Sam, *The Influence of Robert Venturi on Louis Kahn*, Washington State University Master of Science in Architecture: May 2008, http://citeseerx.ist.psu.edu/viewdoc/download?doi=10.1.1.632.3995&rep=rep1&type=pdf.

Rogers, Robert, "Freud and the Semiotics of Repetition", *Poetics Today* 8, Nos 3-4, 1987.

Ronner, Heinz, and Sharad Jhaveri, *Louis I. Kahn: Complete Work, 1935-1974 1st edition,* Boulder, Co., Westview Press: 1977.

Rosenau, Helen, *Vision of the Temple*, London, Oresko Books: 1979.

Roth, John Paul, *Structures for Thought: Forms from the Works of Architect Louis I. Kahn in Relation to Psychological Principles of Integration,* University of Oregon Master of Architecture Thesis: 1978. Found in the Jonas Salk Archive, Box 540, Folder 13.

Rowe, Colin, "Classicism and Neo-classicism in Modern Architecture", *The Mathematics of the Ideal Villa and Other Essays*, Cambridge, MA, MIT Press: 1976.
—*As I Was Saying: Recollections and Miscellaneous Essays*, Caragonne, Alexander ed., Cambridge, MA, MIT Press: 1996.

Rykwert, Joseph, *On Adams House in Paradise*, New York, Museum of Modern Art: 1972.
—*The Idea of the Town: The Anthropology of Urban Form in Rome, Italy, and the Ancient World*, Princeton, NJ, Princeton University Press: 1976.

Salk, Jonas, *Anatomy of Reality: Merging of Intuition and Reason*, New York, Columbia University Press: 1982.
—"Horizons into the Future", *Art and Antiques*, December 1990.
—*Man Unfolding*, New York, Harper and Row: 1972.
—*The Survival of the Wisest*, New York, Harper and Row: 1973.

Scholem, Gershom, *On the Kabbalah and Its Symbolism*, New York, Schocken Books: 1965.
—*Zohar, the Book of Splendor*, 7th edition, New York, Schocken Books: 1974, c. 1949.

Scully, Vincent, *Louis I. Kahn*, New York, George Braziller: 1962.
—*American Architecture and Urbanism*, New York, H Holt: 1988.
—*Architecture: the Natural and the Manmade*, New York, St Martin's Press: 1991.
—*The Earth, the Temple and the Gods*, New Haven, Yale University Press: 1962.
—"Frank Lloyd Wright and the Stuff of Dreams" and "Louis Kahn and the Ruins of Rome", *Modern Architecture and Other Essays*, Neil Levine ed., Princeton and Oxford, Princeton University Press: 2003.

Serres, Michel, *Rome, The Book of Foundations*, Stanford, CA, Stanford University Press: 1991.

Smith, Norris Kelly, *Frank Lloyd Wright: a Study in Architectural Content*, Englewood Cliffs, NJ, Prentice-Hall: 1966.

Snow, CP, *The Two Cultures and a Second Look*, Cambridge, UK, Cambridge University Press: 1964.

Solà-Morales I Rubio, Ignacio, "A Lecture in San Sebastian", *Arquitecturas Bis* 41-42, January-June 1982.

Solomon, Susan G, *Louis Kahn's Trenton Jewish Community Center*, New York, Princeton Architectural Press: 2000.

Steele, James, *Salk Institute.*, London, Phaidon: 1993.

Stoller, Ezra, *The Salk Institute*, New York, Princeton Architectural Press: 1999. Additional contributor: Daniel S Friedman.

Summerson, John, *Classical Language of Architecture*, London, Methuen: 1963.

Swanson, Randy Stuart, *Four Laboratory Designs Considered as Mediative Representation*, PhD dissertation, University of Pennsylvania, Philadelphia: 1993.

Tafuri, Manfredo, *Theories and History of Architecture*, New York, Harper and Row: 1980.

Tyng, Alexandra, *Beginnings: Louis I. Kahn's Philosophy of Architecture*, New York, Wiley: 1984.

Vallhonrat, Carles, "Tectonics Considered Between the Presence and Absence of Artifice", *Perspecta 24*, Cambridge, MA, MIT Press: 1988.
—"The Invisibility of Tectonics, Gravity and the Tectonic Compacts", *Perspecta 31*, Cambridge, MA, MIT Press: 2000.

Vattimo, Gianni, *The Transparent Society*, Oxford, UK, The Polity Press: 2005

Venturi, Robert, *Complexities and Contradictions in Architecture*, New York, Museum of Modern Art: 1966.
—*Iconography and Electronics Upon a Generic Architecture: A View from the Drafting Room*, Cambridge, MA, MIT Press: 1996.

Vidler, Anthony, "The Third Typology", *Oppositions 7*, Winter 1977.

Vivoni-Farage, Enrique, *A Measure of Silence: A Theory of the Transformation of the Wall*, PhD dissertation, University of Pennsylvania, Philadelphia: 1985.

Whitely, Nigel, "Banham and Otherness: Reyner Banham and the Quest for an Architecture Autre", *Architecture History*, Vol. 33, 1990.

Wiseman, Carter, *Louis I. Kahn: Beyond Time and Style–A Life in Architecture*, New York, WW Norton: 2007.

Wurman, Richard Saul, *What Will Be Has Always Been–The Words of Louis I. Kahn*, New York, Rizzoli: 1986.

ILLUSTRATION SOURCES

INTRODUCTION THROUGH CHAPTER FIVE

© 2018 Barragán Foundation, Switzerland/Artists Rights Society (ARS), New York:
FIG. 104

© 2018 The Barnett Newman Foundation, New York/Artists Rights Society (ARS), New York:
FIGS. 159, 160

© F.L.C./ADAGP, Paris/Artists Rights Society (ARS), New York 2018:
FIGS. 149, 183

© Matt Wargo:
FIGS. 30, 134, 191

Aaron Rose/Museum of the City of New York:
FIG. 193

Architectural Archives, University of Pennsylvania
—Anant Raje Collection: FIGS. 167, 171
—Cortland Hubbard: FIG. 112
—George Pohl: FIGS. 97C, 155, 174, 179, 188
—Gottscho-Schleisner Collection: FIG. 89
—John Nicolais: FIGS. 66, 73, 81, 84, 86, 87, 95, 137, 139, 147
—Lawrence Halprin Collection: FIG. 109
—Marshall Meyers: FIGS. 142, 143
—Matt Wargo: FIGS. 36, 47
—Mildred Schmertz: FIG. 126
—Paul Philippe Cret Collection: FIG. 49
—William Whitaker: FIG. 133

Arne Maasik:
FIG. 175

Art & Architecture Collection, Miriam and Ira D. Wallach Division of Art, Prints and Photographs, The New York Public Library, Astor, Lenox and Tilden Foundations (from *The Castellated and Domestic Architecture of Scotland from the Twelfth to the Eighteenth Century* by MacGibbon and Ross):
FIG. 144

Art Institute of Chicago:
FIG. 154

Arthur Rosenbaum:
FIGS. 23, 68

Artres/MoMA (Art Resources/Museum of Modern Art):
FIGS. 57, 127

Bibliothèque Nationale de France-from De Culto Divino (1678):
FIG. 161/PP 110-111

By permission of the Rita Bronowski Trust:
FIG. 3/PP 162-163

CO Architects:
FIGS. 107, 108

Edizioni di Comunita (from *Ignazio Gardella* by Pier Carlo Santini):
FIG. 93

Franco Cosimo Panini Editore:
FIG. 42

Franklin D. Roosevelt Library:
FIG. 8

Google Maps:
FIGS. 2, 166

Historical Society of Pennsylvania:
FIG. 6

Images of Jonas Salk used with permission of the family of Jonas Salk:
FIGS. 3, 8, 98/PP 162-163

J.N.L. Durand (from *Précis of the Lectures of Architecture*):
FIG. 4

J. Paul Getty Trust, Getty Research Institute, Los Angeles (2002.R.41):
FIG. 149

Jeffry Kieffer:
FIGS. 56, 65, 80, 83, 85, 94, 98, 119, 120, 121, 122, 128, 151, 152, 153, 187, 189, 190/PP 102-103, 158-159, 164-165

Jonas Salk Papers, Special Collections & Archives, UC San Diego:
FIGS. 19/PP 146-147

John Ebstel Photos/Keith De Lellis Gallery:
FIGS. 52, 113, 124, 125

Louis I. Kahn Collection, University of Pennsylvania and the Pennsylvania Historical and Museum Commission:
FIGS. 1, 5, 7, 12, 13, 14, 15, 16, 17, 18, 20, 21, 22, 24, 26, 27, 28, 29, 32, 33, 34A, 34B, 34C, 35, 37A, 37B, 37C, 37D, 38, 40, 41, 45, 46, 48, 50, 53, 54, 55, 57, 59, 60, 61, 62, 63, 64, 69, 70, 71A, 71B, 71C, 74, 76, 77, 78, 79, 82, 88, 90, 91, 92, 96, 97A, 97B, 97D, 99, 100, 102, 103, 106, 110, 111, 114, 115, 116, 123, 129, 130, 131, 132, 135, 136, 140, 145, 156, 163A, 163B, 163C, 164, 168, 169, 170, 173A, 173B, 176A, 176B, 182/PP 82-83, 166-167

March of Dimes:
FIGS. 9, 10

Mark Cartwright of *The Ancient History Encyclopedia* (www.ancient.eu):
FIG. 185

Mary D Waller (from *Chladni Figures: A Study in Symmetry*):
FIG. 44

Penguin/Random House UK (from *Etruscan and Roman Architecture* by Axel Boëthius):
FIGS. 31, 51, 72

Penguin/Random House US (from *Zohar–the Book of Splendor* by Gersholm Scholem):
FIG. 157

Piranesi:
—(from *Le Carceri d'invenzione*):
FIG. 177
—(from *Observations on the letter of Monsieur Mariette with opinions on architecture, and a preface to a new treatise on the introduction and progress of the fine arts in Europe in ancient times*): FIG. 181

Ramée–*Architecture de C.N. Ledoux:*
FIG. 25/PP 20-21

Raymond Meier/VS+Company:
FIGS. 178, 180, 184/PP 120-121

Ribapix:
FIG. 67

Richard Saul Wurman:
FIG. 146

Rizzoli (from *The Paintings and Sketches of Louis I. Kahn* by Jan Hochstim):
FIGS. 101, 117, 158, 186 (all original drawings, whereabouts unknown)

Sue Ann Kahn:
FIGS. 11, 39, 43, 118, 138

Salk Institute for Biological Studies:
FIGS. 75, 105, 148, 192

Universal Jewish Encyclopedia:
FIG. 162

University of Chicago Press:
FIG. 150

University of Virginia Special Collections Department:
FIG. 165

Viollet-le-Duc (from *Entretiens sur l'Architecture*):
FIGS. 58, 141

Yale University Press:
FIG. 172

APPENDICES

Jonas Salk Papers, Mandeville Special Collections, UC San Diego Library by permission of The Jonas Salk Legacy Foundation:
PP 147-157

The Architectural Archives, University of Pennsylvania:
PP 159-161, 163

ACKNOWLEDGMENTS

This book and almost any book on the work of Louis I Kahn is dependent on the resources available from the Louis I. Kahn Collection at the University of Pennsylvania. I want to thank curator William Whitaker and assistants Nancy Thorne (retired) and Allison Rose Olsen for their work in obtaining documentation for this project. But one must also acknowledge the numerous founders and supporters of the collection, which was threatened with dispersal because of the indebtedness of Kahn's office after his death in 1974. The history of this effort has been recorded by the second curator of the Kahn Collection, Julia Converse, in the first large book on Kahn's architecture and urbanism, which is the catalogue of the 1991-1994 traveling retrospective of the architect's work. Jonas Salk was one of the supporters of the founding of the Louis I. Kahn Collection. I also want to thank one of his three sons, Dr. Peter Salk, MD, PhD who as President and Director of the Salk Legacy Foundation allowed me to access, in early 2014, his father's papers in the Mandeville Special Collections Library at the University of California at San Diego, La Jolla. Access there was facilitated by Lynda Claassen and her staff. Amanda Faustine, Communications Coordinator at the Salk Institute, also aided this project by providing several images gratis.

A debt of gratitude must be paid to Professor Kenneth Frampton of the Columbia University Graduate School of Architecture, Planning and Preservation, who reviewed my work and made a key publishing recommendation. Prof. Frampton wrote one of the key essays on Kahn's work. Thanks to Sue Ann Kahn for allowing me to publish some of her father's sketches, which are crucial to an understanding of his work. If this book is dependent on the resources of the Kahn Collection in Philadelphia it is equally dependent on the editing work and suggestions of Anna Danby, Director of Publishing at Artifice, and the work of the key graphic designer on this project, Rachel Pfleger. Justin Lewis meticulously reviewed the text. Duncan McCorquodale must also be acknowledged. He allowed me entrée into this publishing effort.

Relatively late I met Richard Saul Wurman during one of his visits to New York City. I thank him, as well, for permission to include one of Kahn's sketches in this publication. Richard, as a member of Kahn's office in the late 1950s and early 1960s, published the first significant book on Kahn–a book on the architect's drawings. Twenty years later he also published a major compilation of Kahn's sayings and writings. I thank Professors David Chapin, Alan Feigenberg and historian Robert Twombly, who invited me into their special class at the Spitzer School of Architecture at the City College of New York in the Fall of 2014, which celebrated the one-hundredth anniversary of Jonas Salk's birth. Jonas Salk was both a CCNY and NYU graduate. The class was devoted to the study of the Salk Institute and Kahn's unbuilt Levy Memorial Playground on New York City's Upper West Side. Thanks to Amar Malla, Senior Project Design manager at the NYC Department of Design and Construction and former architect in Chandigarh, India for a contribution to this project. Also, at DDC I want to thank Program Director Richard Brotherton for conversations over the years on Kahn that kept "the fires alive".

To my friend of over forty years, Sr. Mario Noriega, urban designer and city planner of Bogota, Colombia—I am indebted to his 1979 invitation for me to lecture at the University of the Andes which re-ignited my passion for Kahn's work. In the early 1980s, on two occasions, I visited Prof. Vincent Scully at Yale University to share my earlier research on Kahn's work. Prof. Scully published the first book on Kahn's work and career in 1962. Since that publication he was a forceful advocate and explicator of the architect's work. This book is dedicated to Prof. Scully, who passed away in November 2017.

Artifice Press Limited
81 Rivington Street
London EC2A 3AY
United Kingdom

+44 (0)20 8371 4000
office@artificeonline.com
www.artificeonline.com

Designed by Rachel Pfleger
Edited by Justin Lewis

British Library in Cataloguing Data. A CIP record for this book is available from the British Library.

ISBN 978-1-911339-35-9

Printed in the United Kingdom by CPi Colour.

Cover: Darren Bradley/OTTO

Artifice